Dear Gina,

keep becoming that wh... you a... become ...tha... is your...

MW01166347

"Rarely do we as Americans really get to hear, and thus really get to understand, what leads a child to violence. Even more rarely are we ever really forced to reckon with the horrors that our nation's criminal justice system inflicts on children in our name. Perhaps most important, we never really learn what it is that we can do to rescue our nation's children from the hell that is our prison system—what they need from us so that they can feel loved and feel like the human beings they are. With raw passion, beautiful prose, and stunning power, Mario Bueno's memoir gives us all of these things. It is a must read for the entire country."

—Heather Ann Thompson, Pulitzer Prize-winning author of
Blood in the Water: The Attica Prison Uprising of 1971 and Its Legacy

Reformed

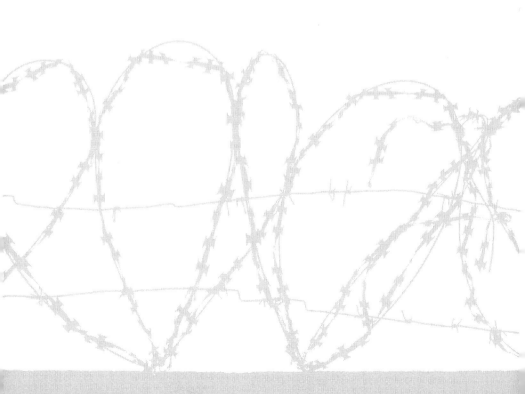

Reformed

Memoir of a
Juvenile Killer

Mario Bueno

Phoenix Rising
1759 W. 21st Street
Detroit, MI 48216

Published 2018 by Phoenix Rising

Printed in the United States of America

ISBN: 978-1-943290-42-0
Library of Congress Control Number: 2017961436

With deepest gratitude, this book is dedicated to
Dr. Joan Duggan, the Mother of Detroit's Comeback,
for mentoring, guiding, and counseling a group of broken men
closer toward their purpose so they can give back to the community
they once harmed. And to Tracy for creating the space of
healing and restoration for both Samuel and myself.

"When there exists no enemy within,
the enemy outside can do you no harm."
—*Old African Proverb*

CONTENTS

FOREWORD

"It's a pleasure to meet you, Mr. Blanchard," said Mario, sporting a navy suit and a smile. We exchanged handshakes and pleasantries as I entered the large conference room in the office of Mike Duggan, the Mayor of Detroit. At the time, I was the Director of Youth Services for Detroit, leading a multi-million-dollar campaign to provide 5,000 plus summer jobs for youth. Additionally, I was launching a city-wide elementary school soccer league and co-leading President Barack Obama's, "My Brother's Keeper" (MBK) initiative for Detroit. Mario was interested in learning about youth services and the preventative measures being taken to derail the school-to-prison pipeline.

As the conversation continued, I learned that Mario had only been released from prison three months earlier after having served nineteen years. Whew! I was impressed by his intellect and gentlemanly conduct. Of my seven brothers, three are deceased and three have served time in prison, so I appreciated Mario's authentic eagerness to aid the youth of Detroit.

Since our first encounter, we have developed a fond respect for each other's work. I've watched Mario leverage those earlier connections that led him to the mayor's office. Later he became Legislative Aide for the Michigan House of Representatives, earned a Bachelor's degree, started his own nonprofit, LUCK, Inc., and secured over a quarter million dollars to fuel his efforts. I know plenty of people with a fraction of Mario's accomplishments who have never experienced a day in prison. With his extensive experience guiding men within the incarceration system, mentoring youth, and helping returned citizens reintegrate into society, it's evident why Mario is named the Reform Expert.

It's a critical time in American history. The conversation of how we can uproot our communities to enhance the lives of people who suffer from systematic issues is at the forefront of the human rights conversation. With respect to reform, this book will serve many in three categories: prevention, rehabilitation, and reintegration. I'm looking forward to national impact from the Reform Expert, Mario Bueno.

Shawn T. Blanchard

Author | Speaker
CEO of Lions Dream, LLC
Philanthropy Advisor at SnapSuits

CHAPTER 1

A BOY'S PAIN ... A MAN'S WORLD

August 6, 1995, approximately 5:00 p.m., Nick's House

IT WAS EARLY on a summer evening when the sounds of ice-cream bells and kids on bikes filled the streets of Pontiac, Michigan. While other sixteen year olds from my high school were studying for their ACTs, I was brokering a gun deal. "It's broke, lil' bro," said Nick, my oldest sister Sandra's boyfriend. "Sorry, no can do." He stood in the doorway of his house waiting for me to tell him my plans, looking straight at me like a poker player. Nick was sixteen and my sister fourteen when they got together five years earlier. He was a short white guy with a smile that could, and did, help him scheme and scam his way through life. Though he worked his craft of carpentry and remodeling, he was also skilled in drug hustling. Nick was gifted but lacked discipline, which was rooted in an unstable childhood of abuse and trauma. Neither of us had a relationship with our father. At that pivotal moment on my timeline, we had a "little brother, big brother" connection that filled a void, however dysfunctional.

"I don't care. I don't plan on shooting him," I replied. Nick looked over his shoulder, making sure that my sister Sandra was not behind him. Sandra was about three months pregnant at this time, and her values had already begun to change. She was settling, not wanting to be around the wild group of girls she once hung around. In addition, she was also trying to keep her boyfriend, Nick, and her little brother, me, out of trouble. "I can't let you go into robbery with a broken gun, bro," Nick whispered. "You know he is more than likely carrying a gun that works." I understood his point, gave him the customary handshake and embrace, and left.

Up to that point, I had robbed others by force, blade, scheme, or a pellet gun that looked real. At a time and age when my pain screamed louder than my purpose, I was looking for any excuse to rob this local marijuana pusher named Samuel. In 1995, the street code was defined by movies that glorified "cultures of honor" like *Menace to Society, New Jack City, American Me,* and *Blood-In and Blood-out.* If you were part of the "game," then you were fair game.

I began as a low-level marijuana pusher at thirteen, buying ounces of weed from Sandra's earlier boyfriends and making dime bags as a way to triple my money. It was during a time when my parents struggled with loving themselves, as many do, so a space existed that allowed for the negative influences of the world to woo me, while creating a perception that the world was not safe; thus, the "I must do it alone" state of mind was founded. The formation of this attitude began much earlier though. Before both of my parents remarried, they were consumed in an ugly divorce that transcended into a custody battle. As a four-year-old, I witnessed my father being violent toward my mom all for the intended purpose of preventing her from taking me away.

"Bitch, you will *never* take my son away from me," he shouted as he manhandled her. Even as youngster I knew my father loved me. I have fond memories of kicking a soccer ball around together when I was just two years old, of him tossing me in the air, putting me in the backpack as he jogged the rugged terrain of the back trails of the neighborhood. But the sight of him brutalizing my mom terrified me.

"Daddy, daddy, no! Get off of mommy! Daddy, *no!*" I screamed as I punched his buttocks in an attempt to save her. To my horror, I watched him hold her down as she broke through the glass of my second story bedroom window. Thankfully, he didn't push her all the way through, though he could have. At the time, I didn't know if my mom was hurt or not, but in the middle of my sobbing and yelling, he stopped and looked down at me. His angry face turned sad with the realization that he was not just hitting his wife, but also his three-year-old son who felt every blow in his tiny, gentle spirit. He dropped his hands and walked away, his head down in shame. I stared at my mommy as she cried.

"Mommy, are you okay?" I asked. She pulled herself away from the shattered window, slid off my desk and stomped, all five-foot-two of her, out of my room into the hallway and picked up a gigantic rectangular cardboard box. At that age everything looks much bigger, but I remember her straining to grasp this box as she grunted, tossing it down the stairs, smashing my father in the back of his head as he made his way down.

I was never the same after that incident. Every other weekend my father would try to pick me up for weekend visits, but I would hide in the closet, frightened of the anger that I had witnessed.

I have often wondered what was in that box, so one day, decades later, I asked my mother. "Your father's clothes," she explained. "We were separating, and he was moving out. He was trying to take you away from me. You are correct in your memories, but it's the order you got wrong. Your father and I were upstairs, and you and your sister were down stairs. He was beating me up. He walked away and that's when I picked up the first thing that I saw. It was the box of his clothes. That thing was so heavy," she burst into laughter, finally now able to laugh at that which had made us both cry. "You were downstairs, which is why you remember seeing me throw the box at him. And, yes, then he ran up the stairs after me, and I ran into your room. You chased him up the stairs and..." She stopped and looked down. "You stopped him from beating me up." I could see that she now understood the effects their feuds had on me, though she didn't at the time.

In time, I grew to once again trust my father's embrace. We developed a healthy bond as he served as my soccer coach and my sister's softball coach. He spent his days at work and his nights involved in our extracurricular activities.

These two images of my dad, a loving father but abusive husband, created a house divided that could not stand. That little boy never stopped fighting to save his mommy. I couldn't save her then, and in the years to come, I couldn't save her despite my prayers to a silent God. Thus, an inner battle had been waged and buried deep within my psyche; the bitter fruit of which we would all eat from during my adolescent years and, to a degree, for the rest of our lives.

My father took my mother to court every year in an attempt to win custody until finally, after six years of battling, my mother remarried and moved Sandra and me to Miami, Florida in 1987. I was nine. "I'm pregnant, and I just got married," blurted my mom one day as we were eating dinner at Taco Bell in Pontiac, Michigan. "We're moving to Miami. What do you think?" I chomped down on my Taco Supreme, stared out the window and shrugged. What could I say? The only way the courts would allow her to take my sister and me away from my father was if she were to remarry. Since she was already pregnant, she and her fiancé got married at the courthouse without telling us. Her new husband was to finish his medical schooling in Florida, so we were dragged along.

When we left for Miami, it destroyed my father, and, to a certain degree, the strength of our relationship. I wrote him often and yearned for his presence. I did not understand what was going on at the time, but now, decades later, I understand how drug abuse and pain influenced my mother in her decision-making. She despised my father so much that her pain and anger blinded her to the fact that taking my sister and I away from my father would not only hurt him, but it would jeopardize our destinies; for the effects of a fatherless home are far-reaching.

I never did develop a father-son relationship with my stepfather. How could I? As I reflect, I now question how a man could have a nine-year-old boy's best interest in mind by taking him away from a healthy relationship with his biological father. He operated out of self-interest from the inception, and the residual effect was a disconnection between a father and his only son, a disconnection that would prove deadly.

In that move was the seed to my destiny, for along with the disconnection to my father came my mom and step-dad's cocaine abuse, and, invariably, a disconnection to the whole, to life, love, security and safety. Cocaine was the theme of the 80s, and the dealing of it was heavily based in Miami, Florida. My mom started using drugs when I was in fifth grade, though I didn't know that at the time. When she was high on cocaine, she became paranoid. She carried a chrome .38-caliber pistol around the house on her hip tucked inside the waistband of her pants as she peered out the windows, thinking people were breaking in. This was my normal day at the age of eleven. My older sister Sandra knew what was going on, and she responded as most teenagers would: she rebelled. She began to run away and stay at the house of friends who hid her. As my mom's cocaine use and subsequent paranoia became more frequent, she claimed to see my sister in trees and on rooftops. She would yell at the top of her lungs, "Sandra! Sandra! Sandra, is that you?"

As an eleven-year-old, I was afraid and confused. I questioned others in an effort to understand. "What's wrong with my mom?" I would ask my stepfather, but he would just shrug his shoulders and walk away. Others blamed Sandra's running away for the depression and paranoia in my mom. I believed that story for almost two years, until one day I overheard my aunt say something shocking to my cousin Tone.

"It's my fault. I wish I would have never given her cocaine." That one piece of information was the switch that began the transformation of sadness into anger. I no longer blamed Sandra. Now I blamed my mom. I felt betrayed. I had trusted her and felt like she had sold me out, and Sandra, too. This sadness that transformed into a destructive anger would ravage all in its wake.

Eventually, my mother and stepfather moved us back to Michigan when I was twelve, but by then, my father had remarried and rekindled a sense of family, of belonging, of companionship with another woman and her daughter. At first, this did not affect me as much as it did my sister. Of course, had my father's second wife had a son instead of a daughter, I'm sure I would have felt replaced as my sister felt.

During their engagement, my father's soon-to-be wife won me over, an eleven-year-old boy, with food, sweets, and laughter. After the wedding, however, the wooing quickly ceased, and her treatment of me involved a lot of mental and emotional abuse. For example, when I tried to call my father, she wouldn't pass on my messages, which he would then respond with, "You never call me anymore." She also frequently chastised me for the smallest of childish infractions. Worst of all, she drove a wedge between a father and a son, a wedge that became the driving force of pain for many years.

At thirteen, in the middle of eighth grade, I had a paradigm shift from victim to victor mindset. Or so I thought. Up to that point in my life, my father had always taken me to get my hair cut once a month, like clockwork, except for the years we lived in Florida. Once we moved back to Michigan, though, my parents were divorced and I only saw him every other weekend. We bonded during these trips to the barbershop. Though my father and I were close, I kept the drug abuse and dysfunction a secret. As I reflect, I understand that I had personal motives for doing so. First and foremost, I was loyal to my mom. I knew that my dad would use this to attack her in court or in public. At the tender age of twelve, I *knew* this, for I had witnessed it. Second, I didn't want to live with my father because of the abusiveness of his second wife and the freedom that I experienced at my mom's. I hung around with guys who were gangsters, drug dealers, and serious men of the street. That lifestyle held allure for me. Thus, I had to keep it a secret, or my father would use it to gain full custody.

As my mom's drug abuse worsened, however, my visits to my father's became more frequent, which only created a larger space for my stepmother's abuse. Since her abuse was merely verbal, I could deal with a non-loving, non-familial combatant over witnessing the decay of my mother's being, her essence, her spirit. Those weekends were an escape from death, from hell. For me, death and hell were interchangeable. Both lacked the love of God, which is the energy of life.

Though in a sense I was jumping from the fire into the frying pan, I did not understand this until my father began deviating from his normal fatherly tradition. "I'm taking you to get your haircut! You hear me, boy?" had been ingrained in my mind since the age of four after my mom cut my long curls off to spite my father. I yearned for and embraced that fatherly possessiveness, of ownership. I loved it. To know that from which you came and to whom you belong provides a foundation for the shaping of your vision for who you are to become. When a child does not know who they are, then anything can be ascribed to them. My father fought for me for many years, until finally, his fighting spirit grew weary. "Son, I'm sorry, but I can no longer take you to get your hair cut. Your mother raised the child support again, so I cannot afford it," my father staring out the car window, unable to look me in the eye. I nodded my head, reassuring him that it was okay, as I tucked away my anger. My father had been remarried now for about three years. I knew that his new wife and stepdaughter vacationed lavishly and went on shopping sprees. Later I found out that his wife was also suffering from the affliction of cocaine abuse and alcoholism.

The denial of a haircut by my dad was the denial of a crucial piece of nurturing that I desperately needed. We used to spend hours bonding on those days. He would breathe life into me during these moments. I yearned for his fatherly guidance and support to provide me with the safety and security needed for the development of my young mind, as I was escaping from the sadness and dysfunction under my mother's roof. Up to this point, my father had provided a shade of protection from the dysfunction that awaited me in my mother's home. The loss of that father-son connection slowly killed that little boy's sense of security, safety, and love.

I grew to hate being at my father's, but I shook it off so that I did not have to deal with seeing my mom high. The hair cut incident led to other monetary "restrictions," such as my father not paying half of the tuition charged by the Pontiac Catholic school they were sending me to. With the monetary restrictions mounting as a feud to contest child support, attitudes worsened. I continued to visit my father through the middle of the eighth grade, until one day he reprimanded me, telling me that I needed to be nicer to my stepmother. He had just gotten home from his eighty-hour work week. On that day when he reprimanded me, however, I didn't even look up from the television, and he walked away, figuratively and literally. At that very moment, at the age of thirteen, I vowed that I would leave my father's house and never come back. Years later, when he was trying to make amends, he confessed that she was using cocaine heavily behind his back and wiped out his bank account.

Once I realized that I could no longer seek my father's abode as a place of refuge from the horrors of home, a seed was planted within my mind, a belief system that said if I am to make it, if I am to be strong and not be hurt, then I must do it alone. I told myself that day that I would not depend on anyone anymore. No longer would I feel this vulnerable, naïve, or weak. No longer would I allow *these people*, as I now categorized my parents, to hurt me. No longer would I depend on them for the safety and security I so desperately needed. A seething anger grew into a mindset of putting money over miracles. I stopped praying to a God who I could not see and began to pursue a false god who provided me with basics to feel secure, safe, and powerful by having control over who or what could hurt me.

With this intention set, I started dealing drugs, and within a few years I digressed to robbery. I robbed both customer and supplier. It was easy for me to rationalize my aggression and violence toward such people. The pain of despising my mother was easier to handle as aggression and anger. That is how I learned to cope. Life was hard, and I blamed my mom, an addict, for much of this pain. Thus, robbing my customers was easy. I didn't respect my mom, so why would I respect my customers? The pain that I felt for my mom grew into a murderous rage at her drug dealer.

His name was James. At least I assumed James, her longtime friend, was the one who was pushing it to her. He had been the neighborhood dope man for decades, doubling up at General Motors at the same time. Starting at around the age of fourteen, I fantasized about killing James. I did not have a plan, just a seed of desire rooted in pain. By sixteen, I had the car and the means, but by then, my desires and values had changed. I wanted money *and* revenge. My big plan was to rob James of his money and his life . . . just as he robbed me of my mom. But first I needed to be sure that he was the one. On several occasions, I parked at night down the street from his house, waiting to see if my mom would come over to buy drugs, but she never came. It wasn't long after that someone else took care of James for me.

James lived in a small house in the heart of Pontiac. His girl was a professional heister who boosted the highest end name brand clothes, suits, jackets, and jewelry. She had been arrested over ten times, but she was good at what she did. You name it, she had it: Gucci, Prada, Italian Suits up to $10,000. She and James were comfortable and in their own little Bonnie and Clyde type paradise until late one night, as James exited a poker game where he, the money magnet, had won more than his opponents thought he deserved. James was robbed, killed, and hung on a fence right outside that after-hours club in Pontiac. He hung there, as an example for others not to shine too much. I no longer had to hunt James down.

In a way, I had stopped searching for him anyhow. By that time, it was more about business than a personal vendetta. At sixteen, if it didn't make dollars, then it didn't make sense. So, when Samuel, the neighborhood dope man, crossed my path, there was no question that I was going to rob him. I had robbed others by force and by gun; however, the guns that I had used were always pellet guns or filled with blanks, even though they looked and felt just like a real, loaded gun. I was aggressive, so the fear I ignited within my victims—drug dealers and buyers—would paralyze them. This time, though, I was robbing a high-level drug dealer who was six foot seven to my five-foot-seven boyish frame, so I didn't want to take any chances.

"I can't let you go into this robbery with a broken gun, lil' bro," insisted Nick. It made sense. What if Samuel had a gun? I couldn't go into this unprepared, so I left in pursuit of my sword, my destiny, my proverbial rite of passage bestowed upon male adolescents in acknowledgement of their transition into manhood. Or so I believed. I would take that bag of dope and money from Samuel. I would strip him of his safety, his security, just as it had been stripped from me, for we can only give what we have. I was a lost boy, angry with an unseen Father (God) for not answering his prayers to heal his mother and angry with a seen father for abandoning a boy who was quietly drowning in his emptiness.

I left Nick's house with scrambled thoughts on how to get a pistol quickly, and then it hit me. I reflected on what had happened years ago when I was thirteen. My mom was visibly more paranoid that day than usual. Her eyes were wide, and she was grinding her teeth. I hated seeing her like that. I hated not being able to help her, to heal her. It must have been some bad dope because she kept my baby sisters' ages one and two, and me, trapped in the car for hours parked in the driveway of our house. She kept pointing to the windows of our upstairs, asking, "You see? You see them?" I'd been living with the stress and anxiety of her constant paranoia for so long that talking my mom down had become a normal part of my life. I finally convinced her to let us go into the house.

Once inside, she sat on the couch with the gun out staring at the dark path of stairs. Most of the time I could not tell if she was hallucinating. There were odd happenings in our home. It had been formerly owned by the Catholic Church, which it used to house nuns and priests. When we moved in, Sandra stayed in the basement where she would conduct séances with an Ouija board for hours upon hours with groups of "believers." Some schools of thought say that such things are nonsense, while others would argue that such practices open portals to other dimensions.

What I can say is that I did, personally, experience unexplainable things, from the sound of opera singing so high-pitched that it was almost deafening to broken glass shattered inside the kitchen with not one object moved out of place. Thus, it was challenging to differentiate between my mother's paranoia from prolonged cocaine abuse or demonic hauntings. Either way, I lived in constant fear. My stepfather was neither a crutch to lean on nor an emotional support. He showed no interest in nurturing my sister or me.

As she sat there with her gun in hand, bags under her eyes from lack of sleep from having two toddlers, I worried. She did not look normal nor was she acting like her usual self. I remember that we argued. I'd been feeling sad that her paranoia had become a normal response, but that day my sadness turned into anger. I'd had it. I wanted to go upstairs, but she wouldn't let me. "There is no one up there!" I yelled at the top of my lungs. As I attempted to go up the stairs, she raised the gun, pointing it at me. I raised my chin. "You gonna shoot *me* now?" I said it in a low tone, seething with anger. I grabbed the closest thing to me, a toy lawn mower that my little sister played with and threw it at a large glass-covered painting. "Shoot me!" I yelled, over and over and over. "Shoot me! Shoot!" as tears poured down my face. I was tired of the paranoia and the quietness of a house that oozed sadness and death instead of joy and life. I was tired of being left behind to witness my mother's downward spiral into depression and numbness.

She lowered the gun and chuckled. I grabbed the phone and ran upstairs, dialing my grandma's phone number, frantically crying, "Mama, my mom is paranoid and pointed the gun at me. Please tell Papa to come at take the guns from her." Within the hour, my grandfather, Papa Mango as we called him, left work from the General Motors plant and raced to our house. He removed both of the guns that day.

Her erratic behavior continued all the way through my tenth-grade year until finally, after her body and mind could take it no longer, she sought help. She curbed that addiction but began to use alcohol to numb her pain. Some years later it was revealed to me that it was not only my mother who suffered from cocaine abuse, but my stepfather, as well. My mother kept it quiet and compounded the dysfunction until one night, while she nursed one child and spoon-fed another, my stepfather stayed out all night with no justification as to his whereabouts. That was the seed of separation that not only divided the essence of their marriage, but also tore apart the very foundation my mother attempted to stand upon. My mother was never the same after that.

So that day, August 6, 1995, it hit me. Maybe my grandfather still had some of those guns. I could get one of those guns for the robbery, so I raced to a payphone to call my call my cousin Tone. Tone was eighteen years old then and had a passion for baseball. Tall, strong, and built for the majors, Tone would have made it to the pros if he'd simply had the mentorship, the fatherly guidance that we both needed, but his father and mother chose sex, drugs, and alcohol over him, just as many of the baby boomers did. Instead, he was dealing drugs, pursuing women, and abusing alcohol and drugs, just like me.

At that time in 1995, beepers (pagers) were our main source of contacting others with payphones as our conduit of verbal communication. He was home. I explained to him my plan to rob Sam, the dope man, as those who knew him in Pontiac, but Tone didn't give me the answer I wanted to hear. "You don't know where the guns are? What the fuck!" I shouted.

He quietly listened and then said, "I don't think Papa (our grandfather) even remembers where he put them," said Tone. "But my boy Jay has some guns for sale. I will hook it up if you take me with you, and we can split the money and dope." I thought about it for a few seconds.

"Okay, but don't go pussy on me. Where you gonna be at?"
Though Tone lived with my mom's parents in Pontiac, as most
Sundays, he was going to my mom's house in West Bloomfield to
visit with the whole family, as was our custom. Now that my mother
was cleaning herself up, this opened the doors for my grandparents
to come by and visit more frequently. My mom was very close to
her father, Papa Mango. "Alright," I said, "but Sam wants to meet
soon, so I'm going to meet you out at my mom's house so we both
can be on the phone when you talk to Jay. That way there won't be
any misunderstandings, and he won't be spooked about me calling
or showing up without you."

At this age, my grandparents had started separating my cousin
and me. Maybe they saw the dark path that I had been on over the
past several years. In eighth grade, I earned an academic scholarship, withstanding my mom's serious cocaine addiction and my
father's profound absence, but I was also growing increasingly hostile and apathetic. By ninth grade, I quit trying to succeed academ-
ically. I sought refuge from my pain by chasing money rather than
pursuing inner growth and achievement. My pain for what *was*
outweighed my hope for what *could be*. In an attempt to salvage
my future, my grandparents came to my mother's house to take me
to live with them in the summer before I was to enter ninth grade,
just as they had done for my cousin, but my mother wouldn't allow
it. As I reflect, I believe it would have been an acceptance of her
failure as a mother had she relented. Now, three years later, their
only recourse was to separate us, since I could no longer be saved.
Along with the fact that my father stopped communicating with
me, this was yet another loss at a pivotal time in my development.

Now at my mother's house, in the privacy of my room, my
cousin and I called Jay. "Yo, waddup? This is Tone. Yeah. You still
got those pistols? Yeah. Well, for my cousin and me. Yeah. Well, I
can't go with him to pick them up, so I am sending him. Consider

it for me. Don't worry about getting paid. We got you." Because my grandparents did not like for my cousin and I to hang out, I had to leave him there with the plan to come back before the meeting with Samuel.

I kissed mom on the cheek before running out the door. She was giving a dinner party to some guests, the Allende family who had recently moved from Puerto Rico. Mr. Allende was looking to establish his own medical practice in Michigan, seeing as his youngest daughter had been accepted to the University of Michigan. They had two daughters, Brenda, nineteen, and Zulma, twenty-two. I looked at the nineteen-year-old and just shook my head. She was gorgeous but clearly out of my league with her full-ride to the University of Michigan. She even had a Spanish accent and a body to die for, but I was just an eleventh grader angry at the world so I did not even consider wasting my time. Little did I know how important she would become to me.

August 6, 1995, approximately 7:00 p.m., Jay's House

It was a beautiful, late summer evening. As I walked up to Jay's door, I noticed a massive construction project in which new apartment buildings were being built. Bulldozers were parked throughout the area with piles of dirt to the left and right and leveled land anticipating its development. I reached Jay's apartment door, and it opened as if he had been watching for me through the window. Jay was an athletically built white guy with a charismatic smile that welcomed me in.

"Tone has spoken highly of you," he said. "You are welcome in my home, lil' brother," speaking to me like Nick did, as if he was some mentor sent to guide me toward the light. I saw the guns laid out on the table as I scanned the rooms, doors and exits without him even noticing. My heart was racing, but through Ishinru, a Japanese style of street fighting, I had been trained to use my adrenaline as fuel, and I always carried a fighting blade with me. My father introduced me to Ishinru after I was repeatedly suspended from school beginning in the seventh grade for acts of aggression and fighting. Serendipitously, this was just before he took a three-year absence from my life. My sensei developed into a father figure, as a void was left unfulfilled. I trained voraciously, both inside the dojo and out, and by the age of fourteen, I was no longer allowed to fight kids my age because of the level of aggression with which I fought. From fourteen to sixteen, I only sparred with older, trained men, and specifically, the lead instructor. Ishinru consumed my life during that time until the streets won out. It was my "why," my reason for living, for moving on. When you have a *why*, then you can get through any *what*.

But the ability to harm objects or people was not a good mixture for a troubled teen fueled by self-consuming anger at being abandoned and traumatized. I began to lash out at my mom by punching holes in the doors and walls. I would yell, "Kill yourself!" as I destroyed things in the house, no longer the victimized youth who had not heard from his God. No, I became a victimizer who sought power and money as a means of control. In reality, it was as a means of safety and security, regardless of how delusional or futile my attempts were. The straw that broke the proverbial camel's back for my mother was when she arrived home from running errands late one day, thus preventing me from making it in time for Ishinru training. I began yelling at her and punching holes in the walls. "You are never allowed to go to martial arts again until you change your attitude!" she shouted. "You are just like your father!" This was a mantra I had heard a thousand times over. Once Ishinru was taken from me at age sixteen, I went downhill quickly, for I had lost my *why* . . . and, the only positive male role model in my life.

Keeping my Ishinru training in mind, I watched Jay's chest as he breathed, looking for signs of extreme nervousness or excitement as I asked him various questions. By sixteen, I had already been in many situations that had gone "wrong," and I learned the signs to look in highly stressful situations that could lead to conflict. I had learned from my Sensei, who had both street and structured fighting experience, that heavy breathing could be a sign of deception or anticipation of action, for the body is fueling the veins with oxygen and adrenaline. I had to spec this guy out for myself, as I had never put much trust in my cousin Tone's judgment. He had always been a bit of a sucker even though he had grown up in the small, hardened inner city of Pontiac, Michigan. He had been sheltered and coddled and was naturally naïve, a dangerous mix in an anti-social environment like Pontiac of the 80s and 90s.

"I only have experience with revolvers," I told him, which was a half-truth, in reference to the revolver that my mother would carry throughout the house as she held my little sister, paranoid from the cocaine.

"Bro', you want the .45 caliber pistol for robbing this guy. That way if he pulls a strap out, you won't lose. This .45 will tear him in half," said Jay.

"How much you want for the .45?" I asked.

"These are my roommate's. He wants $200 for the .45. Tone said he would take care of the payment, so don't worry about the money," Jay said.

"Good. This mothafucka is huge, and he's the dope man, so you know he's strapped," I theorized, blinded by the facades of movies like *Menace to Society* and *New Jack City* that glamorized the dope game, and, invariably, the stick-up game. It's as old as sweet American Pie, from the days of the pilgrims to the days of Baby Face Nelson and Al Capone. My culture's paradigm said it was okay by the street code to rob the drug dealer: "You in the game?

Then you fair game. Period." That was my core belief at sixteen. I'd already been selling dope for three years. I had *become* a menace to society.

"Well, lil' bro, you about to get 'Shootin a Mothafucka 101' by big bro" Jay," he said with a cigarette in his mouth and a huge grin. I looked him in the eye, wondering if I'd have to kill him, as well.

At sixteen, there were two images of Mario: One image was that of a "good" kid who had a lot of potential but just hung around the wrong people. I had just completed eleventh grade with an average GPA. The teachers either hated me or loved me. I have always had a desire to make others smile and, in that pursuit, I have made many relationships. "You have charisma," most of the elders would say. My mother, desperate to find me a means of salvation, placed me in West Bloomfield High School, an affluent school in the suburbs of Oakland County. The principal today, Mr. Watson, had just come out of graduate school and was then just a history teacher. He quickly became popular among both staff and teachers. I gravitated toward his sincerity and genuineness, which provided the security and positive male mentorship that was lacking in my life. He used to take me out to Ann Arbor on weekends to play basketball with his brother and other older, pillars of the community type men. The teachers and parents around me saw potential, but all I could see was pain.

On the other hand, the other image, among my peers, was that of the dope man who didn't take shit from anyone, regardless of age, position, or strength. Many loved me, but just as many hated me. I made the boys envious because the girls gave me added attention, and because I was literally a salesman, I mingled with the Jocks, the Jews, the Chaldeans, the Preps, and the Trailer Parks. I was an anomaly: I was the only Latino who spoke like he was "black," was fluent in Spanish, and who socialized with literally every social group. Yet, I looked at them as either customers or "marks" who had been fed with a silver spoon.

My family did not speak of the sadness and dysfunction that occurred behind our walls. At the time, I didn't know that many such families existed, families who projected an image of wholeness but who were completely broken. The "well-off" families were battling demons just as we were, just on a different economic level. My parents were no different in that they were simply trying to cope with the stresses of life, but as I express these thoughts I cannot help but re-center my being with the mantra, "Let he who has not sinned throw the first stone."

Jay and I walked outside his apartment building to a vacant area where the construction had been in progress. He shot the .45, deafening me for a moment. The gunshot forced his hand to jerk back. This let me know that there was power behind that machine. "You want to make sure that you're firm in your grip. Don't let him grab it from you," he instructed as if he'd had experience. He unloaded it, repeated the process and shot it rapidly again. He sped up the pace until I got the process down through observation.

"Now, it's your turn. Show me," he said and handed the butt of the pistol to me. I reach out for what seemed like a mile, an eternity, almost as if I was having an out-of-body experience. In that fraction of a second, I knew that my life would never be the same, and not for the better, yet I couldn't stop the trajectory of my actions nor of the bullets; both were on a path toward unending pain, heartache, and confusion.

Bang! First shot. *Bang!* Second shot. My heart rate increased. "*Aim*, bro'. Remember, it's either you or him!" *Bang, bang, bang, bang, bang!* The deafening noise continued until I finished the clip. The emptiness within was filled with a false sense of self, of ego, of pain transformed into anger as I sought control, sought power. And, indeed, I felt powerful beyond measure. I felt like I could make it on my own.

CHAPTER 2

VENGEANCE IS MINE

August 6, 7:23 p.m., Jay's Apartment

A S THE SUN SUNK LOWER on the horizon, I watched the cloud of dirt that arose from the gunshots. "I'm ready now. I need to make a call," I said as I reached for my pager to retrieve Sam's cell number. Only drug traffickers and doctors had cell phones back in 1995. I paged Sam from Jay's phone.

"This Sam. Who dis?" Sam said with his signature opener.

"Waddup? It's Mario. I'm ready to meet," I said arrogantly, always using my real name, never a nickname as most hoodlums adopted for protection from both law enforcement and victims. I wanted people to know who I was. I wanted to make my mark. As a youth, I simply did not want to be hurt anymore, but unfortunately my only avenue to do so was to hurt others. As the renowned teacher, speaker, author, and former prisoner Shaka Senghor says, "Hurt people *hurt* people" (Senghor, 2016).

Although I was supposed to take Tone with me, I theorized that he would probably just get in the way. As I reflect twenty years later, I realize that it was my greed that allowed the meeting to not include Tone.

"Meet me at Northern in about fifteen minutes," said Sam, as he hung up the phone without a goodbye. Northern was our local high school. I looked up at Jay.

"It's on," I said. Jay handed me the .45.

"It's loaded bro! Don't shoot your dick off," he said with a grin, a lit cigarette in his mouth. I grabbed the .45 and put it in my waistband.

"I'll be back," I said as if to quiet my own uncertainties. Sam and I had never met at Northern or any remote place. It was always in the parking lot of a party store or restaurant. This bothered me and raised my level of unease, for now I wondered if perhaps he was planning to rob me.

August 6, 8:05 p.m., Pontiac Northern parking lot A

As I circled the school, I could see people playing tennis and walking the track. There were two parking lots on the premises. One parking lot had cars from the tennis players and joggers. The other one was up on a hill, behind the school, intended for teachers and staff; this one was empty and away from the earshot of those enjoying the facilities.

I parked in the busy parking lot, lowering myself in the seat as I watched the tennis game, the jogger, the dog walker. I parked strategically, at an angle, so I could see the entrance of both parking lots. Finally, after what seemed an eternity, Sam pulled up beside me in his signature white Jimmy with tinted windows and shiny, chrome rims. He got out of the car and walked over to my window with his six-foot-seven-inch long frame. "Waddup, doe?" he asked and handed me a small brown bag that had about a half ounce. "This is the stuff. I have the pounds in the car. See if you like it," he said in reference to the sample bag. I opened it up as I peaked at his waist, trying to see if he was carrying a gun. "Don't forget, I want

$2,500 for each one," he said. When he told me what he was going to charge me per pound, I was offended. *I'm going to take that shit from him,* I arrogantly thought. I looked up from the sample bag with a bud of marijuana in my hand, holding it up to my nose as I looked him straight in the eye and winked.

"Of course, big bro," I said with a grin. "Okay, I'm gonna roll a lil' somethin' up outta' this bag. Let's go up to that parking lot to make the exchange," I said and motioned to the parking lot that was overlooking the tennis courts and track. He peered over his shoulder and squinted to see the location.

"Bet," he said as he made his way back to his car. I pulled out some rolling papers and a magazine from the center counsel. "This shit is like taking candy from a baby," I murmured as I played 2pac's song "Dear Mama." I calmly watched the white Jimmy crawl its way to the top of the other parking lot as I rolled a joint. I lit it, took a long puff, and then blew it toward the windshield.

August 6, 8:21 p.m., Pontiac Northern parking lot B

I pulled up to Sam, numb from the joint, hopped out of the car and opened Sam's rear passenger door to access the stash. I felt like I was moving in slow motion. There was a large bag. I opened it as Sam started to say something about the quality of the weed. "It's good shit, huh? I got it . . . " The sound of my heartbeat drowned out Samuel's words. I had never been so scared in my life, and yet it was this fear that always pushed me through whatever was before me. Finally, after acting as if the quality of the weed was question-able, I reached behind my back and pulled out the .45-caliber and raised it, pointing it in Sam's direction. All in one motion, Sam stretched out his long arm toward the gun as I pulled the trigger one time. *Bang!* I pulled again. *Click.* The gun jammed. "Fuck," I mumbled as I scrambled toward the ground, making my way around the back of the Jimmy, anticipating a gun battle. I frantically tried to unjam the gun with no success. I flipped the gun around so I could use the handle as a makeshift weapon. My heart was pounding, and my palms were sweaty as my fight instinct kicked in. I tried to peek through the limo tint back window, but I couldn't see a thing.

Suddenly, from my peripheral vision, I was startled to see an explosive sprint by Sam toward the tennis courts. I walked a few steps in that direction as he peeked over his shoulder. "And don't come back!" I shouted as I pointed the jammed gun in his direction. I ran to the driver's side door that was hanging open, pulled the keys from the ignition and threw them into the bushes about thirty feet away so that he couldn't give chase. I grabbed his cell phone, charger, and a bag of CDs and tossed everything into the large dope bag in the back, then jumped into my car and drove off, peering into the rearview mirror as I thought, *like taking candy from a baby.*

August 6, 1995, approximately 9:00 p.m., Jay's Apartment

Knock, knock, knock! I beat on Jay's door, breathing heavily. Jay finally opened the door. I barged in and threw the .45 on his couch. "The gun jammed," I yelled. "You almost got me *killed!*"

"What do you mean?" Jay responded in disbelief.

"I pulled out the strap and told him not to move, but he lunged forward, so I shot one time, but then it jammed. He ran away, so I couldn't get him. Now it's gonna be war. You just signed our death warrants," I snapped, breathing heavily. "If he comes for me, I come for you. So, the way I see it, you better step up to the plate," I growled as I glared at him. Pure bitch. "Give me that .25 caliber I was looking at earlier." I grabbed the .25-caliber from him and hurried off. Samuel would be back to settle what I had started.

Of that I was sure. And when he did, I would be ready. I had a plane to catch for Miami in the morning and a bag of dope to sell before then. I would deal with him later.

I left Jay's house feeling liberated. Drugs had significantly deteriorated the relationships within my family, and in some twisted sense of a subconscious reasoning and rationalization, I felt a sense of retribution and power that led to a false sense of security. It was as if my actions had spoken for the twelve-year-old boy who could not protect himself from the world around him.

I then drove to my Uncle John's house, my father's brother. My uncle was a Pontiac city councilman at the time, and I needed to get a speeding ticket "taken care of," so to speak, before I left for Miami. Since the ticket was from a Pontiac police department, I figured it was worth a shot to see if he knew the officer. Plus, this was the excuse that I used to take off from my mom's house in such a rush. He was my excuse and my alibi, literally. My uncle and his family were later called by my defense as alibi witnesses. The time that the prosecution claimed I was robbing Samuel, I was actually already at my uncle's house. It was merely an argument of timing. My uncle and his family were forced into hiding for quite some time when the news revealed that he would be an alibi witness for my case. Sam's family had put out death threats to anyone testifying on my behalf. When the threats became credible, the county sheriffs came in the middle of the night to carry them off into protective custody. My aunt hated me for years because of this frightening experience.

On that peaceful Sunday evening when my father's family would gather and have dinner, I sat on the TV room floor watching the Simpsons and discussing the ticket with my Uncle John. "So you think you can get this thing thrown out?"

My Uncle John was always funny and loving. "We'll see, little Mario," he said, smiling as he usually did. His world as he knew it could be crumbling to pieces, but my Uncle John wouldn't let you know it. He was poised and calculating with an emotional intelligence that befits any leader. I sat there with my uncle and his family, my older sister Sandra and her boyfriend Nick, now a father-to-be, watching television and making small talk. After about half an hour, I said my goodbyes and made eye contact with Nick, communicating in a way that he would understand to meet me outside.

I waited in my car as Nick finally made his way outside. My eye contact conveyed secrecy, thus, I knew that he would be nonchalant about coming outside. He walked up to the driver's side window as the car was running. "Bro, I robbed that guy, and I got some pounds in the back. You wanna get rid of it for me?" He squinted.

"How much you want for them?"

"Give me $1,250 a pound."

"How long do I have to get you the money?" he asked, always careful with the details.

"I come back from Miami in ten days. You have ten days," I said, sensing a newfound respect coming from him.

"You got it," he said with a grin. "Come by later tonight to drop it off. Just beep once, and I will slip out the back door so your sister doesn't know what we are doing," he said, always cautious about my sister Sandra.

With business taken care of, I drove off to pick up my girlfriend Theresa. We then drove to my house to pick up my cousin Tone who had stayed behind when my grandparents returned to their home in Pontiac. As I approached my house, I turned off the headlights and quietly pulled into the driveway. I honked once, and Tone slipped out the front door and jumped in the back. "Wassup? Why didn't you come and get me earlier?" he demanded. I slowly drove off, turning the headlights back on.

"He wanted to meet right then and there. I was still deep into

Pontiac with Jay showing me how to use the strap," I said casually. I noticed his body language loosen up a bit, but he was staring out the window. I could see he was upset.

"Who wanted to meet?" Theresa asked as she lit a cigarette. "And for what?" she said, raising one eyebrow.

"Nothing, babe," I said, pulling out a bag of weed as we parked in the lot of a little neighborhood park. "Here, roll this up," I said and handed her the bag of weed and papers.

It was a warm, late summer night, and we were three teenagers disconnected from ourselves let alone our families. We each had a story of pain and struggle with being just kids. I replayed "Dear Mama" on Tupac's CD. We could all relate to pain with our moms. Theresa finished one joint and lit another. She took a long puff as I watched her gorgeous silhouette with the brightness of the moon behind her. So much potential and, yet, so much pain. Theresa lived with her middle school principal. We called her Mrs. "G," but Theresa used the affectionate term Uma. Everyone who met her said that Mrs. "G" was an angel on earth. It was said that she could never have children because she was a guardian angel, protecting and caring for thousands of children. Theresa passed me the joint and noticed that I had been staring. "What are you thinking about?" she asked, grinning ear to ear.

"You're beautiful," I said. She blushed, as usual, and started to roll another joint.

"So, what happened?" whispered Tone from the back seat. I passed the joint to him and blew out.

"He reached for a gun so I had to," I whispered, trying to lip the words more than speak them.

"You had to ..." he said, making a motion as if firing a gun so that Theresa wouldn't hear. I nodded.

"Who reached for a gun, Mario?" Theresa said.

"Nothing, baby, don't worry about it," I said, trying to dismiss her fears.

"I'm afraid, Mario. I don't want you to go to jail," she said, as I began to laugh hysterically.

"Babe, I ain't going to jail. Now light that other joint." We hung out listening to music, smoking, and talking about life's twists and turns.

A little later, we dropped Theresa off at Mrs. G's house where she was living at the time. Our goodbye was intense. Theresa and I were in love at a time in our lives when neither of us had a loving home life. Thus, the effect we had on each other was significant. I was to leave for Miami the next day so our goodbye was a little longer than usual. I got back into the car. "She still thinks that you are going to Puerto Rico?" Tone asked.

"Yeah," I said and shook my head in regret. I started dating Theresa after I had plans to go to Miami to meet with a cute crush I had met earlier that year. There was no sense in canceling a trip to Miami. I slowly drove us home as we listened in silence the words from Tupac's hit *Me Against the World*. It was fitting.

August 6, 1995, approximately 11:30 p.m., Mom's
House, West Bloomfield, Michigan

Tone slipped past me as I walked into my mother's bedroom where she was watching the local news on TV. She never even noticed that Tone had been gone. The caption on the television read, "Black male shot and killed behind Pontiac Northern High School." I crumbled inside. "Good night, mom. I love you," I said, as if I hadn't noticed the television.

"Do you see why I do not like you hanging out in Pontiac anymore, Mario?" my Cuban-born mother said in her heavy accent.

"Aw, don't worry, mama. Ain't nothin' gonna happen to me," I said stoically as I leaned over her bed and kissed her forehead. "Goodnight, mama."

"Goodnight, *mijo*." As I walked down my mother's hallway, I may as well have been walking toward the death chamber. I felt to my very bones that heaviness was sure to come upon me, a heaviness that was sure to break me.

"How did all this happen?" I uttered to myself. "If Nick would have just given me the broken gun," I reasoned in disbelief. I became nauseous from the realization that I had just taken a man's life.

I got back to my room and sat on my bed, staring off into the moonlight that shone through my window. Tone was lying on the floor next to my bed with a pillow and a blanket.

"Wassup, cuz'?" asked Tone.

Still in shock, I mumbled, almost inaudibly, "He's dead. He was shot."

"What's up? What did you hear?" he asked, sitting up with a frown.

"Mom was watching the news. It showed a black man getting shot and dying behind Northern," I said, panic now turning into relief. I'd left Jay's place with a .25 caliber pistol and an understanding that war was sure to be fought in the streets. Now with Sam dead, there would be no war. He shook his head.

"That's fucked up, bro'. What're you going to do?"

"Fucked up? Are you crazy? Now there won't be a war," I responded. Tone looked at me and sat there in thought.

"You're right," he conceded. "Now you don't have to worry about him coming after you." I sat on my bed, smoking weed until Tone passed out. I laid back and contemplated the night's events. I thought about what I had done and was proud. I did it just like Gumby and Mario Sierra had done it, just like Rauly and Fat Matt. I did it like all those guys that I looked up to. I did it *Menace to Society* style, one of my favorite movies at that age. I did it . . . alone. I could be safe. I could be secure because I could make sure of it. I contemplated the other dope dealers in the neighborhood. "Yup, they'll be next" I whispered to myself.

"What? What's up?" my cousin asked half asleep.

"Nothing, just thinking out loud." We lie there, numb to the world.

August 7, 1995, Off to Miami Per the Santera

The months leading up to taking Sam's life had been relatively tranquil, for the most part. I was a sixteen-year-old adolescent "in love" with Theresa, my beautiful seventeen-year-old Italian girl who brought peace to an otherwise turbulent world. Even though we slept, ate, and breathed each other's presence, I was young and playing the field. Having met a beautiful Cuban girl while on a family vacation earlier that year in Florida, I had wanted to visit my family in South Beach, Miami that summer so that I could see her again. My mother was against it because I was constantly in trouble or under investigation by some law enforcement agency, whether it was an allegation of robbery or larceny or assault or fighting. I was routinely suspended from school for fighting. She felt that I did not deserve it, yet my behavior was a reflection of my environment, not my essence.

My mother was finally convinced to allow me to purchase a ticket to Miami after a visit with her *santera*, a Puerto Rican "witch doctor" named Lucy, known throughout *el barrio* of southwest Detroit for possessing the gift of foresight. Her mother was also known to possess the gift of prophecy, though she passed away giving birth to Lucy.

In March of 1995, late on a cold winter night, my mother asked in a polite but forceful way to accompany her and my little sisters to Detroit. She was trying hard to get herself back on track. Both she and my older sister, Sandra, were moving forward. Sandra had enrolled in college (she had yet to be pregnant), and my mother had stopped using cocaine and was going to work several days a week. My father was also making a valiant attempt to reintegrate himself back into my life after divorcing his second wife, a relationship that entailed drug abuse and dysfunction. Yet "Little Mario," as I had been dubbed years ago, was an arrow that had been shot into the sky. There was no turning back from this destiny; this path of pain and struggle that was pulling me to an awakening of my purpose.

What remained of him was a boy lost to the whims of his emotions. Angry, indignant, embittered, he no longer trusted the world around him. He no longer held respect for authority, for such respect is commanded first from parents and primary caregivers, and, then, and only then, is that respect transferred to other figures of authority. He was still the four-year-old boy who held memories of anger and hatred between the two people he loved the most, memories of his father pushing his mother through the bedroom window as they fought.

What remained was a young man in pursuit of his rite of passage regardless of how or what, but simply a passage. What remained was a boy looking for any patriarchal figure, real or imagined, who would stand to oppose *him*, try *him*, and throw *him* through a window. What was left was a boy at war with ghosts from the past who haunted his heart and mind while destroying his purpose, a boy who saw his father in other men, the one who abandoned him, the one whose word was *not* his bond, his nemesis. What remained was a lost, young man who made money his god and anger as his fuel.

"*Chico, ven conmigo,*" Lucy said in her Puerto Rican accent, distinguished within the Latin community. "Come with me, boy." Puerto Ricans are the closest bloodline to Cubans. She was already heading through the kitchen. She looked back and said emphatically, "*Coño! Ven ahora!*" "Damn it! Come now!" Her request surprised me. I jumped, leaving my little sisters on the couch. I walked swiftly passed my mother and murmured, "What the hell the crazy lady want, ma-a-a-n?" in my rude vernacular. She remained quiet as she walked toward the television room to accompany my sisters.

At this point in my mom's life, she was trying to get everything back in order, including me, but while she was working and my grandmother was taking care of my little sisters, I was running gambling tables in the basement. Moving from Pontiac to West Bloomfield, a more upscale neighborhood, simply expanded my marketplace to a higher-end population. I loved the profit margins.

Later, I found out that my older sister, Sandra, now nineteen and more stable, was so worried that I was going to harm someone or be harmed that she called every local and state law enforcement agency within Michigan trying to get me help. With every call, they responded the same: "He must first commit a crime."

"He's committing them every day. Ya'll just ain't caught him," she would exclaim, slamming down the phone.

Now, desperate for any healing, even spiritual, my family turned to Santeria to "cleanse" me of my inclination for wrongdoing. I played the game and walked down the long, dark stairs of this home located in southwest Detroit. I entered a small, dark room that had a candle lit in the middle of a table. On the wall, I saw a picture of the Sacred Heart of Jesus and on the table stood a stack of old, very used Tarot cards. She began to shuffle, staring directly at me . . . and me at her. She blinked first. They always did, even when I was sixteen.

She shuffled again and again, and then slammed the cards against the table. "*Cut,*" she demanded. I was surprised, both at the aggressive way in which she banged the cards on the table and her tone.

"We playing poker?" I said with sarcasm, a defense I have used most of my life when angry or greatly disturbed about something.

"I take dis berry, berry seereesly. Ju undustand?!" she said in her broken English. Having no top teeth in her mouth made it even more difficult to understand her.

I just stared at her. I did not have much respect for women those days, and now, as I struggle to understand the importance of small things such as not raising your voice to a woman, I am beginning to understand that my tendency to be disrespectful toward women was rooted in how I responded to my mother's struggle to cope with life's ebb and flow, ups and downs. She would be paranoid, holding my baby sister and peeking out the windows all night, all day. I became so angry by fifteen that I would tell my own mother, "Kill yourself. Do it! Shoot yourself. All you are doing is killing yourself slowly. You are killing all of us!" I look back in both sadness and disgust because I was so judgmental. She was simply trying to survive . . . as we all are.

"Oka-a-y-y-y-y," I responded as I cut the deck. She glared at me, and then proceeded to lay out the cards in order. She stared at each card, slowly, methodically. She looked up at me, with fear in her eyes, and quickly gathered the cards and reordered them. Head down, periodically shaking her head, she was clearly having a discourse with herself over what she had just witnessed. Having socialized with Sandra's older male friends and boyfriends since the age of twelve, I had learned how to sense energy, especially fear. She was genuinely afraid of what she had seen.

"Is everything ok?" I asked the *bruja* in Spanish. She looked up with a tear in her eye. This time she gently laid the cards down and said lovingly, "Cut, please," as one tear slid down her cheek onto the table. At that moment, I sensed pity and sorrow and thought, *What the hell is going on?* She put her head down, staring at each card as she slowly, with purpose, laid each card down.

"You buy your drugs from a really big, black man, correct?" she asked me. I looked at her as if she was stupid. She repeated the question more forcefully.

"Boy, this is very serious. You do not understand, damn it! Nor what is going to happen!" she said softly, with tears in her eyes. Now she had my attention. I looked at her intently, deep down into her soul. I paused. Although a prophetess, she was also of the streets; thus, she understood the pause to mean that I was not about to discuss my drug trade.

"You buy your drugs from a really tall black man, about six-foot-six, like one of those basketball players. He is older than you. You are going to kill him. It will be over money and a lot of drugs." I just gave her the same blank stare I had begun learning at the age of eleven when my grandfather played poker against me—yes, *against* me, for he always kept his winnings and vice-versa.

During her "consultation," she said that there were energies at play that were trying to manifest my demise in the form of me taking a man's life and going to prison, but that she was going to make sure this did not happen. She emphatically expressed that I was being called to do something great but that "evil energies" were working to thwart that which God has destined. What I did not understand at the time was that she was giving me a preview of my *why*, of my reason for living, my reason for continuing day-in and day-out in the belly of the beast.

There was only one problem with this prophecy. At the time, I was buying my drugs from a short white guy around my age. So, I just knew she was full of shit. *Okay*, I thought, *I'll play the game.* So I continued to act as if I was listening intently.

"You must leave here as soon as possible. You are trying to go to Miami, correct?" Aha! Now she had my attention.

"Yeah, I wanna go to Miami to see *mi familia*," I said in Spanglish. At that age, I barely spoke Spanish, yet I understood it well, a cultural norm among many first- and second-generation Latino immigrants.

Now I knew that my mom was in on this bullshit. She must have told this toothless old woman that I wanted to go to Miami over the summer, and she was trying to get me to behave by scaring me with this story. I laughed to myself.

"I am going to tell your mom to send you there as soon as possible." I walked up the stairs feeling great! I had just landed a vacation in Miami.

She guided me to her bathroom at the top of the stairs. The tub was full of clear, clean water. As I stepped into the small bathroom, I noticed that she had her hands over the water as she prayed. She began to pray loudly, with bass in her voice, as if it wasn't her. I was taken aback by the authority in her prayer, this *bruja*, witch doctor, as I'd heard her referenced behind her back, in a whisper as if she could hear you even though she was nowhere in sight. She stood in front of me with her eyes closed, dipped the branch into the water, and then tapped me forcefully with the branch using her left hand, her right hand grasping my head as she prayed, calling upon the Holy Spirit.

At one point in her "cleansing," there was an apex. Her voice grew louder and louder, until she began shaking and speaking in tongues. That was when I thought she had taken it a little too far. Of course, I was the cynical teenage gangbanger who was pissed off at the world, at the system, at authority, at anything reminiscent of an authority figure or model. Of course, this was purely subconscious, and I was unconscious. I completely dismissed the *bruja*'s warning upon exiting her premises. All I knew was that I was going to Miami.

But I did walk out of that house feeling lighter, which translated into a change in behavior. Over the next several months, I lost the desire to hustle. I usually spent the profits as they came in but kept a few grand for start-up capital to buy a nice amount of dope wholesale from Pontiac and then sell it retail to the suburbanites. Theresa and I lived off that money for the next several months. We were completely consumed with each other that spring and summer of 1995. With the world around us falling apart, we lost our pain, our heartaches, our reality, and ourselves. We smoked, chilled, and enjoyed the spring and summer.

It's been said that, "Ignorance is bliss." Even though I had just received a prophecy from a soothsayer, I turned my back on this gift as if removing a pebble from my shoe, as if *she* was the inconvenience. Listening to her was merely a means to pacify my mother.

Getting in trouble with the law prevented me from leaving sooner that summer. From petty larceny at Meijer for stealing liquor to small robberies in the neighborhood, police detectives would routinely contact my mother in pursuit of interviewing me. But I never got in trouble because I would never talk. Between the police departments in Pontiac, West Bloomfield, Farmington, and the police in the schools in those areas, I was a hot commodity, so to speak. It was the norm for law enforcement to call my mom and request to interview me for "such-and-such" investigation. I was involved in everything and anything that could make money.

August 7, 1995, Off to Miami

The next morning, I awoke in a daze. I rubbed my eyes and thought about what happened the night before. I looked down at the floor and saw my cousin. I looked back at the ceiling. *Fuck . . . it wasn't a nightmare* was all I could think. I shook it off. *Fuck it; if you're in the game, then you're fair game,* as Mario Sierra used to say, one of my sister's boyfriends who was the leader of a notorious Pontiac gang, *Latinos In Action.* I hopped out of bed and rushed to get ready.

My mom barged in to make sure that I was up and ready. "*Coño,* hurry up. You are going to miss the plane!" she said as I kissed her on her cheek. Mom was so much better in those days. She was working three times a week at the business she helped create with her husband, and she was staying away from drugs and alcohol. She slipped here and there, but it was nothing like the days of the past. By that point, though, it didn't matter to me. I had prayed my prayers as a twelve-year-old boy, begging God for help. I was sure that even God had abandoned me, and that pushed me to lean even further on me, and only me, for that emotional safety and security that every child needs.

Before we left for the airport, my mother, not trusting what her son was capable of, forced me to pull my pants down to make sure that I didn't have any drugs on me. My baby sisters were laughing hysterically as I playfully yelled back at my mom, as she demanded that I pull my pants down. "Do it now!" she yelled. She was panicked that I would try to smuggle marijuana on the plane and get caught. I smiled inside. I figured she would do as much, so I had put it in my carry-on, which was already in the trunk of the car.

On the way to the airport, my cousin sat in the back of the van with my little sisters, who were five and seven and excited to send me off on my trip. I waited until I arrived to the airport to put the two ounces of marijuana in my crotch. I kissed my mom and sisters and gave them a huge hug. I ran off toward the terminal in excitement and anticipation to come back. I couldn't wait to rob more drug dealers. Like taking candy from a baby. Just as they had harmed me, just as I was alone in my sorrow as they fed my entire family poison, so, too, would I poison them with the venom of my anger and vengeance served on behalf of the young boy I once was. This is the danger of the human mind: the ability to rationalize and justify any behavior in order to live . . . to cope. This ability is the slippery slope that we must remain cognizant of.

CHAPTER 3

BROKEN

August 9, 1995, approximately 7:00 p.m., South Beach, Miami, Florida

I SPENT THE first TWO DAYS in Miami relaxing and catching up with my Aunt Aida, Uncle Alberto, and cousin Albertico. On the third day, I spent the morning and afternoon with the Cuban girl, Lupita, who I had met while on vacation with my family. We ate, talked, walked, and laughed, but it was clear that there was not much between us. We had a crush on who we imagined each other to be instead of the reality of who we were. I spent the rest of that day walking the South Beach strip, listening to the beats of 2Pac and Biggie as I reflected on what had happened back home just a few days before. I did not think about my victim or his family . . . not once. *I* was a victim, so was my narrative that shaped my existence. *I* was the one in pain. *I* was the one who needed to protect myself. I . . . I . . . I . . . I had a victim mentality coupled with an unquenchable anger. Instead of thinking about my victim and his family, I focused on my next target.

"There is a problem at home. Your mom said to call this number," said my Tia Aida in Spanish as she handed me a small piece of paper with the number of an attorney in Michigan who was awaiting my call. My heart plummeted, and my breathing became heavy as I dragged my feet like cinder blocks toward the bedroom where I had been staying for the past few days. As I sat on the bed, I stared at the number and then at the phone. Finally, I dialed.

"Yea, this is Mario Bueno. U-h-h-h-h-m, I don't—"

"Son, we have been expecting your call. Just hold one second please," said a gentle, female voice.

"Mario!!!" came a near deafening shout. "I'm Jerome Sabbota. Call me Jerry. I've been waiting on your call. Your mother has retained me to represent you. The prosecutor's office is currently drafting your indictment for felony murder and armed robbery." There was dead silence for about ten seconds.

"Look, m-a-a-n-n-n-n, I'll call you back," I said as I slammed down the phone. I frantically dialed my cousin's beeper number and punched in the emergency symbol 911, a normal code back in 1995, indicating, "Call back ASAP."

August 9, 1995, approximately 8:00 p.m.

After pacing the floor for what seemed an eternity, the phone finally rang. I snatched up the receiver. "Hello?" I asked, breathless.

"Mario?" I heard my cousin's voice at the other end.

"Yea, what the *fuck* is going on?!" I yelled through the phone.

"Don't come back. The cops think you did it," he said, breathing heavily. "I'm going to take off, on the run." I was really confused. I couldn't for the life of me imagine why he would take off if the cops thought I had done it.

"Are you fucking stupid?!" I exclaimed. "They think I did what?! I didn't do anything," I responded in a panic, thinking he may be calling from a recorded line. I hung up and frantically dialed the attorney's number once again. How could I not come back? Besides, his statement was loaded with the implication of guilt on my part.

"Yes . . . , u-h-h-m-m-m . . . ., this is Mario . . . , again," I mumbled sheepishly. The same tender voice responded.

"It's okay dear. Hold one second." As I waited for what seemed to be an eternity, my heart pounded as I scrambled to think of what to do next. My first thought was to run. I would take my cousin Albertico's gun, my money, and a small bag and just run. I theorized that it would be easy to get to South America from Miami.

"Mario?" shouted Jerry through the phone. A long pause ensued. He was loud enough, but I was lost in thought. I was scrambling to figure out why my cousin had told me to not come back. "Mario, you there?"

"Oh, yes, sir, I'm sorry," I replied, snapping my attention back to the call.

"Yeah, I figured you'd call back soon enough." I could hear the grin in his voice, as if he had bet his life that I would call back within five minutes. I remained silent, and so did he for a minute. Finally, he said, "So here's is the deal. I was a prosecutor for the Oakland County District Attorney's office for twenty-five years. For the past fifteen years, I've been a very successful defense attorney. Because of my relationships within the prosecutor's office, they sometimes give me a courtesy by informing me that my clients are being charged with something. Your mother has retained me to represent you, so it makes you my client. It turns out that you are being automatically waived from the status of a juvenile and are being formally charged as an adult for felony murder, armed robbery, and felony firearm in the murder of Samuel James." He paused.

I couldn't mentally repeat the words that he had just uttered. I couldn't comprehend the meaning of those words, let alone the weight of their meaning. I was in a daze, almost like having an out-of-body experience. We remained silent for another minute. Finally, he exhaled, and raised his voice a few notches. "Do you know what this means, son?"

"No," I mumbled. I was completely frozen, staring at the floor, in a room over 2,000 miles away from anyone I was close with. I felt completely empty inside. I was, once again, alone.

He continued, almost yelling. "It means that they don't give a fuck that you are only sixteen-years-old. It means that they are trying to send you to a fucking adult male prison for the big L. *Life!* It means that they want to send you with the big boys, so I need you to be completely honest with me. In order for me help you, I need you to trust me, to trust that I am on *your team.*" I paused and then exhaled.

"He reached for a gun, so I shot him," I finally said.

"Okay, so he had a gun?" he asked. I paused.

"Yeah, he had a gun," I responded.

"So, you seen that he had a gun?" he asked for clarification. I thought about it. He had to have been carrying some heat. He just had to.

"Yeah, I seen a gun," I rationalized, thinking that this would be my salvation.

"Good. Good. I just got a guy off in Pontiac on manslaughter for shooting a guy in the back after the guy robbed my client during a drug deal," he said. I knew whom he was talking about. It was the cousin of one of my drug connects, a former boyfriend of Sandra's. He wasn't lying. He sure did get him off. He was selling a guy two pounds of weed and the guy tried to run away with the product. Jimmy shot the guy right in the back and killed him, which is technically first-degree felony murder. This carries a natural life sentence. He got him off with manslaughter and only did seven years in prison.

"Come back to Michigan in the morning. I told the prosecutor's office to pull the cops back from pursuing you because I am walking you into the precinct myself tomorrow afternoon. They gave me that courtesy, as well. Get some sleep kid. You're about to fight the battle of your life," he said as hung the phone up.

My thoughts went directly to my girl, Theresa. I was sure she must have told on me. The only other person who knew anything was my cousin, Tone, and I knew for sure he would never have turned on me. I assumed that the police must have scared her into turning against me. I was so naïve.

August 9, 1995, approximately 11:30 p.m.

I was scheduled to take an early flight back the next day. My older cousin slept outside my door to make sure that I would not make a run for it; thus, my plan was thwarted. In retrospect, he saved me from impending pain. Had I taken off, the loneliness of breaking all ties with what I knew would have been harsher than the razor wire I was soon to experience. I didn't share any of what happened with my family in Miami, and no one asked. I think they were afraid of what the answer might be. I tossed and turned all night. I did not understand what was about to happen, but I had a deep, inner feeling that my life would never be the same. I couldn't get the attorney's word out of my mind. "Life . . . Life . . . Life." I pressed two pillows against my head. I couldn't make it stop. I fell asleep that night with the knowledge that I was going to prison for life. Yet, I lacked the understanding of what this meant. Thus, I was afraid.

August 10, 1995, approximately 8:00 am, Miami International Airport

My Tia Aida embraced me tightly. Then, pushing me back, gripping each bicep, she looked at me with her tear-filled eyes. "*Prométame que volveras a verme!*" she said. "Promise me that you will return to see me!"

It was not until years later that I reflected upon this conversation as I silently prayed in my cell. At that moment, Tia Aida was breathing a different *life* into my soul, my mind, my being. She was planting a seed of strength. She understood this, but I had no clue. She was tossing a mustard seed of faith onto a soil that was ripe for sowing. I never did get to see her again. She passed during my incarceration, as many of my family members did.

August 10, 1995, approximately 12:30 p.m., Detroit Metropolitan Airport

As I took that last step off the airport terminal, I saw my poor mother, head tilted, eyes running with tears, as she repeated, "Why, Mario? *Why, mijo? ¿Por que?* Do you understand what you've done, *mijo?* Do you know what you have done?" I said nothing. I just stood there lacking the fortitude, the knowhow, the character, or the understanding to nurture my mother or anyone else. Looking into her eyes, I knew that I had broken her in half, and that realization destroyed my very essence. It ripped into pieces any love, comfort, or solace that remained in me. At that very moment, I knew what it meant to destroy someone who you truly loved. We walked the rest of the way down the airport hallways in silence; mother and boy, together, facing another challenge... another obstacle... and, terrified at the unknown peril that awaited them.

August 10, 1995, 1:30 p.m., Law Offices of Ribitwer & Sabbota, LLP, Bloomfield Hills, Michigan

Looking at my mother and me, Jerry, my new criminal defense attorney, said, "I'm sorry to meet you under these circumstances, son, but you have now been formally indicted for felony murder and the accompanying felonies. I called the prosecutor's office and told them that I would personally be turning Mario into the Pontiac police station this afternoon so that they would not come looking for him at your residence or on the streets." My mother began sobbing. Jerry attempted to comfort my mom by explaining the process that would soon begin. Part of the terror in any situation is the not knowing.

As we made our way to Jerry's car, once again I thought about my girlfriend, Theresa. She had to be the one who told on me. I was fuming. I knew it had to be her because it was between her and my cousin, and surely my cousin wouldn't betray me. He was family.

August 10, 1995, approximately 2:00 p.m.,
Pontiac Police Station, Michigan

With one tear rolling down my cheek, the officer guided my first finger to be inked and printed, then another. From behind, my mother gently unfastened the clasp on a black-beaded necklace that hung from my neck that held a silver cross medallion. Suddenly, in a moment of pure irony, symbolism, or fate, the beaded necklace broke, and the cross fell to the ground, as my tears flowed more rapidly. All three events felt like they happened in slow motion. Sobbing and groaning, my mother quickly fell to her knees as she grabbed the silver cross, kissed it, and whispered, "I will never abandon you. I promise you, I will never abandon you."

In the distance, almost surreal and far-off, through my mother's uncontrollable sobbing and the officer trying to verbally console her while fingerprinting her son for murder, I vaguely heard my attorney speaking. "Don't say a thing. They already know not to interrogate you without me present or one of your parents. Now that I'm here, it will be me, but keep your mouth shut."

The officer allowed for one last hug. My mother put her arms around me and whispered, "Be strong *mijo*. I am here for you." As tears rolled down my face, I understood then, too late, of course, what she had been saying for several years. "*Mijo*, once you are in the system, I will not be able to save you." And, yet, how is salvation defined? I thought about that as the officer gripped my arm and guided me away from my mother. I heard her sobbing, moaning, groaning as I walked further into the police station. Her cries grew fainter and fainter as I stepped inside the cell with chipped paint and walls completely covered in gang graffiti, obscenities, and other foreign things that did not belong on a wall. I exhaled and sat down on the bench. The steel door banged shut as a huge set of jingling keys locked the door that would shut me away from my world and everyone in it for the next two decades.

Approximately 30 Minutes Later

Detective Kerry, a twenty-year police veteran with years of experience as a detective, entered the holding cell about half an hour later. Sitting inches away from me, we stared straight at the graffiti-filled wall. "Sometimes things happen, Mario, that we did not intend to happen. This is what we believe happened here. We know that you are a good kid. We think you just fucked up. We also know that you weren't alone. Who was with you? Jay? Tone?"

Immediately, I responded with, "Tone had *nothing* to do with it." I instinctively protected him, at the sacrifice of self, for such a statement implies incrimination. That was one of the proverbial nails in my inevitable coffin. The homicide detective continued with his questioning as I gazed at the ground.

"Don't you get it, son? If you play like a tough guy, then you are going to get sent upstate with the *tough* guys," he said, with frustration in his tone. I looked up slowly.

"I'm used to being the tough guy. It's what I am good at," I said as tears rolled down my face. As a twelve-year-old boy, all I yearned for was to be loved by my mother and protected by my father. By then, I was no longer thirsting for my mother's love. No, I wanted to be respected. I was no longer hungering for my father's protection. Now, I was going to stand guard of my own heart, mind, body, and soul. I would be the one to protect me. "You are the detective. Get to detecting." I was a gangster, bottom line. And a snitch-rat I was not, so much so that my nickname among the sheriffs became *Baby Face Nelson* because of my crime, gangster response, and my baby face look. Detective Kerry glared at me.

"Ok, play the tough guy. I love those kind," he said as he stomped out of the holding cell and slammed the iron door. I sat there confused and empty, trying to figure out what to do. I always had an answer . . . until now. I sat there for about an hour, until they came and shackled my ankles and my wrists. "We're taking you in front of the judge now. You are about to be formally charged with the murder of Samuel James," the detective said in a somber tone. Again, I was numb to the words, for I had no frame of reference to understand the gravity and weight of their meaning.

Sitting in the courtroom in the jury booths, I sat cuffed, one convict in a chain of many, being formally charged and arraigned, all Blacks and one Latino, me. My charges were read aloud: "Felony murder, armed robbery, and felony firearm." I heard them, but they did not truly resonate. At the age of sixteen, what does truly resonate on such a tender mind and immature perspective on life?

After the judge affirmed the charges and remanded my case for preliminary examination, the assistant district attorney asked the judge, in an affirming tone, "Hold him in the juvenile facility, correct, Your Honor?"

"No, remand him to the Oakland County Jail," said Judge Bradley as he looked over at me with disdain. The prosecutor jerked his head in my direction then back at the judge. At the time, I knew no difference. To me, that was not unusual, for nothing that was happening was usual. I would later learn that I was the only juvenile in Oakland County Jail. There were numerous sixteen-year-olds charged with murder as adults, but the judicial norm at the time was to house juveniles in the juvenile facility that was designed to house youths. Thus, the noted head jerk by the prosecutor.

A few years later, my father revealed to me that Judge Bradley was a political foe of my grandfather. My grandfather migrated from Ecuador in the 50s, and as work conditions did not favor the workingman, or the immigrant, my grandfather saw an opportunity to both help his fellow man, and in his mind's eye, pursue his purpose. He became a leading figure in the Civil Rights battle of the 60s, and, as with all success, he attracted friends . . . and foes. Judge Bradley happened to be one of those foes. And, in his last failed attempt to incur pain upon his perceived political enemy, Judge Bradley landed me in that Oakland County Jail cell on August 10, 1995, knowing that I would be placed in solitary confinement, for the law demanded such protective measures for youths, those "super predators" as Hillary Rodham-Clinton once eloquently dubbed us. We were to be separated from the adult offenders until post-sentencing. Judge Bradley buried a sixteen-year-old boy within a six-by-nine-foot coffin. What Judge Bradley did not know was that I was a seed. As with every seed, germination requires disruption and a cracking of the seed exterior so that it may go through the painful process of becoming. His proverbial burying of me in a deep, dark place was the beginning of my painful path towards the unveiling of my destiny . . . my purpose . . . my *why* for being.

Of all of the institutions in our society, prisons retain the greatest similarity to their early nineteenth-century forms. Their method for dealing with problematic prisoners or "special needs prisoners" is usually the same: solitary confinement. In 1995, the *Automatic Waiver Law* allowed a prosecutor to automatically waive me in as an adult for the purposes of charging and trying me. Yet, until I received a conviction and a *sentence* of adult confinement, the law also required that I remain separated from adults until that time. There is a saying that I soon learned in prison: "Long-term solitary confinement will produce one of two fruits: a scholar or a schizophrenic."

August 13, 1995, Oakland County Jail

Three days had gone by since the judge had ordered me to be housed in Oakland County Jail. I was in the large, bullpen like cell of the Health Care Department. These cells were intended to hold prisoners for a few hours as they awaited a medical appointment before transfer, yet I had been there for three days.

Bang, bang, bang! I heard on the window above me as I slept on the floor of the cold, brightly lit cell. I looked up. There were three large holding cells that held ten to twenty prisoners as they waited to see the doctor or dentist. The last large holding cell contained the women. There were large, thick windows between the cells that allowed for us to communicate; however, the last cell had darkened glass to protect the privacy of the women, but I sometimes witnessed blurry tits being pressed against the smoky windows as the men hooted and hollered for more.

"You got a m—?" as the man in the larger holding cell next to me asked, using his fingers as a pistol. He was a tall, skinny, white-skinned Latino who had tattooed sleeves up to his neck. He didn't dare say the big "M" word, in other words, "murder," as if it was taboo or bad karma to say out loud. I shook my head up and down in acknowledgment to the fact that, yes, I had been charged with murder.

"Keep yo' head up, young dog," he replied, shaking his head in disbelief and sadness for my conditions. I was being held in a temporary cell, on the floor, and my youthful appearance must have made me look like a baby. As I reflect, and as I look at the sixteen-year-olds around me today, I realize that I was just a baby, at least mentally and emotionally.

By the fourth day, I was moved into the back of the Health Care Department where those who have been classified as having a need to be temporarily isolated are housed, usually, for detox from alcohol and drugs, or a temporary holding for protective custody reasons. There were only four single cells. The back hallway that held the cells was dark and spooky. One light flickered on and off. It was quiet for the most part. There were small televisions outside the cell windows with microphones inside the cell for the prisoner to hear the television, and it was positioned outside the cell, in front of the cell window. This allowed us to see and hear the television without having it in our cells.

I walked into the cell with my bedroll that consisted of two blankets, two sheets, two bath towels, and two washcloths. This was all that I had to my name. I walked into that cell not knowing that this would be "home" for the next 387 days, as I fought my murder charge. I sat on the plastic mat that lay upon the concrete bed that was built into the structure of the cell, connected to the wall. I leaned over, put my face in my hands and vomited all that was in me. I stared into the toilet as tears rolled down my face. I leaned back against the wall and sat. *How did I get here?* I thought, as I shook my head in disbelief. I was sober now. I had not been sober for any extended period of time in over two years, and I was only sixteen. The weight of the world had crushed my spirit, but now, I had to be sober to deal with it. This frightening reality had me nauseous to the point of losing twenty pounds within the first thirty days. My emotional turmoil prevented an appetite and kept me in a constant state of nausea. I was broken, spiritually, mentally, and emotionally. I now realized why I had been smoking weed, drinking, and chasing money as my god: I was sad and hurt. I was still that twelve-year-old boy who was angry with a god who remained silent during the darkest moments of his life, a god who said nothing as his life was torn apart by pain, anger, violence, dysfunction, and drug abuse. I sat there on that cold, dark cell still angry with that same god.

I definitely do not recommend solitary confinement for youths, or for anyone for that matter, because it separates him or her from the knowledge and understanding that they are in need of love, of connection to the whole. It separates them from the awareness that they are an important piece of a divine puzzle with a uniqueness planted within. As it says in the Bible, "All things happen for the good for those who love God and are called to His purpose." I believe this to be true. While it may have been a provision of the Lord for me to endure the harshness of an adult prison, it begs the question, "At what cost?" What is the residual effect of such an experience on an impressionable mind? What will be the fruit for our communities when youths who were imprisoned as teens come home after twenty, thirty, or forty years of confinement? What quality of life will these men possess? These are questions worth answering, for one may only give what one possesses. Thus, for the sake of pure self-interest, I often ponder what will these *boys turned men* possess? What are we, as a society, providing these fallen youths, besides a concrete jungle, a hardened environment that resolves conflict with aggression and violence?

CHAPTER 4

AN AGREEMENT MADE
THROUGH A BROKEN SPIRIT

August 14, 1995, Oakland County Jail

I DON'T KNOW HOW LONG I'd been lying there. In this solitary, there was no daylight, just a persistent fluorescent light that enabled staff to see inside the cell. "Rounds" (guards walking cell to cell) were supposed to be done approximately every thirty minutes because statistics show a spike in suicide attempts and rates for those confined to solitary confinement. I was heartbroken and desperate. Even though I had spurned God repeatedly before all this happened, I turned to prayer. Suffering brought me to my knees, helping me be more open to what the spirit was saying, better yet, what I was supposed to learn from the pain. Pain is simply a message, a tug, a tap on the shoulder of the flesh and of the ego to remind us that in humility and quiet one may hear whispers of direction, glimpses of purpose, the *why* that helps us get through the *what*. And, it is the *why* for which we live, for which we breathe.

The last time I prayed, I was but a boy, begging God to heal my precious mother from her struggles. I prayed incessantly during those times for two long years. It was a lifetime in the mind of an eleven-year-old boy. But my prayer went unanswered and that boy forgot about his God. A boy who set childish ways aside too early and who began picking up the values and habits of the ones he looked up to; a boy who set aside the humbling effects of praying on one's knees and replaced it with an aggressive, criminal mindset, forcing others to bow before him. The Bible commands us to "Honor thy mother and father." Why is this so important, because God said so? No, that is dogma. It is because a child's relationship with his or her mother and father, or the lack thereof, will greatly influence how he or she responds to authority, to the community, to the world at large. Why was I resistant to authority? Why was mere position not sufficient to garner my respect as a youth? Because I had lost all respect for my parents. And, this loss of respect was my tragic choice from my immature mind that could not bear the weight-load of my pain. At the core of me, I felt abandoned. To survive, I turned angry.

When a child does not honor his mother and father, it is unlikely that he will honor other facets of authority, such as teachers, police, and elders, and, invariably himself or his peers. For this reason, it is written, "Honor thy mother and father" period. It is not written, "Honor thy mother and father *if*. . . ." It says to honor them with no conditions. The greatest tragedy of a child losing respect for authority is that these youths are then disconnecting from the very resources that exist to serve their needs and guide them into their purpose: the wise elders around them disguised as "stupid teachers," "dumb old neighbors," "white or Uncle Tom policemen," as the list of disconnecting belief systems goes on, passed on culturally through systemic shortcomings. My parents struggled with life and with their own standards. Thus, the lack of a conscious presence by my parents created a lack of standards for me. I lost respect for them, and in that process, I lost respect for myself. The youth of today are harboring pain and trauma that has transformed into anger, a stronger energy, that pushes them through their immediate needs and threats. And yet it is a path of self-destruction, for it adopts a victim mentality that can only give that which it possesses: more victims.

In a cell that mirrored a dungeon in hell, I remember crawling to my knees, crying out to the heavens in realization of the depths of my sin, of my falling short. I beat my chest and begged Samuel, my victim, for forgiveness. Finally, after gaining a clear mind and remembering the boy who sought his God, I became bold as I looked up, pounded my chest and begged God, no, I *dared* God, to make a deal: "If You, Lord, who is all powerful, all knowing, choose to save me, then, I, Lord, will spend the rest of my life helping kids like me." Tears poured down my face as I looked to the heavens. I crawled onto the plastic mat that would become my bed for the next nineteen years. I used one blanket as a pillow and hugged the other blanket, still longing for the peace, comfort, and safety that I had yearned for so many years, as I cried myself to sleep, just as I did long ago, alone then and alone now.

I awoke hours later from a loud *smack*. I jumped and snapped my head around to look at the source. I saw the cell door slowly closing as a sheriff walked away. A Bible was on the ground. I was raised Catholic and went to Catholic school for about six years of my childhood. Ironically, I had never read the Bible. Go figure, huh? I just followed blindly. It's easier. It doesn't require thinking. I opened the Bible to Genesis and began to read. I began to read a manual, a book on how a product works, according to the manufacturer. I read with a hunger, a thirst that was so deep that I read the entire Bible within the first three months of my imprisonment. I could hold down fluids, but I could not bear to take in food. I was merely hungry for the understanding of God's Word. I was starving to know His Will for my life.

I created a system of reading the Word. I would read chapters of the Old Testament, in sequence. In addition, I would read chapters of Proverbs, Psalms, and the New Testament. I structured it like school so I could study the classes in rotation throughout the day. In addition, a deacon from the Prince of Peace church in West Bloomfield, Michigan would visit me every Saturday morning to study the Book of Job. Since he was a representative of the church, I was able to visit with him for limitless hours in the attorney booth. Otherwise, I was allowed only one visit per week, besides my lawyer, for thirty minutes, behind a small glass window. So, envision the meaning of these visits to a sixteen-year-old held in solitary confinement for twenty-four hours a day, seven days a week, with constant exposure to light, noise pollution, apathetic guards, and hardened criminals. For me to receive a visit, a real visit that entailed a friendly smile, an embrace, a shake of the hand, an uplifting, positive conversation along with a prayer and a blessing was, for me, a reminder of what truly mattered in life, before walking back to my cell for another 165 hours.

Upon hearing the news of my incarceration, Lucy, the *bruja*, had done another reading in my name. She said that this had to happen so that God could use me to help many youths. I embraced this new prophecy during that time in the county jail, for your story can either empower or disempower you. Telling myself that I was going to be used to save many hurting youths like me empowered me to get through the mental and emotional hell of facing felony murder charges.

To this day, I am not sure who was the vehicle by which God delivered the Bible that fourth day in solitary. There was one older guard, in particular, who would prop my door open that first week and talk *with* me, not *to* me. He reminded me of my grandfather. We spoke a lot about life, God, regret, mistakes, and the future. I realize now that he was making sure that I did not commit suicide.

Many who worked inside the prison knew that it was uncommon for a youth to be placed in such harsh conditions.

August 21, 1995, Back to Reality

Smack! Two thick stacks of paper landed on the table in the four-by-four-foot holding cell that was designated as the "attorney booth." The room barely fit Jerry, my attorney, let alone the two of us. My weekly clergy and attorney visits occurred in this claustrophobic habitat. "Here is your amazing cousin for ya," chuckled Jerry as he set one foot on a stool. The fact that Jerry had been a former prosecuting attorney for twenty-five years afforded him the influence to obtain the statements that led to my indictment without a motion for discovery or a pre-trial hearing. The two stacks of papers contained in it three statements, three nails in my coffin, two by my cousin, Tone, and one by his friend Jay.

"Your cousin sold you down the river. And the story that they are telling is *not* the story you told me," he said as he glared down his nose through his spectacles. Tone had stretched the truth against me instead of for me. He made it look like I had thrown the pistol in a lake to protect his friend. Of course, he excluded the fact that he had helped set up the gun deal and was supposed to go with me to rob Samuel.

I stayed quiet, weighing my options. I was scrambling for an out. *I should have killed both of them,* I thought bitterly. As I reflect on it now, I understand that it was love for my cousin that had made it impossible for me to fathom that it was he all along who had betrayed me and not my girlfriend, Theresa. Later, through discovery, I sat in my quiet cell reading the transcripts of the interrogations and interviews by the homicide detectives who were building the case against me. I found two interviews in which the detectives accused Theresa of knowing the truth. "His cousin Tone says that you were a part of the conversation," was the assertion. But she never Bitter. She never broke. It turns out that she was the strong one. She stayed loyal to me as a girlfriend, and then for the next twenty years, as a friend, even though it cost her. Many of her loved ones berated her for "supporting a murderer." She visited me often, especially in the early years. She supplied me with a love that reached beyond walls, beyond fences. Tone, on the other hand, not only betrayed me but also turned his back on me. He never sent me a dime or even a letter for the first eleven years until one day I finally received a written apology: "I am sorry, bro'. I wish I would have been there for you." I never responded. What was there to say?

Jerry continued to glare at me, waiting for a response. "I did not know who you were, Jerry. You can't expect me to admit to a murder over the phone to a person I'd never met," I responded. I could see understanding come into his eyes.

"So, what *did* happen?" Jerry asked, leaning forward. I slumped a little in the chair, having to go back to a place that I no longer wished to go, having to explain myself to a man that I barely knew, though it was starting to feel like he was my favorite uncle or something. I was not accustomed to having to explain myself to anyone. It was a bitter taste in my mouth to be questioned for acts that, in my egocentric prism, were proper rules of engagement based on sub-cultural norms. I had done what I thought to be ethical within the confines of an otherwise unethical world.

"I met up with him to buy a few pounds of marijuana, but instead, I robbed and killed him. When I pulled my gun out, he reached out, like stretched out, to grab the gun, and I pulled the trigger one time. He ran off really fast. I didn't even think he was hit, he ran so fast," I said, as I stared into Jerry's eyes, trying to measure his true internal response.

"So, what part did Tone play in all of this?" Jerry asked with one eyebrow raised.

"Tone set up the deal with Jay for the purchase of the guns, and, in exchange, I set up the drug deal. Tone was supposed to go with me, but I didn't have enough time to pick him up before the meet with Sam," I said stoically.

"So, Tone did not go with you?" Jerry asked, confused.

"No," I replied dryly, seething inside, fixed on Tone's betrayal.

"So, who was with you? There is an eyewitness saying they saw two people drive away from the crime scene in the same car. The car that matches the description of the vehicle that you were driving," Jerry said in a disbelieving tone, as if I was lying to him.

"Look, I was *alone*, you get it? I don't know what else to tell you," I snapped and looked away, absorbed in thoughts as to how I was going to kill my Judas.

"So how come there was blood in the driver's seat?" Jerry asked.

"He was sitting in the driver's seat, and I was standing near the rear passenger door, with the door open, and as I looked inside the big brown bag that had the pounds," I explained, "I pulled the gun out and shot."

"So, you didn't even know for sure that he was shot?"

"No."

"Did you go there with the intent to kill him?" he asked, squinting his eyes, peering deep within the burrows of my soul.

"At this point does it matter?" I asked in frustration. I slipped back to that moment in time that felt like eternity, yet I could not stop the events that were unfolding as Jay loaded the gun for me.

"Shoot that fucker right in the head and don't hesitate, or he will get you first, lil' bro," Jay had counseled. I had walked inside Jay's house for a pistol to conduct a robbery, and I had walked out with a vision of murder. I walked out with a mindset, a mantra, of *I gotta get him before he gets me*. This is the danger of allowing just anyone to speak into the mind of a youth, because the inner self-talk that a youth harbors becomes the creative energy that forms his external reality. At that moment, a seed of murder was planted within a soil that was rich in pain and anger, rooted in a lost faith. I waited for Jerry's response. He shook his head. I continued.

"I thought that Samuel was jumping out of the car with his gun, so I ducked around the car and held the .45 like a hammer, waiting for Samuel to bend the corner with his pistol, but he never did. Instead, he ran really fast toward the tennis courts. That's why I didn't think he was shot. Then I took the .45 back to Jay's house because it jammed."

"So, you gave the murder weapon to Jay?" he asked in disbelief.

"Yeah, but I didn't know that it was a murder weapon at the time. So, I traded it for a .25." I said in response, as if it was common sense. Jerry changed topics.

"So, what role did your cousin play in all of this?" he asked again. I exhaled.

"The initial agreement was that my cousin would tag along and split the dope and cash if he could produce a gun on short notice. Sam called me and wanted to meet right then, but I didn't have time to go and get Tone, so I went alone. I didn't give him half the stuff, 'cuz he didn't go with me. I see now that was a mistake," I mumbled, seething in anger.

"Will you roll on your cousin, or Jay, for a deal?" Jerry asked with an eyebrow raised as if he already had a deal on the table. I looked up as he peered down through his tiny, gold-framed glasses.

"Na-a-a, I ain't a rat. You do what you gotta do, and I'll do what I gotta do," I spit out with venom. It made me nauseated to consider the reality that I had been betrayed by my own cousin, a brother who had been raised by my side, a brother who, not only *would* I die for, but to a certain degree, did. When asked by the homicide detective if my cousin Tone was with me that night, I had responded that he had nothing to do with it. That response placed me, at a minimum, within the confines of the conspiracy and placement at the scene; it was incriminating. Thus, I threw myself upon the proverbial sword as my brother's keeper, as we defined it in the street. Yet, I found no reciprocity, no loyalty, and no honor among thieves. I vowed that I would kill him. Not his friend . . . but *him*.

Jerry chuckled as he stood. "Alright, be the tough guy, but I need you to understand that in this game, the tough guy always loses. Gotta tell ya my professional opinion, chief, so never take it personal," Jerry said as he grabbed the doorknob to the tiny, arcane attorney booth. Jerry was like an old mob attorney who had been jaded by a system that was stacked against the offender, so why bother trying. "A few more months in that cage, and you'll change your mind. They all do," he said as he looked at the filthy walls around us. He walked away from a boy who was trying to be a man, once again, by going solo, doing it all on my own.

As the deputy escorted me back to my cell, I thought about how much my life had changed since taking Samuel's life. I went from South Beach, Miami to twenty-four-hour lock down, solitary confinement, three meals slid to me through a door, and charged with felony first-degree murder that carried a sentence of natural life. It was still hard to believe that *this* was the end of the story, the end of my life, my fate, and, yet all that existed around me said the opposite; it said that life, as I knew it, would never be again.

I walked into my six-by-nine cell, sat on my concrete slab and thought about all of the signs that my cousin had displayed in the months leading up to this murder. My love for him had blinded me to the reality that he was not a friend but a foe. I ignored the blatant acts of disloyalty and disrespect as "him just not knowing any better," yet, as I sat there on that slab of concrete, I understood: *La envidia te mata.* "Envy kills you." I had ignored the threats of a snake until it was too late. "Never again," I said under my breath.

I sat reminiscing about the previous months. That summer in July of 1995, I got arrested at Meijer for stealing a gallon of vodka from the shelf. I customarily purchased all of my alcohol in Pontiac where the Arab stores would sell to an infant, but I was out in Commerce and headed to a party in the opposite direction of Pontiac. A family of off-duty police officers chased me into the parking lot where I fought all three of them. Because I had nothing on my record, the police called my mother. She was obviously upset and tried to punish me even though she was still drinking and occasionally doing cocaine. The next day I ran away to my girlfriend Theresa's where I stayed for a week. I negotiated my return to my father's house who was recently divorced and purchasing a new residence. I lasted about two weeks there after taking his car late one night to meet with Theresa.

Before leaving, I ran to the stove to light a joint and then ran off. Mistakenly, I left the stove running gas, so when my dad received a call from my mother at 3:00 am saying, "I have a bad feeling that Mario is in trouble," my dad, at first argued, then got up to check and smelled gas. He found the stove on, but I was not in my bed and nowhere to be found. Since he smoked cigarettes habitually, he became convinced that I had tried to kill him.

Upon returning to my dad's, I crept up the stairs reeking of alcohol and marijuana. As I reached the top step, the light flickered on, and my dad was standing there in his robe, looking like a maniac. He jabbed me in my abdomen with a wooden, major league-sized baseball bat.

"Where the fuck have you been?" he demanded, looking like a madman.

"I went to see Theresa, Dad, I swear," was all I could muster. I thought for sure he was going to swing as horrific memories of him attacking my mother flashed through my mind. By that age and mentality, I could have harmed my father, fought back, but I didn't want to. I saw on his face first anger, then confusion, and, finally, relief.

"The gas was on, and you were gone. I didn't know what to think," he said, lowering the bat. "You almost killed us, son. Had your mom not had one of her crazy 'feelings' then I would have woken up and lit a cigarette, just like I always do. This entire house would have blown up," he said as he shook his head and walked back into his room.

I went to bed, and as I lay there, I vowed to myself that I would never purposefully harm him. I knew I could, and I knew that a deep part of me, my innermost subconscious that witnessed him assault my mother, wanted to.

The next morning as I lay there hung-over from the alcohol and the emotional confrontation, the phone rang. "When I get home I'm gonna break your fuckin' legs with that baseball bat," I heard my father growl in a low voice through the phone. "There was vomit all over my car, and it's ninety degrees outside. Do you know what that smells like? I hope you like being fuckin' grounded," he snarled as he slammed down the phone. I had never been grounded before. My mom would sometimes say that I was grounded for a week and then forget the next day. I had no structure, no respect for authority. I lay there as I thought about my options. There was no way that I could be so far from Theresa and be grounded, so I called my mom.

"I want to come home," is all I could muster. There was a long pause at the other end.

"Well, I am not going to come and get you," she said.

"I will have Papa come and get me," I said confidently. No matter what, if I called my grandpa, he would come and get me from wherever. Ever since that day he came and took those guns away, he had treated me differently. He was more patient and less critical. As expected, I called and Papa came and got me, but once again, trust had been broken between my dad and me.

Weeks later as my father stood on the other side of that one-foot-by-one-foot window, he told me, "You broke my heart that day son. That day that I came home from work and found the house empty, your room empty, your drawers empty. You broke my heart that day." Tears flowed down my face, tears rooted in a twelve-year-old boy's brokenness and abandonment. He reached out to the glass. "I would never harm you, my son. I love you. Why didn't you call me first? Why didn't you call me first?" he said in a low voice through the small opening in the middle of the glass that separated two worlds whose realities were like night and day. He was referring to me not calling him from Miami when I was made aware of my impending murder charges.

"I was ashamed. I didn't know what to say," I replied. I had been conditioned to do it alone and to take my sense of security and safety into my own hands.

"Son, I know that I have failed you in the past, but I promise, I am here for you. I will never leave you. What can I do to help you? What if anything?" he whispered.

"There is only one way to save me," I said, staring into his eyes, knowing that at his core he was a good man who would not be able to follow through with what needed to be done. "Jay (I mouthed it and shook my head no) C-A-N-N-O-T testify," I said, using my finger as if pulling a trigger. "This shit is chess, not checkers. They told on me, so fuck 'em. I could send them away forever," I told him, pushing my father past any limits he had ever considered. My father looked me in my eyes, pursed his lips, and shook his head up and down.

"Don't worry, son, I won't let you down. I promise," he said. He put his hand up to the glass window as I followed. "I love you, son. Do *not* lose the faith."

"Visits are over. Everyone line up by the door. Now!" yelled the large, bald, white deputy. I watched my father walk away and thought about his loneliness as a father and my loneliness as a son. How could we love each other so much, yet, hardly even know each other? I didn't know the devil my father wrestled until, during one visit, he expressed, "I thought your step-father took my place," which shed some light on his own inner turmoil of abandonment as a father. A reality I never considered until he opened up for one of the first times. I only knew that when I needed him most, he wasn't there, and I didn't know how to call out in my pain. How could a boy tell a man that he needed him; that he yearned for his presence, his guidance, his love, when the boy's environment had only taught that such thoughts and feelings are not reciprocal in this unsafe world? Despite all this, I walked away feeling optimistic that my dad would be there for me. *He won't let me down this time,* I told myself. The big court date was in a few weeks, and if my dad took out Jay, then I would be home free.

As I walked back to my cell, I argued with God. "You didn't answer me when I was a kid begging you to heal my mother's addiction. How can I place my trust in you now?" As I laid my head on my pillow and wept, I whispered to myself, "He cannot testify."

Finally, it was the big day. I walked into the 50th District Court courtroom in downtown Pontiac holding up the waistband of my pants to keep the shackles and belly chains from yanking them down. After losing twenty pounds the first thirty days in solitary, I was a whole 145 pounds soaking wet. *Clank, clank, clank.* The chains that bound my ankles and wrists rang out as I was escorted into the courtroom from the back chambers.

As I walked in, I glanced at the large crowd who were apparently Samuel's friends. They glared at me with anger and hatred, as was to be expected. The homicide detective seated me in the chair, but I was pulled back up to my feet when the judge entered. "All rise, the Honorable Judge William Waterman of the 52nd District Court now presiding," yelled the bailiff. I stood holding my pants up as the judge motioned for us to sit.

I settled my nerves and glanced over my shoulder to look for my family, my supporters. I noticed that there were quite a few more deputies in the courtroom than usual. I saw my mom, dad, and sister, and I looked into my dad's eyes for any sign. "Use any means necessary," I had emphasized to my dad, "to be sure that Jay doesn't testify." I winked, and he nodded with a grin. *He did it.* (Exhale) *I'll be home by dinner.* "I have received notice that there have been death threats coming from both sides of this sad, sad situation," said Judge Waterman. "Let me take the time to explain how seriously I take this matter. If I find out that anyone, *anyone*, has threatened anyone here outside of this court, then I will personally be offended and take full measure of the law in my hands. Now, if you are not a blood relative of the victim or the defendant, please stand up." Approximately fifteen young African-American males stood up on the prosecutor's side of the courtroom and three people stood up on the defense's side. "Thank you for your honesty. Because of the seriousness of these threats, only blood relatives will be allowed to be in here. I thank you for your support and would ask that you place your energy in supporting the mother, sister, and children of Samuel. Officers, please show them out of the courtroom," the judge gently expressed. "Is the prosecution ready for their first witness?"

"Yes, your honor, we are ready to proceed with our first witness," said the prosecutor. I held my breath for what seemed to be an eternity. Everything was going in slow motion as I waited to see who would be my accuser, who would take the stand. The courtroom doors closed, and I slowly looked over my shoulder. Jay glided past me with the bailiff guiding him to the witness chair as the prosecutor yelled out, "The people call Jayson Apple to the stand." I stared at him coldly, but he could not bring himself to look at me. I looked back at my father and shook my head. He responded with a reassuring look and a wink. I was seething. I shook my head in disgust. Once again, he had let me down.

"Raise your right hand," said the clerk as he swore Jay in before his testimony, as is the court tradition, a façade of factual finding that allows one to bear false witness against his neighbor. "Do you swear to tell the whole truth and nothing but the truth, so help you God?"

"I do," said Jay. Once his swearing in was complete, Judge Waterman spoke to him.

"Son, do you understand that what you are planning to testify to is incriminating? Do you understand that the prosecution, if they so choose, can use what you are going to say against you?" the judge asked Jay several times. Jay looked down at his feet and nodded his head. "Son, the court reporter can't record a head nod. Was that a yes or a no?"

"Yes, sir, I understand," said Jay, clearly scared out of his mind. I could see that he was trembling. In his tape-recorded statement, Jay never even mentioned Tone or me coming back and giving him the murder weapon; thus, a good indication that I hadn't known that Samuel was shot. Homicide detectives had found Jay in his apartment with several firearms, ammunition, and no license for selling arms. The phone call I made to Samuel's pager and Samuel's subsequent call to Jay's house phone from Samuel's cell phone was more evidence pointing to Jay as the killer. When detectives questioned Jay initially, all he said was that I came over, and he sold me a gun. He said that he never saw me after that point and he never mentioned his friend, my cousin, Tone, in his statement.

The judge, once again interrupted the process, and asked, "Son, you do understand that you have a right to remain silent if your testimony incriminates you? Do you understand this, son? Do you understand that you could be charged with a crime, or crimes, if your testimony incriminates you?" the judge spoke slowly and softly as if to a child. Years later, I ran across a guy who had hung out with Jay the night before this testimony. He said they did cocaine all night as Jay complained about having to testify against "some kid over a murder" or else he would "get charged with some guns." Yet, when my attorney cross-examined Jay about his "truthfulness" and whether he had received any promises or deals in exchange for his testimony, he emphatically denied it, as also did the Prosecutor. Jay testified against me that day and sealed my fate. "Are you sure that you still wish to testify, son?" The judge made one last effort to adequately counsel Jay, even offering to postpone the proceeding until he could be appointed his own counsel.

"No, no, your honor. I want to testify," Jay almost mumbled.

"Speak up, son, my reporter cannot hear you."

"Yes, I *will* testify now," he said with a newfound bass in his voice. I shook my head softly, squinted my eyes, and looked over my shoulder. My father pursed his lips and put his head down. Jay went on to testify to his version of events. He told just enough to get my case remanded over for open murder and for him and Tone to escape a murder indictment.

A week later, my father came to visit. With his head down and tears in his eyes, he said, "My son, I know that you can't understand why I chose not to do what you wanted me to do, but it goes against all that I am. I pray that one day you'll forgive me, son, that you will forgive me for failing you. I love you, son. There is good in you. You will get through this, but you must get though it with faith in God, not in man," he said. I nodded my head. I didn't understand then, but what my father did was try to correct his former incorrect choices that had led to our current situation. It was his bad decision-making coupled with my mother's that had created the monster that stood before him. And it was up to him to augment and ignite the process of transformation that my mind and my soul desperately needed.

CHAPTER 5

DEAL OF A LIFETIME

January 1996

I WAS TRANSPORTED from Oakland County Jail (OCJ) to the courthouse by the homicide detectives because I still could not, at least I was not supposed to, be around adult offenders. Although charged as an adult by the prosecutor, I had to be convicted and then sentenced as an adult by a judge. Until then, I was to be kept away from adult prisoners as long as I was at the Oakland County Jail. The sheriff deputy at the courthouse was responsible for placing me in the holding cell until the judge was ready.

On this particular day, the deputy opened the door to the main bullpen where approximately fifty adults were packed in like mice. I looked at the holding cell and back at the sheriff. "Get in!" he ordered. At that split second, I reasoned that this officer was either setting me up for a hit, as there had been many threats made on my life and that of my family, testing me, trying to get a reaction out of me, or he was just ignorant of the fact that I was not supposed to be in there with adult offenders. At the risk of sounding like a coward, I said nothing and prepared for battle. I walked in, chest out, and sat at the open spot on the bench with my back to the wall and slowly scanned the room, staring at each man. Approximately ten to fifteen minutes passed, the regular interval for rounds at that time, with no incident. Then, as luck would have it, a new officer came in and recognized me. It was Officer Lopez, a longtime friend of the family. "Mario! What are you doing in there?" he said as he frantically opened the cell door. He grabbed my arm forcefully, yet in a manner of fatherly concern. "Why didn't you say something?" he says, as he guided me to the smaller, empty, adjacent cell. I walked into the cell, turned around, and grasped the bars as I looked into his eyes. "It's not my job," I replied. I reasoned that there was a time, quickly approaching, at which point I would be propelled long-term into this cage of men where violence and aggression is law, and the only one who could save me was me. Period. So, I may as well start this process now.

Fearing another hung jury, the prosecutor offered my attorney a deal: testify against my cousin or his friend, or both if I wanted, and I could get out at the age of twenty-one.

Some would argue that such an offer, such a deal, would be the epitome of karma coming back to bite Tone and Jay on their asses. Others would argue that justice must be measured according to one's due and in equal proportion to society's expectations. The homicide detectives truly wanted my cousin and Jay to pay for this crime as well, and to a higher degree because they were adults. The primary reason I was offered a deal was that the evidence actually pointed to Jay. This increased the chances of another hung jury at minimum. A "deal" would result in three convictions: Jay, Tone, and myself. Most people would equate this deal to that of salvation, and for my foes, a dish served cold.

My parents cried, however, as I explained to them that I could not, in good standing, accept such a deal. First, it would break my grandparents' hearts for Tone to be sent away for anytime, let alone life. Tone was their "son," their baby boy, their favorite. Second, I was the one who had made the choices that led to Samuel's death. I am the one that killed Samuel. Thus, it is written in the Word, "God will not be mocked, as a man sows so shall he reap." Regardless the intensity of that that bitterness, or its longevity, I had to eat from the bitter fruit that I sowed. I understood that I could run from correction no longer. My faith told me that I had to answer for Samuel's death; and, that "answer" would entail some much-deserved suffering.

"I beg you, son, to reconsider, to think about what you are doing, what you are saying. Son, you may never come home," my father cried out in pain. As my mother and father pressed their hands against the smudged, one-foot-by-one-foot thick glass window that prevented any contact, any touch, all I could see was tears and heartache. All remained was pain for what was and regret for what should had been. My mother yelled in her grief, ordering me to take the deal. "You *save* yourself, Mario! Do you hear me? You must *listen* to me! I cannot live without you," she wailed. I looked through the glass, tears rolling down my face as I pressed both hands against the glass in unison with my parents. I understood, just for a second, the depths of their love for me. They had always loved me, though I had become blinded to it by my own heartache. I stared into my parents' eyes, into their pain.

"I failed you Mom ... Dad. I promise not to fail you again. I did this. I must carry this cross. My faith tells me that God is in control," I said as I lowered my head. The past six months in solitary had entailed a spiritual growth that I never knew existed. I *knew* that God was in control, though I could not explain how.

"You haven't failed us, son, you hear me! Pick your head up. Don't lose your faith, son. The Lord is with us," my father snapped back at me, trying to speak life into my heart and soul. I lifted my head to see tears flow from my father's eyes as my mother clutched her chest in pain, holding the cross that had fallen on the ground during my fingerprinting.

Just then, the sheriff yelled out, "Visits are over. You have two minutes to clear the area." Thirty minutes once a week... for nearly a year. The remainder of the time was spent in solitary confinement. As I reflect on this experience, as I write these words with tears flowing from my heart, I am taken aback at the atrocities we as a society impose upon our children. It is written, "A society may be measured by the way it treats its most vulnerable." I had a total of twenty-four hours of non-contact visitation with my parents, at the age of sixteen, during that one-year period in OCJ's solitary; the remaining **8,736** hours were spent in solitary.

February 1996, "Health Care" Department

For the first eight months in the Oakland County Jail, they continued to house me in the Health Care Department. Due to the extreme isolation, the back four cells were generally used for detox or prisoners who needed to be isolated temporarily. Now, twenty years later, studies are revealing the long-term effects of solitary confinement on the psyche and adjustment; however, these studies are concentrated on adults. Mental health professionals speculate that the jails have become a repository for the severely mentally ill and its effects on staff and other prisoners creates for an unstable environment that is hidden from the public eye. Often referred to as the criminalization hypothesis, this trend is thought to be the unintended consequence of policy modifications (Teplan, 1990). There exists much empirical data through scientific research that expounds on the long-term implications of isolation through solitary confinement. "There is not a single published study of solitary or super-max like confinement in which non-voluntary confinement lasting for longer than ten days, where participants were unable to terminate their isolation at will, that failed to result in negative psychological effects. The damaging effects ranged in severity and included such clinically significant symptoms as hypertension, uncontrollable anger, hallucinations, emotional breakdowns, chronic depression, and suicidal thoughts and behavior" (Haney, 2003). The long-range implications for adolescents who experience solitary confinement, however, specifically longer terms in isolation, are much more extreme when it comes to attempted and/or successful suicide rates.

The depths of despair felt within the confines of solitary are deepened as a youth. Lacking the coping skills of an adult, I struggled internally to survive. They would only let me out of my cell every three days for a shower. In that I found my refuge, my safe place to cry aloud to God. Sitting on a dirty shower floor in the County Jail, a "juvenile killer" as the news had dubbed me, I begged God to take my life and end my misery. Out of each 168-hour week, I was locked in my cell about 164 hours. I spent the end of my sixteenth and nearly my entire seventeenth year in solitary.

I remember the constant stress and fear of not knowing. At sixteen, you don't know much, but the criminal justice system is a frightening maze of stop-and-go proceedings for any adult, let alone an adolescent. For the most part, it's merely a sham, a façade of the pursuit for justice.

That year, the Oakland County Jail had amassed eight juveniles who had been charged as adults by the "Holier Than Thou" district attorney. These juveniles were being expelled from the Juvenile Detention Center across the street where they were being housed as juveniles, all the while facing adult charges in adult court. Their judge had seen fit to house them in the more comfortable conditions of the juvenile facility, but for behavioral reasons they were sent to the county jail to be "disciplined." They were, for the most part, gang leaders who were embracing their reality: they were going to prison for a long time. Thus, their hope was minimal, and their reason to behave non-existent. The Juvenile Facility, not being able to manage these influential, lost leaders, sent them to the adult county jail where the staff incorporated different rules of engagement: they will beat your ass, regardless of how young you are.

Again, I don't recommend solitary confinement for anyone, especially youths. It is a form of torture that has not yet proven to be rehabilitative. To "re-habilitate" is to restore a person to "normality." The first problem with solitary is that the youthful offender is coming from an environment that was everything but "normal." Second, the youth is constantly "becoming," evolving, maturing physiologically, emotionally, socially, and, hopefully, spiritually. To place this youth in solitary is to stunt that growth. The youth becomes a dwarf to the social norms expected of them by social standards. The youthful offender adapts to their environment more than the adult, and therein lays the problem: their environment goes from aggressive and violent to hyper-aggressive and hyper-violent. Invariably, this Culture of Honor becomes a "normal life."

The only reason I survived and, yes, even thrived, while in the county jail's harsh solitary conditions was because I had the blessing of love, support, and stimulus from people who sincerely cared about me and my welfare. I had people *feeding* me the substance I needed for my mental and spiritual evolution, whether it was my father sending me college-level books through my uncle; the city councilman, who visited me (off the books) in the attorney booth that allowed him to hug me, hold me, and cry with me; Chaplain Jim Richards who came every week to debate the highs and lows of Job from the Old Testament; my loving mom who would park outside of Oakland County Jail wailing aloud to a God who remained silent at a time when every cell in her body was being challenged to go on, to survive for a better tomorrow; or Theresa who would write me daily, hourly, begging me to call her. "You are coming home, right Mar?" she would ask, all the while running up insurmountable phone bills with the hope that I would be home soon to help.

"Yes, my love, don't worry. I'm coming home," I would reply, as tears silently wet my shirt as I sat cuffed to the payphone near the deputy's desk. This was a privilege granted me every few days "*if the officers had time*" as it was clearly explained to me on day one. Theresa provided me with intimacy, that blessing of having someone out there who actually needed me, wanted me, and yearned for my voice and letters. This provided the energy I needed, at times, to keep going. It was another *why* that helped me get through my *what*. Many young offenders do not have this benefit.

I had a fertile mind, and they planted and nourished seeds of mental and spiritual strength and growth. I had fallen into the depths of despair, and, yet, in this quiet brokenness I began a rebuilding process that would lead me toward my purpose. This is *not* the case for most people, especially youths, placed in long-term solitary confinement.

March, 1996, "Juvenile Rock," Oakland County Jail

Now, after eight months in solitary within the Health Care Department, I was being told, respectfully, to pack my stuff and get ready to move to I-Center, dubbed the "Juvenile Rock," to be housed with other juveniles being held in solitary. The Health Care Department, four cells of solitary, and the Juvenile Rock, eight cells of solitary, are all in the county jail. The cells in Juvenile Rock are also solitary, though they have bars, taking away the complete solitary state. Most of the staff had developed an affinity for me because of my youthfulness, the harshness with which I was being housed, and simply because they had gotten to know me. I stayed quiet and read all day, and I treated them as I would like to be treated. Some reciprocated, and some did not. The principles that were developing within me through pain and study allowed me to walk with integrity and character. Some would scoff that I was a fraud or the "perfect prisoner." In actuality, I was simply experiencing growth as an individual, prefaced by immense pain.

To be honest, I was not looking forward to the move. The cell that I'd been in for the past eight months had a glass window in the door that looked out on a hallway. The I-Center had bars and was noisy. The staff made comments like, "Hopefully, you can talk some sense into those animals," or, "You're gonna hate it there." Words can shape our experience if we allow them. Our experience in any situation will be determined by our attitude. I didn't allow the comments shape my reality.

I-Center was not far from the Health Care Department. You had to travel through several hallways and a couple of check points where we had to be buzzed through. The Oakland County Jail is an impenetrable fortress; the maze of hallways intrigues even the captive. "You aren't going far, Mario. You'll be better off with the younger guys. You will be a good influence on them," said the sergeant. The staff sent the sergeant to be the bearer of bad news because they knew that I would be disappointed. I swallowed the discomfort and quietly listened to what the Spirit was trying to tell me, for in all things lay a reason, a purpose.

I gathered all of my possessions, including a toothbrush and toothpaste, a cup, and a few goodies like chips and cookies and tossed them in the middle of my bed. I then undid my bed sheets and rolled my possessions into a bedroll. I also had a small cardboard box full of books. I laid the bedroll on the box and picked it up. "Ready," I told the Sergeant. By now they trusted me enough to not cuff me.

Once we arrived at the I-Center, the guard pulled out his over-sized keys and opened the "cat walk," a space to walk alongside the single cells, yet still be enclosed. We, one prisoner at a time, were allowed one hour out into the "cat walk" a day. This enabled us to use the shower, the phone, or simply just walk up and down talking to the other prisoners who were waiting for their hour outside of their cage. Most of them could not afford the $15-dollar phone calls, so using the phone was out of the question.

The "cat walk" was as smoked filled as a saloon on a Friday night. One youth who was standing in the catwalk, soaking up his hour of glory and "freedom," puffing a cigarette. "*Mario!!!!*" he yelled with a huge smile. It was Benson, a large, young, African-American kid of just fifteen. Benson had been charged with first-degree felony murder, armed robbery, and conspiracy to commit murder, car-jacking, and a slew of other charges. He and a few other teens car-jacked a suburbanite white guy. They killed him and kept his body in the trunk as they rode around for days. "What you doin' here? You wit us now?" he said with a smile only a mother could love.

Benson, like the other juveniles who now comprised the eight-man juvenile rock, had passed through the Health Care Department. With permission from the staff, I had welcomed each one with a small bag of commissary items and verses from the Bible. I remembered how I had felt, alone and broken down, when I first arrived at the county jail. Of all places of confinement, the county jail is by far the most inhumane. To place a youth in long-term solitary confinement is incomprehensible. Thus, it soothed my own inner pain to relieve that of another. This was a path; a destiny of ministry that began in the depths of hell called solitary confinement and continued on the catwalk of I-center, a path that would continue throughout the prisons of Michigan.

As I walked down that smoke-filled, paint-chipped, darkened catwalk on I-center, I understood for the first time how this giving and receiving thing worked. I had given something to them. In return, I received warm welcomes and smiles from all my "brothers." They were giving that which I had given unto them: love, respect, and hospitality. It was in this moment that understood, completely, the two-sided coin of Karma. While some may refer to Karma as a "bitch," others look at her as a pretty little angel that is making way for purpose and destiny. I got it! If I give love, then I get love. In the bowels of hell on earth, i.e. the Oakland County Jail, a Universal Principal of understanding took root that was destined to produce an abundance of fruit. I was determined to sow "good" seed, for I desired "good" fruit.

Life in I-Center consisted of absurd TV shows that kills one's brain cells with absolutely no educational stimuli. With most of the juveniles being on some sort of psychotropic drug, usually Seroquel, there evolved a medium of exchange between the juveniles and the second most powerful position in the county jail: "Trustee." Trustees were prisoners serving time for a misdemeanor but who had jobs such as janitorial porter, kitchen worker, laundry porter, and others. These scumbags were the pawns of the guards who had free reign on the facility. Yet, the relationship between the two was more of an, "I won't tell on you if you don't tell on me" arrangement because the guards were more crooked than the trustees. County jails are notorious for unseen atrocities at the hands of prison guards. With its enclosed walls, maze-like structure, and buzzed-in security doors every fifty feet, the Oakland County Jail was a world of its own with rules of engagement and laws of governance that were inherently different than social norms. In the county jail, the deputy is god. Period.

Recently, the kind of atrocities that can, and do, occur were highlighted in the leaked videotapes from Riker's Island of New York that showed sixteen-year-old Kalief Browder being physically assaulted by both staff and fellow prisoners alike. One video shows a guard escorting a cuffed Kalief from his solitary cell to the shower. At one point, the guard slams Kalief to the concrete floor as other deputies rushed in to assist. In Oakland County Jail, the violence perpetuated at the hands of deputies did not differ. "Trustees," so called "trusted" minimum-security prisoners serving their misdemeanor time by working in the jail, would perform every other duty other than that of the deputies and health care staff. Thus, they were out of their cells most of the day, which allowed them to witness these atrocities at the hands of the guards upon the other prisoners who were awaiting trial, conviction, and sentencing before being sent upstate. This old song has been played for centuries, from the house slave to the field slave days, pitting one against the other. The "trustees" were the eyes, ears, and confidants of the prisoner guards with the understanding that such confidence came with protection and sweeteners. Protection, meaning, "You (the trustee) keep your mouth shut, and we (the prison guards) won't set you up," and sweeteners in the form of goodies (food) that was likened to money to the poor. Guards would bring so much food in for themselves that the leftovers would be a banquet style meal for any prisoner.

The first eight months in the Health Care Department afforded me the opportunity not only for self-reflection but also observational learning. The guards watched me, conducting rounds every thirty minutes, but I watched them, the trustees, the nurses, the staff, and the other prisoners. I was a sponge, soaking up every detail, for I quickly understood that such details would safeguard my life, my survival. I observed that some guards joked with everyone, including the prisoner trustees, and even me, but most did not. Most treated us with disdain and distrust. I later learned that "distrust for the prisoner" is at the core of their training. When I learned of the training, I began to understand that the façade of friendship expressed by the prison guard was more of a

puppet-master mindset to control a larger segment of the population by gaining information and knowledge through a cooperative
relationship.

While on the juvenile rock on I-Center, I was able to witness
the spectacle of the present-day slave running behind his masta'
on the present-day slave quarter barracks, i.e., the I-Center cat
walk that ran parallel to the prisoner cat walk. Three televisions
hung from the ceiling of the prison guard catwalk, spaced apart
proportionately so that all eight cells could have a vantage point
to at least one television. When one of the eight was using their
hour per day on the catwalk, there was no conflict in changing
the channels on any of the three televisions. However, when us
juveniles used up all of our "lifelines," so to speak, we would lean
on each other for help. We were each allotted only one hour per
day out of our six-by-seven-foot cells, but sometimes we needed
to get a message out at a different time of day, so we assisted each
other in making calls or sending messages. The rule was that you
had to use up your one-hour slot well before the catwalk closed for
the night, which was 8:00 p.m. After the catwalk closed, we could
no longer have one of our cohorts change the channel. I never
watched television unless there was a movie on. For the most part,
I stayed in my books, thoughts, or prayers as I observed all those
around me. My quietness and my wisdom served as fodder for the
starving young souls around me. I began to minister to them, and
I found meaning and purpose in that service.

On one particular night, the officer's first comment when coming onto the catwalk was, "Don't ask for a *fucking* thing." He stared
into the eyes of seven Black and one Latino youth. I rubbed the
beads of my rosary, staring back. There were certain officers that
you just did not mess with, and this was one of them; but I was
always resistant, even then. Since we needed a channel changer,
one of the youngsters, "June Bug" we called him, whispered down

the juvenile rock, "I need some magazines ya'll. I'm finna make us a channel changer. After I change my channel, I'll pass it down to ya'll so you can change ya'lls' TV." We passed the magazines through the bars cell to cell until about ten of them made it to June Bug.

"June Bug," I whispered.

"Yea, Rio?" he replied. The boys from the "Yac", that is, Pontiac, called me Rio.

"Do me a favor," I said. Even then, I had learned that manners and respect get you much farther when dealing with men of the street.

"Sure, Rio, wassup?" June Bug whispered back.

"Let's wait to see if he does another round, or if a trustee comes around, and I'll ask for the them to change the channel. Let's just see," I whispered back.

"Sure thing, Rio. No problem," said June Bug, as there was no need for an explanation.

We told the time through the television programs. The *Fresh Prince of Bel Air* came on at 4:00 p.m., *Who's the Boss* at 4:30 p.m. and so on. By the TV programs, I could tell that more than forty-five minutes had passed since the officer had done his round. It was a Sunday, so that was not necessarily uncommon, but to leave us juveniles alone for any length of time was volatile. That bunch was always up to something.

I forgot about the television and, instead, began to make myself my nightly hot cocoa. First, I wrapped my toilet tissue into a little ball, placed it at the back of my steel toilet/sink and lit it on fire. I always placed the ball of tissue at the back of the toilet so that I could easily knock it into the toilet water when finished or if the guard was coming. I used a pencil to puncture the lip of the small milk carton and tied a small piece of ripped sheet to each end of the pencil as a hanger of sorts and then hung the carton over the flame to heat the milk. I reached into my bag of commissary and pulled out a 3 Musketeers candy bar, unwrapped it, broke it up into small pieces and dropped them into my plastic tumbler ready for the hot milk to be poured on top. This was my closest thing to hot chocolate, a childhood favorite.

As I was breaking up the candy bar, from the corner of my eye I saw a long, fishing pole-type mechanism made from the magazines that we sent to June Bug. *He's in motion.* I dropped the candy bar into the cup and waited to see if June Bug could change the channel to TNT, our favorite channel after 9:00 p.m. because it showed movies. I pressed my face against the bars to whisper, "It's on," but I could already see a row of hands gripping the bars in anticipation of June Bug's stance of resistance. We were rebels without a cause. The television closest to me and June Bug was probably a good ten feet away. The pole stretched and stretched until it began to bow as we all gasped in unison, but it stayed firm enough to change one channel, then another, then another, until finally, the trustee came flying out of nowhere, yelling, "What the *fuck* do you think you are doing?" He yanked the channel changer from June Bug's hands.

"You dumb white bitch," June Bug yelled out. "I will fuck your punk ass up as soon as they break these bars!"

"Shhhhh," I told June Bug. "Don't create a scene!" It was too late.

"Faggot? Faggot? Look who's talking? They gonna fuck your faggot ass all the way upstate," snapped the trustee as he laughed with an evil look. "All you little faggot juvi' bitches are gonna get raped upstate." He broke up our channel changer, piece by piece. "I'll let boss know how much you little faggots appreciate magazines. I'll make sure they come and take all your fucking magazines, you little b—" Before he could fully get the word "bitch" out of his mouth, a little bar of state soap hit him right in the eyebrow. "Ouchhhh!" he yelled as bar after bar of soap came at him like a hive of bees. "Fuck you, you cracker bitch," was the overwhelming battle cry.

I stared at the chaos and just shook my head. I walked the entire two feet to my bed, next to my toilet, and lit the ball of toilet tissue under the milk carton as I continued my nightly ritual of making hot chocolate. The next day, I knew that the guards would shake us down and take anything they deemed contraband. I would lose my lighter, the one that I secretly bought for twenty items costing $.50 each from the very trustee who was now running from soap bars like he was running from bullets. I watched how trustees became puppets to the puppet master guards, and I vowed inside that would never be me.

The first week on "Juvenile Rock" was more amusing than traumatizing. Benson, "Chill Will", Kenta, "Smoke," "Mouse," "Daz" and I were the "permanent residents." The other two cells were used for juveniles facing lighter sentences that were simply acting out in juvenile detention. They never stayed too long. And it was "good" for them because these fellas gave them hell. They would torture these kids. Of course, when I was awake or praying I was able to quiet them down and make them leave them alone, but one can do only so much, especially when these "short timers" had a smart mouth and needed protection from others. I never understood this logic. Occasionally, a belligerent drunken adult who was arrested for disorderly conduct was thrown into a cell to sober up. Though we were in single-man cells that separated all eight prisoners, it was legal for them to place such individuals around us at the time. Or if the guards wanted to torture in a less threatening way, if there was an open cell on the juvenile rock, then they would put the adult prisoners in with us. We were the noisiest of hallways in the entire jail. From water fights to soap fights, the juveniles never left a dull moment.

On most occasions, the televisions would all be turned off as a community punishment for the actions of a few. On one occasion, they put an ornery alcoholic in the first cell on the juvenile rock for his own protection. Turns out he liked to use the N-word for both staff and other prisoners in an old southern way. He must have gotten hit with over a hundred bars of soap those three days, not to mention the cups of water that the youths would throw on him throughout the day. But the mean drunk continued to call them the N-word. I couldn't help but laugh. The old racist deserved it. He wasn't ever seriously hurt. Just a lump or two on his simpleton head. The guards made sure that the young cubs didn't get to him. I smiled at each girlish scream the man would give off with each pelt to his skin by the small green bars of soap that I would soon learn were made by state prisoners "upstate."

The guards in the Health Care Department had been wrong: the next four months that I served on the Juvenile Rock were not bad at all. In fact, as I reflect on it, I realize that it was the beginning of my ministry, the beginning of the fulfillment of my covenant to save youths like me. God used this harsh environment to help me understand my audience, my future students.

We had some good laughs on that Juvenile Rock in the spring and summer of 1996. I had been there the longest, thus, they all called me the "OG," meaning Original Gangster of the Rock, but on a serious note, I played the role of counselor and minister to these youths facing life sentences, though I didn't realize it at the time. The food in the Oakland County Jail is possibly the worst food I have ever tasted in my life. My mom and dad made sure that I kept money in my account so that I could buy commissary food. I explained to my parents our conditions and how the other youths didn't have much. They made sure that I had enough money to help the others in need so that they did not go to sleep hungry. My mom even dropped off a suit for one youth who had been charged with attempted murder.

It was then that I had a stirring in my spirit to help guide young men to the knowledge and understanding of the Lord. I ministered to them during their hour out on the catwalk, praying over them, reading the Word to them and discussing its mysterious power and implications. Every day, one or two of the seven other juveniles would ask me to pray with them, over them, or read the Word to them. I prayed often, and when I did, I could hear other juveniles whispering, "Keep it down, y'all, Mario's praying." I would smile, internally, and give reverence to God for softening the hearts of these youths that had been calloused by the shorthand that life had dealt them. I did not know whether these seeds would take root and grow. I taught them that they were where they were because of who they were; and, if they were ever to get out . . . ever . . . then they would have to begin, immediately, sowing different seeds. I taught them principles . . . first being the principle of harvest: to the measure in which you sow, so shall you reap. And yet, I had not fully understood or embraced that which I was teaching. I still had so much growth to undergo. I was unconscious of the fact that the enemy did not exist outside the window . . . but in the mirror.

CHAPTER 6

SENTENCING

May, 1996, Presentencing Investigation Interview Phase

THE INTRO I RECEIVED from Ms. Cathy Miller was less than warm. She was the lady who held my fate in her hands, the one who was to assess who I was and whether or not I would benefit from the services of the juvenile department or the "services" of the Michigan Department of Corrections. Cathy was a middle-aged, middle-class white woman with reddish brown hair that reached her shoulders. She was educated and smiled a lot, giving off an air of safety and security to her interviewees, however false.

"Mario, I'm Cathy. I work for the Family Independent Agency, and I am responsible for assessing whether you qualify for juvenile placement. The adult probation department will also interview you in the next couple of days. Then we both will give our recommendations in court, sort of like a little trial where both attorneys will ask us questions, under oath, and then the judge will decide whether to sentence you as a juvenile or an adult. What you say can, and will, affect your success in an appeal. I have been told that you are in a position to possibly win an appeal. I will be honest

with you, Mario, Judge Anderson is the harshest judge in Oakland
County, so it does not really matter whether you accept responsibility and admit guilt. He will not sentence you as a juvenile. But
legally, I must tell you that what you say may be used against you
if you succeed in receiving a new trial."

"So, you don't think that he will send me to the juvenile department, ma'am?" I asked sheepishly, tears in my eyes.

"No, I'm afraid not. Even if I went in there begging for you, Judge
Anderson *will not* send you to our department," she said with
almost a nonchalant attitude. There was coldness in this woman.

I walked away from that morning interview confused, spiritually. Having now been convicted of second degree murder, my
only "out" was being sentenced as a juvenile. Surely, God would
not require me to go to an adult prison system. I was consumed
with fear and doubt, feelings that were all too familiar. "God let me
down before, why wouldn't he let me down again?" I mumbled as
I walked down the juvenile catwalk on I-Center. I peeked in the
cells of the juveniles who were asleep and thought about our fate.
I was saddened by the stark reality that God was not coming to
save me, or any of us. They stayed up late, talking and whispering
about their fears in the dark. "Daz, do you think we can make it?"
whispered a youth frightened of the not knowing. I would hear
them as I prayed silently to a God who had yet to respond.

I later learned that earlier that same year Ms. Miller had aggressively fought for the sentencing of a sixteen-year-old who had been
convicted of murder, armed robbery, conspiracy to commit murder, and more to go to the juvenile department. His rap sheet was a
football field long. She won. He went to juvenile. Later, in my personal development through the studying of the social sciences, I
realized that we all fall prey to this unconscious identification with
others "like us," and thereby afford them more opportunities, or
simply respond to them with a slight degree of more compassion

and understanding. I say this because Max, the young man she defended, was white, and so was Ms. Miller. I can't help but wonder if I had been white instead of Latino if she might have been more willing to go to bat for me.

Next was Marcus Mudley, the representative for the Adult Probation Department, who interviewed me for about twenty minutes. The questions were from an interview document that he read off. He was respectful but dry. No emotion. As if it were merely a formality. As if his decision had already been made. I did not take anything positive away from this interview. I was hopeful, yet at that age, the entire process was very confusing.

Despite her discouraging responses, Ms. Miller's interview had left me hopeful because she was honest in terms of my judge. I had already heard a lot of bad things about him, so her confirmation led me to believe she might be compassionate toward my process. And, yet the process is just that, a process . . . a non-emotional, mechanical thing called the *Criminal Justice System*. It is a system that has become so complex that it has developed tunnel vision when it comes to the incarceration of men, specifically minority youths and young adults. All the attention has been placed on the front end of the sentencing with little focus on the long-term implications of warehousing these youths for decades, that is, the back end.

Imprisonment at a young age, especially solitary confinement, creates gaps in the social learning and development of the youth that may never be retrieved. The only remedy is a continuous exposure and commitment to stepping out of one's comfort zone, the inverse of the natural response to the post-traumatic stress that one will invariably experience. This compels me to wonder: what would a person's "comfort zone" be after decades in prison since he or she was a teenager?

June 1996, Presentence Investigation Phase: Sentencing

Finally, the big day came. The courtroom was full of my family, supporters, and long-time friends of my family. Everyone was hopeful, praying that I would get sentenced as a juvenile and sent to a juvenile prison where more resources like education and counseling would be available. The heart of the controversy was that I could only be held, legally, until I was twenty-one. I was now seventeen. Only four years for a cold-blooded murder screamed "injustice," especially during a 1995-96 election year that touted quotes about inmates from the Clintons as "Super predators who must be made to kneel." Especially for a seventeen-year-old who still refused to admit guilt or accept responsibility for his actions, and who was unconsciously harboring the bitterness of blame for the environment from which he came.

Jerry didn't call any witnesses on my behalf. When asked about this, he said, "What for? Judge Anderson read all of your cousin Tone's statements. Remember? He knows that you are guilty, so he believes that you are a coldblooded killer that made his mom commit perjury on the stand." So, there you have it. There was no point. I sat there in the courtroom, slumped in my chair in a bright orange jumpsuit staring directly at Ms. Miller as if to say, "We both know the truth. We both know that you are a liar." I did not even blink. I was as still as a statue, frozen and numb from it all.

"It is in my professional opinion that due to Mario's refusal to accept responsibility for the crime and admit guilt, he is not amenable to treatment. In addition, his refusal to admit guilt will be a distraction to the other juvenile offenders," she said with a straight face in response to the prosecutor's questions. "I strongly recommended that Mario be sentenced to the adult prison system because they offer more services that would better fit his needs." Twenty-five years later I have yet to discover what those services are, besides warehousing.

I was in shock. I looked over my shoulder to my family who were also surprised. Ms. Miller had interviewed them as well. Her advice had been the same: "The judge will not sentence Mario as a juvenile, thus, safeguarding the chances for appeal. This should be your goal. If he admits guilt and begs for mercy, I believe the judge will still sentence Mario as an adult. And, to make it worse, his admission of guilt will negatively affect his chances if he gets a new trial through the appeals court." Marcus, the representative from the adult probation department, had told us the exact number that the prosecutors would recommend: twenty-two to forty years. This was no surprise because the prosecutor's office and Marcus Mudley's were right next to each other. It's a brotherhood, this thing called the "justice" system.

At the time, I felt betrayed by Cathy and Marcus and even the "system," but mostly I felt betrayed by God. Go figure, a murderer angry with an absent God! The audacity I had. Yet, after a year in solitary confinement and a spiritual awakening that had been transformative in nature, I expected a different response from a God who I was sure was now *listening*. Or so I thought. I had changed my thinking. I no longer sought evil but good. I had become a young man after God's own heart, just as when I was a boy. I guess a part of me thought maybe, just maybe, God would have mercy on me since I had sought him with a pure heart. But once again, I felt that God had let me down. I was hurt, scared, and completely *broken*.

July, 1996, Sentencing

Judge Anderson said many things during the sentencing phase but a few things stand out.

He spoke at length about the "expert opinion" of Ms. Miller and how a sentencing to the juvenile department may disturb the rehabilitation of the juveniles around me. He then went on to speak directly to me, staring into the depths of my soul as he chastised me in open court. "You came from a perfect family. You destroyed that. You killed Samuel in cold blood. Shame on you for all that. For all of these reasons, I am sentencing you as an adult. Your sentence is to be served in the Michigan Department of Corrections for twenty to forty years for the murder of Samuel and two years for the felony firearm. May God have mercy on your soul."

As the gavel slammed, I was in a daze. The sheriffs, one on each side, guided me, as if they were carrying me, to the exit as both families, that of the victim's and the perpetrator's cried aloud, one in pleasure, the other in pain, but both heartbroken at the hands of a broken youth. Two lives lost. Two families destroyed.

Feet shackled, belly chains sounding, I paused one foot for a second to see my family though tears blurred my vision. "Keep it moving!" snarled the sheriff, yanking my arm.

My year in solitary brought me to my knees, broke me in half, and rebuilt within me an understanding that the cross that I must bear, I must bear alone. Snitching on guys to get a reduced sentence that would have enabled me to be released at the age of twenty-one was just not the answer. I believe the Spirit of the Living God deep within my soul told me that I would be ok. "You will hurt. You will suffer. But you will be strengthened." I prayed earnestly day and night, imploring God for strength of spirit and wisdom of the mind. As the devil whispered to me, "The storm is coming," the Word that fed my soul and strengthened my heart whispered back, "I *am* the storm." I no longer prayed for freedom. I now prayed for the strength and wisdom to accept His will over mine.

CHAPTER 7

SEPARATE BUT NOT EQUAL

August, 1996, The Ride "Upstate"

"GOING UPSTATE" is a proverbial saying for being transferred to the State Prison System, which was, and is, generally in upstate rural areas. The talk among the juveniles about going upstate was full of anticipation, fear, a commitment to survive no matter what, and excitement for getting out of the horrific confines of the Oakland County Jail. When one of the juveniles previously sentenced and transferred upstate came back for a pending case, he described a place much different than the county jail. "M-a-a-a-n, they got tape players and televisions that you can buy, but you gottta have yo' peeps put funds in yo' account. You can buy food to cook. They call those 'cook-ups.' They got microwaves and yard time that you can go out in for hours. We ain't locked up all day like here." We were excited, indeed.

I had promised myself that if state prison were like the county jail, then I would take my own life. At that age, I could not fathom living twenty-two years under those conditions. We were a bunch of kids, feet dangling through the bars, as we talked about what prison would be like, what we were going to do first and how we would survive. "I'm stabbing the first mothafucka that talks about fucking me. I don't care how big they are, I will stab 'em."

"We'll have each other's backs. Don't even sweat it." Such was the rhetoric that could be heard among us boys trying desperately to become men, for our lives and the quality thereof depended upon such conversations, such commitment to self-preservation, the first law of nature.

At a time when kids should be planning their college classes, we were on I-Center in Oakland County Jail, Pontiac, Michigan planning our entry into Michigan's most notorious prisons. Instead of class registration, we were already being slotted for certain packs, for we would be pigeonholed because of race, ethnicity, color, religion, sexual preference, or courage. Yes, courage, for if you cannot stand on your own and withstand the assault of the enemy, you will be taken advantage of, repeatedly, until you are of no use. And if you do survive, at what expense did salvaging the sanctity of your body come at? What is the residual effect of the mind of an adolescent housed in long-term solitary and in long-term imprisonment with adult offenders? The brokenness has a ripple effect that transcends boundaries, decades, and, yes, even generations.

While it was nice to be around others, there was always a reminder of where you were and what you could expect at any moment. Anything. From what I have been told, the staff in Oakland County Jail are just like any major county jail: hardened, apathetic, and calloused by the job. It is understandable, since it happens even to doctors, so why not for a position that requires, for the most part, a mere high school diploma or GED? Yet I did not come to this understanding, or across this information, during that year as a youth in the county jail. I only knew that it made me feel sad, alone, and even more hopeless for any chance of redemption, both for me and for mankind.

In prison, where the fences are rimmed with razor wire and the walls are high, there was complete autonomy from the checks and balances that would otherwise prevent abuses and atrocities that are usually seen only in the movies. What pushes people to be so callous, so unforgiving, and so cruel to an otherwise vulnerable population? This is a population already oppressed by the shortcomings of life. If a wise man leaves an inheritance to his children's children, then what does a crack-head? A murderer? A career-criminal? A serial-rapist? Or, most common, what is the "inheritance," or the long-term implications, of a fatherless home? Of not ever knowing your father, where you came from, or what model or blueprint should you follow? What frame of reference has been handed down to you? We all need a reference point from which we can map out a vision.

Vision is so important. The Bible says, "Without vision the people will perish." And perishing they are. Almost nine out of ten young black and brown men that I have spoken to from our inner cities lack a vision, goal, or target for which they are aiming. The saddest part is that it is clear that no one has ever held such a conversation with most of these youths. Most of them grew up with no structure or stability in their lives. Subsidized housing rewards young black and brown women for two things: having as many kids as they can and not having a male in the household.

If one searches just the slightest bit through our country's history, we witness that the slave masters were able to "condition" the female slave into being a "good slave" after breaking the spirit and body of the male in the presence of his woman and children so that they may *see* the brokenness and thereby *believe* the brokenness. The condition of a society may be witnessed by the quality of the dominant male force in that region. In most traditional cultures, the male serves as a foundation upon which to build the family. Without a solid male foundation, a family—incomplete in its structural foundation—will invariably fall. The dividedness in our nation, governments, communities, neighborhoods, schools, homes, and, sadly, our children is merely a reflection of the dividedness that exists within man. Within the men I now lived around; and, within me.

Upstate with the Big Boys

Saying goodbye to the Oakland County Juvenile Rock was oddly sad. It was probably rooted more so in fear, considering the fact that I had no clue what to expect upon entering the Michigan Department of Corrections Adult Male prison system. Us "Yac Town Boys," a term that was short for Pontiac, had truly bonded. We promised that we would protect ourselves at all cost. The message was clear: a violation would lead to a slippery slope fueled by the evil forces clearly present throughout that culture. The prison culture embraces fear, violence, and aggression as the means by which conflicts are resolved and monetary gain is achieved. This is simply the normal way of life within that lost city.

The criminal mindset is only heightened in the prison culture. In fact, it is magnified exponentially. It is that of a primitive way of being rooted in fear of losing that which one has left: his pride. Though even that is an illusion of control. We don't really possess anything, nor may we be possessed. As I was able to literally sit and reflect for hours, days, months, and years, it slowly became clearer and clearer: in the end, there is not much that really matters other than what you have done for one another. That joy is a residual reminder that it is through giving that we truly do receive.

The School to Prison Pipeline

I remember being belly chained and paraded around the courtroom, pale from the long-term solitary confinement. Then, I had felt ashamed, guilty, and afraid as I was walked throughout the Oakland County Court Halls in public, begging God to save me. Now the shackles were transporting me to the Michigan Department of Corrections. Once again God stayed silent as I begged for help ... for strength. That anger fueled my focus and determination to survive no matter what. There was no more plotting or scheming. I had been found guilty and sentenced. "If by chance these chains fall off," a sheriff told me, "please run so that I will have an excuse to shoot you." This was followed by peals of laughter.

My life paralleled that of Odysseus in that I, too, was on a voyage of twenty years trying to get home only to be tossed from island to island, continent to continent (prison to prison). At the time, I had no idea where or what "Ionia" was. I would later become intimate with the prison industrial complex. A once-upon-a-time agricultural epicenter turned ghost town, Ionia was now home to eight prisons from level one (minimum security) to the only level six (super maximum security) in Michigan. It was also home to the political system's powerhouses: the districts of the Republicans who controlled the appropriations and corrections committees included Ionia and the surrounding areas that benefited from that region's prison boom. Between the two, they wielded massive political and financial power through the federally-incentivized prison boom of the 80s and 90s. Prior to 1980, only 36% of prisons were located in rural communities and small towns (Beale, 1996). According to Beale, only about four new prisons were built each year throughout the 1960s and 70s; yet during the 80s, four mutated into a yearly average of sixteen, until, finally, it reached its peak at *twenty-five* new prisons being built per year in great ole' America in the 90s. "Between 1990 and 1999, 245 prisons were built in rural and small-town communities—with a prison opening somewhere in rural America every fifteen days (Beale, 2001).

I committed my crime at a time when it was more profitable to send me to the present-day plantation fields called prisons that were now scattered throughout the agricultural ghost towns of Ionia, Carson City, Kincheloe, and the likes, than to sentence me to the rehabilitative environment of a juvenile facility. It came down to dollars and cents.

This massive prison boom into rural America translates into "dramatic consequences for the entire nation as huge numbers of inmates from urban areas become rural residents for the purposes of Census-based formulas used to allocate government dollars and political representation. What resulted was a rural rise to middle class as the urban areas continued to grow while their young minority males remained at their expense. The economic restructuring of the 1980s entailed the acquisition of prisons as a conscious development strategy for financially depressed rural communities (Huling, 2002).

"Hundreds of small rural towns and several whole regions have become dependent on an industry which itself is dependent on the continuation of crime-producing conditions" (Huling, 2002, pp. pp. 1-2). In addition, the federal administrations and legislatures of Bush, Sr. and Clinton—yes, our beloved Bill Clinton—provided financial incentives for each state that put in place the passage of legislation for stricter laws that resulted in longer sentences. Harsher sentencing practices like the infamous "three strikes law" and the "lifer drug laws" were passed by state legislatures and enforced by local governments.

The racial disparities among those most severely sanctioned by these new laws and policies are startlingly similar to those found in student discipline data. In 1998, black youths with no prior criminal records were six times, and Latino youths three times, more likely to be incarcerated than whites for the same offenses

(Poe-Yamagata & Jones, 2000). While comprising one-third of the country's adolescent population, they represented two-thirds of all youths confined to detention and correctional placements (Poe-Yamagata & Jones, 2000). Four out of five new juveniles detained between 1983 and 1997 were youths of color (Hoyt, 2002). Thus, the proverbial seeds of the *school-to-prison pipeline* was sown with mostly poor, minority broken families left behind as the victims.

Many observers, advocates, and educators have crafted the terms such as *prison track* and *school-to-prison pipeline* to describe these dual trends. Such phrases depict a journey through school that becomes increasingly punitive and isolating for its travelers. Many will be taught by unqualified teachers, tested on material they never reviewed, held back a grade, placed in restrictive special education programs, repeatedly suspended, and/or banished to alternative out-placements before dropping or getting pushed out of school altogether. Without a safety net, the likelihood that these same youths will wind up arrested and incarcerated increases sharply. Adult prisons and juvenile halls are riddled with children who have traveled through the school-to-prison pipeline. Approximately 68 percent of state prison inmates in 1997 had not completed high school (Briefing Fact Sheet, 2014). Seventy-five percent of youths under age eighteen who have been sentenced to adult prisons have not passed tenth grade. An estimated 70 percent of the juvenile justice population suffers from learning disabilities, and 33 percent read below the fourth-grade level (Justice, 2001). The single largest predictor of later arrest among adolescents is having been suspended, expelled, or held back during the middle school years.

We have a criminal justice system that profits from the spoils of this "War on Drugs" and "War on Crime" façade they call their mission through corporate back-dealings and curried contracting.

The war on drugs, disproportionately skewed with black and brown men, clogged the courts to the point of breakdown. In 1980, there were more persons incarcerated in federal prison for drug crimes than for all other crimes put together. America's shift toward a prison economy needed a vehicle by which to transport its desired population from the streets into the prison beds: drug policy and enforcement. America's drug policies criminalized a generation of African-American men. Today, on average, blacks receive sentences that are 4.25 percent higher than those of whites (Burch, 2015). Sentenced twenty-two to forty years for a second-degree murder charge that carried only eight to twenty-five years, I experienced the sentencing disparities first hand. Time and again, I ran across white defendants with similar cases and convictions that differed only in sentencing, often receiving only the seven- or eight-year minimum for the same charge, while brown and black prisoners received sentences like mine.

Thus, began the prison boom of the late 1980s and the 90s. Funding was specifically provided for the building of the prison industrial complex as we know it today, and the prisons were strategically placed in white, rural areas. In Michigan, where most prisoners come from the tri-county and urban areas, during this time period there were approximately twenty-five prisons in Michigan's Upper Peninsula and fewer than twenty in the Lower Peninsula. These prisons filled an economic vacuum where the farm lands lay fallow, reflective of the pulse of their local economies with the majority of the residents being on welfare. In fact, there was a huge article in a Lansing newspaper some time ago that highlighted the fact that "Ionia was officially put on the map" because Wal-Mart had arrived, and the article was specifically aimed at praising the prison industrial complex that had brought the economy of Ionia back to life. Wal-Mart was that symbol of success.

"Trust me, sir, you do not need an excuse," I replied to the sheriff gripping my arm who had joked about me giving him an excuse to shoot me. "We both know that." This set off more laughter, but I glared deep into his eyes until I could imagine the feel of the grip of my hands around his throat. He stared back then stopped laughing.

"What the fuck are you looking at?" he growled and walked away.

"Not a damn thing," I said under my breath. I had heard of the atrocities that befell prisoners who were driven upstate by the Oakland County sheriffs. One victim told me that the sheriffs took him out into a corn field and forced him to his knees for an hour with a shotgun to the back of his head as mosquitoes bit his face and arms. "Move, boy. Move just one inch so I can pull this trigger." Thoughts of it tormented the youths waiting to be transferred upstate. My fear was quickly turning to anger as once again I was adapting to the immediate needs of the environment. I learned an important principal that day: "If you stand for nothing, you'll fall for anything." I kept this in mind as I contained my anger.

August, 1996, Day 1, Riverside Quarantine

As I made my way up the sidewalk of Riverside Correctional Facility, the Michigan Department of Corrections' quarantine for the twenty and under prisoner population, one small half step at a time, the chains that wrapped around my ankles and connected to my waist muted the noise and the screams. I paused for a second to give my ankles relief from the pressure of the leg shackles. Then I could hear them.

"I'm fucking you tonight, boy. Yeah, white boy, I'm gettin' that pink ass," yelled a prisoner from a window on the third floor. I couldn't make out where it came from between the blinding sun and the darkened windows covered by makeshift curtains. I just shook my head and thought *I guess he'll be my first victim.*

Although I was afraid, I had been trained to use that freely produced adrenaline to fight, to push, to advance and to win no matter what, no matter whom, no matter where. "You can't just keep trying to fight everyone you argue with, son," said my father in his usual talk whenever I was suspended from school. So, at the age of twelve, during the summer entering my eighth-grade year, my father took me to see "Sensei Moshier" as I was to address him. This was one of the greatest visionary acts that my father did for me. "Martial arts aren't easy, son, but if you don't quit, you will love it," he said. "And, more importantly," he continued, looking into my eyes, you will learn how to control that temper that you inherited from me," he said, with love in his eyes. When we walked into the makeshift dojo that was really an attached garage, I was taken aback. There were four rows with at least eight to ten people in each row throwing punches in unison with a snap and a yell. *"Kia! Kia! Kia!"* It was cinematic, reminiscent of the Karate Kid.

I trained with Randall L. Moshier, a Fifth Don in the Arts of Ishinru. Sensei Moshier was a six-feet-two inch, 220-pound professional power-lifter who could bench 525 pounds at his meets. He had reddish brown hair and was thirty-five the year that I was imprisoned. He had been an eleven-year-old white kid with a dream of becoming the greatest fighter he could be and to live his life training others. That kid lived, ate, and breathed martial arts for twenty-five consecutive years, even after a falling out with his Sensei and mentor. "Success has enemies," Sensei Moshier would later say in relation to that falling out that held back his career. He was a fifth Don when he had a falling out with his Sensei, the only one who could test him for a higher ranking. Thus, Sensei Moshier was stuck being a fifth Don for the last ten years of his career.

Sensei Moshier continued to chase his dream and opened a dojo with his wife and two stepchildren, all of who were black belts trained under him. I walked into his dojo not knowing any of this, not understanding how much this one man would impact my life. "Hello there, Mr. Bueno," Sensei Moshier said, showing my father respect and honor.

"Hello there, Sensei," replied my father. He reached out and they shook hands and embraced. I watched quietly, wondering why I had never met this man. Sensei Moshier walked with an air of confidence, not arrogance. Sensei Moshier walked in power and precision, with intention and purpose.

He turned toward me and said, "So this is the lad?"

"This is he, Mario." It was clear that they had spoken already about me.

"So, son, you like to fight in the streets, huh?" Sensei Moshier asked me, chest out, eyebrow cocked, and rose with a piercing stare. I shook my head back and forth as if to say no. "I can't hear you, son," he said with power yet with compassion. My eyes got watery. I put my head down. I fought a fight within every day, a fight to believe, a fight to have the faith to go on, a fight to understand why would God abandon me and not heal my mom. What else could possibly come forth from such a bitter tree but bitter fruit? "It's okay, son," he reached out and grasped my hand. He leaned forward and whispered, "It's okay son. You are safe here." At this point, my father still had not known of my struggles within my mother's home because I kept it from him.

Safe I was. After training for almost ten weeks, Sensei Moshier called me to fight. "You are going to fight Cave Man. He is a purple belt, and he is kind of big, but his heart isn't as big as yours," he said as he tightened my gloves. "He's the one over my shoulder with the purple belt on," he looked at me and must have seen the fear. He grabbed my chin. "Look at me. Do you hear me?" I nodded yes. "He doesn't have the heart that you have. In life, that is all that counts: heart and effort. Now go show him how much heart you have," he narrowed his eyes as he continued, "Do you *hear* me?" I shook my head up in down, clear of the fear that once paralyzed me. He sowed a seed of belief in myself that day. I walked onto that mat. I stood five-feet-five-inches against this six-feet-three-inch "Cave Man."

The signal was given to begin. "*Ajame!*" I ran toward him and began to punch him in the face repeatedly, driving him into the garage door. I blacked out, so to speak, as I took all that rage and anger and unleashed in the form of wild punches that were landing.

Sensei Moshier had been yelling, "*Ush, ush,*" which means "stop" in Japanese, well before he grabbed my uniform collar and tossed me across the dojo. Sensei then yelled at me in front of the entire class. "When I say *ush,* boy, you stop. You got that? Otherwise you can leave and never come back!" I walked away from that class saddened, thinking that I had ashamed my Sensei. But, later, my father called me in excitement.

"Hey, boy!!! Your sensei called. He said that you have the heart of a lion! He said that you beat the crap out of Cave Man, that tall fucker! Moshier said he's gonna make you into a champion," he exclaimed. I loved hearing my dad be proud of me.

Shortly thereafter, my father and I stopped speaking to each other. Over the next few years, Sensei Moshier filled a void in my life by providing both meaning and mentorship, while my father struggled with his own internal and external battles.

My training gave me some small comfort in face of the threats coming out of Riverside's third floor window that day. The threat also made me recall the taunts of a sergeant in the Oakland County Jail. Because I was a juvenile housed in an adult facility, any services that I received had to be "specially" handled. The sergeant was apparently upset that he had been ordered by the captain to arrange and supervise a haircut. As I received my haircut, the sergeant stood behind me and taunted me in front of an attractive female deputy who stood beside him. "I can't wait til' this lil' bitch gets found guilty and slapped with a life sentence so we can send him upstate where they will rape his little bitch ass and mommy and daddy can't save him anymore." He went on and on as the female giggled. Even at sixteen, I knew that this guy was just trying to show off, but I quietly tucked away his warning and made myself a promise. *This will never happen to me. I am a warrior.* Well, now it was time to put up ... or, shut up.

I continued walking towards my new home, Riverside Correctional Facility, as my leg shackles grew tighter around my ankles causing me to slow down and pause. The taunts grew louder. "Yeah-h-h-h-h, white boy-y-y-y, I'm fuckin' that pink ass tonight." The August sun beat down on my pale white neck, the residual effect of a year in solitary. I paused for one moment at the first step to the prison entrance and squinted up at the third-story windows. I smiled as I whispered, *"I am a warrior."*

"Let's go Bueno!" snapped the deputy behind me. I put my head back down, ignored the taunts and walked into what appeared to be the staff entrance of what was to be one of my many homes. I was guided into an enclosed cage. The door locked behind me.

"Remove all articles of clothing. If you have any jewelry, turn it in now. Any contraband, toss it away now," said a fairly attractive female corrections officer of about forty. Another young black prisoner had arrived from a nearby county also shackled and in the company of his hometown sheriffs. We stood naked as staff walked by on regular intervals. The implication was that this business as usual. From the onset, we were humiliated into the understanding of *who* was in control. I waited for about twenty minutes until I finally asked if we were going to be given clothing. "Don't worry about that. This is not time for you to ask questions," snapped the corrections officer. The most crucial control that the department must maintain is of the mind. There are over 1,200 prisoners in any given prison in comparison to the approximately 120 staff during any given shift. Prisoners literally run the day-to-day operations.

Thus, the imperative nature of running a prison is in controlling the *minds* of the population. Correctional institutions are designed to safely, for both society and the prisoner, house and secure the imprisoned. Yet, imagine a world where we invested in our own safety, as a community, by educating the imprisoned in areas that empower their pro-socialization, ability to resolve conflict and empathize, and workforce development with an opportunity for a livable wage job. Maybe . . . just maybe . . . then recidivism would decrease significantly, just as studies of prisoners being given a post-secondary education prove that a mere associates degree reduces recidivism by over 30% for the imprisoned (Chappell, 2004). I knew even at that young age that my only power was in the control of my own mind; it was in the control of who I saw myself to be. To get through the moment . . . to endure the pressures around me, I would quietly recite as an inner mantra the words of Frankl, "Those who have a *why* to live, can bear with almost any *how*" (Frankl, 2006).

As time passed, vans were pulling up from counties all over Michigan, even from up north. In time, I learned that this was the hub and gatekeeper of offenders twenty and under who were entering the MDOC. Riverside's majority population, however, was twenty-one and over, and it was the level-four population that played for keeps with a lot of violence. Eventually, the cage that we were waiting in was full, holding about fifty of us young offenders, all naked, ashamed, belittled, and "taught who was master" from the onset. I was forced to stand naked in the cage in the lobby of the correctional staff entrance for approximately five hours before I was finally given some clothes. We were in the hands of an apathetic, dysfunctional system that is unknowingly breeding homegrown terrorist through callous, apathetic conditions and a lack of educational opportunities.

My First Lunch in Riverside Quarantine

The youth were predominantly black with a few Latinos and a couple of whites, though the staff that were in charge of "properly conditioning" the newly arrived youths were all whites and mainly women. This was odd to me but reminiscent of the slave days. We were yelled at in every "learning" situation. We were then ushered as cattle to the lunchroom where we were literally given three minutes to eat. We were being "broken" as they do to wild, untamed mustangs. I understood what they were doing and the staff did not like the look in my eyes. Yet, I stayed quiet and observant, understanding that with every action comes an equal, or greater, reaction.

In those days in Riverside, my despair and heartache centered on my loss . . . my woes . . . my life ending as I knew it. I lacked the maturity to understand the ramifications of my actions and the greater loss that, first, Samuel experienced. I robbed Samuel of any opportunity to transform, to evolve, to . . . *become* . . . as God intended him to become. In those early days, I did not consider his family's loss. I was too immature. I was lost in my own sadness . . . in my own loss of not having my mother . . . my father . . . my sisters. I was afraid that I would never return home; never return to see my Aunt Aida. Those fears turned into anger during the daylight hours and into sadness in the darkness of the night when I tasted the salt from own tears and wondered *why have I been judged as a man who knows your laws, Lord, when I have just learned them? Why show me the light just to sentence me to darkness? Why, Lord, show me the way when you have sent me in the opposite direction? Why, Lord?"* But I heard no response aside from the screams of young men being assaulted.

You Never Know Who Is Watching

The first week within the confines of the Michigan Department of Corrections' quarantine for the twenty and under prisoner population was atrocious at best. After our first set of clothing, we were obligated to pick through old, used underwear, socks, and outer garments before shower time. Your stay in quarantine depended upon your sentence, which determined your custody level. The longer the sentence, the higher the custody level, and the higher the custody level, the slower the turnover. This resulted in a longer stay in quarantine.

In that system, there were six levels of confinement, ranging from one (least confined) to six (most confined), with solitary being a separate, most severe form of confinement. In other words, the higher the level, the greater the suffering. At that time, the average level-four bed that housed problematic prisoners and those sentenced to ten or more years took about four months to open up. The lower levels experienced turnover at a more rapid rate, so those prisoners stayed in quarantine for less time.

Over that first weekend, a prisoner approached me in regard to a job that was opening up soon because he was leaving. He was the porter who worked for the attractive lady who had ordered our clothes to be removed on my first day. He said that he had worked for her for about four months and that she only chose level-four prisoners in order to reduce the turnover. He also said that she had watched me throughout the entire intake process and was impressed with my level of maturity. She wanted to know if I was interested in working for her. He went on to tell me that I would have new clothes every day, that I would be out of my cell Monday through Friday all day (in quarantine, prisoners were locked in their cells twenty-two hours a day), and I'd get paid and get extra food. I readily agreed to the job, blessed him and thanked him. He said that she would call me out that week for training. Although I did not view my sentence as salvation, I still praised God each and every day. I was hurt and upset by His decision not to save me, but I also believed that I deserved all that I was getting. So, if I could praise God even under those conditions, imagine how much I praised Him once I got that job.

The events unraveled as he said they would, though I never saw that young man again. Prison is like that. You can have a significant experience with a person never to see or hear from that individual again. The constant transfer of men from prison to prison is strategic to maintain the status quo, for it prevents the unity and solidarity that might lead to an awakening of a higher, collective consciousness toward purpose.

Quarantine for us was deplorable: the cells held two youths with no toilet, and we stayed locked down twenty-two hours a day. You could hear youths beating on their cell door for hours, begging to be let out to use the bathroom. Most would succumb to defecating in a t-shirt, or some other object, and then tossing it out of the window. The urine containers would eventually fill, resulting in youths urinating out the window. The stench that came through the windows on those hot afternoons in late august would curl the strongest of stomachs. I stared out of the window, looking at all of the feces stained t-shirts and shook my head. We were caged as animals and treated as chattel.

I stayed quiet most of the time. I learned that when you are talking, you are not learning, and in this environment, it was costly not to learn fast. Such a cost might lead to a violation of your property, your person, or both. From the day he arrived, one particular young white male tried to speak to anyone and everyone. That is a "no, no" in prison. That first week, I attempted to counsel him privately, out of proximity of the others.

"If I was you, I would stop being so friendly. Someone is gonna take it the wrong way." But he disregarded my advice, my warning. Later that day when we were in the shower room, he was gang raped. It broke my heart to walk out of that shower room knowing what was happening, but at the time, I didn't have the skills or the tools to stop the inevitable.

I was so angry that night as I thought about the conditions that we had been placed, us boys having to become men in accord with how stigmas and stereotypes of prison had shaped our definition of manhood. Most of those youths were becoming savages as a result of a system that didn't care, an institution that is systematic in its implementation of a model that clearly reinforces criminality, generational dysfunction, victimization, warehousing, and illiteracy as a means of maintaining the status quo. A system that is breading homegrown terrorists that are strategically, through systems barring "felons," placed in distinct neighborhoods with the residuals effects being that of a significant deterioration of the moral fabric within that immediate environment (Kirk, 2016).

CHAPTER 8

ARE YOU LISTENING NOW?

August-December, 1996

I SPENT APPROXIMATELY FIVE MONTHS in quarantine, which was completely different than the county jail, where I had been locked in cell twenty-four hours a day, seven days a week. For example, in quarantine, we were taken out of our cells to a lunchroom. It took me a few weeks to acclimate myself to the environment that allowed for social interaction. That year in solitary had changed me, shaped me, and molded me into a being detached from the whole, yet reconnected with the Source. Solitary, ironically, allowed me to be okay with me, with being alone. The origin of the word "alone" is Middle English, meaning, *"All + One."* Solitary, coupled with the Word of God and the enlightening books sent by my parents, forged within me the power to stand, All One, undivided, and indivisible, thus, when the storms would come, I could not be knocked down. Thus, is the power of a foundation. Thus, is the power of knowing *who* you are . . . and *who* you are destined to become.

Quarantine has yard time and day room time, two activities that the prison yard has but in more abundance. Quarantine was slowly getting us adjusted to the prison dos and don'ts so to speak. I had free reign of the place Monday through Friday because of the job I had been blessed with. The office that I worked in was responsible for intake of all new quarantine prisoners. I prepared the intake kits that included their entire prisoner uniform of shoes, socks, underwear, belts, coats, and t-shirts. The position gave me the opportunity to connect with the new men, for that is what these boys were called to become the minute they set foot in the adult prison yard. I breathed life into their hearts and minds. "Mind your business and stay out of the drama. If someone tests you, smash their fucking face in," I would tell the very young, frail youths. They were coming into an adult prison where no one cared about their vulnerability or ignorance to life resulting from immaturity and lack of experience. On the contrary, youths placed in adult prisons—as opposed to placement in juvenile training programs—are "more likely to be victims of prison violence and crime from both inmates and staff" (Martin Forst, 1989). They were walking into an unforgiving reality and it was my duty, my calling within, to remind them of where they have arrived . . . and, what the purpose is for being here, that is: mind your business, read, work out, and stay focused on freedom.

My boss would sit in quiet reflection, as I would minister to these youths. In reality, I did whatever my boss wanted me to. Most of the time, I would do a little work then she would say, "Go to the gym and play some basketball." I would obey, as always. Upon returning, I would find a bowl of cookies and ice-cold milk in the back room where I worked.

I watched the youths around me, kept one eye in a book, and the other on my potential foes. Even then, young men came to me for counsel, for direction. I was younger than most, but I was held in high esteem as wiser because of the principles that the Lord had revealed to me through the reading of His Word. I spoke these principles often and spent a lot of time meditating on the meaning. I don't mean to paint a picture of perfection. I was still angry with the Lord. I felt that my heart and spirit had been transformed and purified. I didn't understand why God would abandon me after my change of heart, so I would read and meditate upon the biblical stories of Moses, Joseph, Job, and . . . especially Jesus, who, above all else, begged God to pass the cup from his lips, that is, take away his painful path towards purpose: "Not my will, but Your Will be done." These stories reminded me that God does not speak just to make us *feel* better. No, on the contrary . . . God's quietness will be so deafening as to stir you to a level of discomfort to where you are so dissatisfied with what is and it will move you to chase that which is stirring deep within . . . at the core of *who* you truly are . . . God.

I now know that purification of heart, mind, and soul is a process that, for the most part, does not begin with joy, laughter, and good times. True purification often results from a life-shattering event that forever shifts your foundation and turns your world upside down. This shift is meant to stop you for a period of time and tell you to, "Wake up!" Many such "wake-up calls" may occur for those whose purpose is yet to be fulfilled. While my greatest wake-up call came in the form of immediate pain through being charged and found guilty of murder, solitary confinement, etc., my growth was just beginning, for it was my *thinking* that landed me where I was.

It takes time to transform one's way of thinking, which has been conditioned by the environment in which they are groomed. As the Hebrew tribe was saved from slavery out of the land of Egypt, so too was I saved from the streets. Yet, they were forced to wander for forty years in a desert as a process of purifying them from the Egyptian culture that resided within them, just as I needed to experience the transformational process of getting the streets out of me.

I still had a significant amount of maturing to undergo, regardless of how much I wanted to help others. It was not enough that I yearned to save young males like me. I didn't possess the skills, tools, and self-healing to guide others to change their *thinking*. At this point, I only possessed brokenness. And, one may only give what one has.

December, 1996-January, 1998, Carson City Correctional Facility

After Riverside, I was moved to Carson City Correctional Facility and spent about two years there. Upon my release from level four to level two, I imagined the anthem, "Who let the dogs out? Woof, woof." I ran around that prison yard like a chicken with his head chopped off: poker table, weight-room, basketball court, and poker table. Oh, did I say poker table? It was a gangsta-hustler man's greatest dream. Except, of course, for the occasional killing, routine stabbings, and fights. I understand now what the rapper 2pac meant when he quoted, "A coward dies a thousand deaths, but a soldier dies but once." The old Mario died back in that county jail, where solitary broke me into pieces; I couldn't die again, for a coward I am not. They could no longer harm me, hence, my apathetic attitude toward an unjust, hypocritical system that no longer had power over me.

In addition to gambling and violence, I had also continued to hustle drugs. My cellmate loved that I trafficked drugs because I had a lot of money flowing around me. I always shared my food with those around me, so we ate well. We purchased meats, cheeses, vegetables, and the like stolen from the prisoner kitchen. I rationalized my drug dealing with the fact that they paid me $20 a month to clean toilets but charged me $20 for a fifteen-minute phone call. Of course, the human mind can rationalize and justify any misdeed.

In the 1990s, the Michigan Department of Corrections was fertile ground for drug trafficking, which was at the root of the criminal element within the prison subculture that was otherwise permeated with extortion, drug abuse, prostitution, armed robberies, and gang violence. The bulk of the drugs always came by way of the corrections staff; however, in the 90s, the rules allowed for property (clothes, jackets, etc.) to be sent to prisoners through the mail. Prisoners run the property room, hence, this provided them with an easy avenue for the smuggling of contraband.

Prisoners still run the property room and most other departments today; however, the amount of personal property that they are allowed to receive from non-contracted (i.e., family and friends) parties is almost zero, making smuggling by means of the property room extremely difficult. All goods and property are purchased through contracted state approved vendors and only through funds in the prisoners' accounts. These internal controls provide the security measures that have greatly diminished drug trafficking within the correctional institutions.

Back then we prisoners engineered some ingenious avenues of smuggling large quantities of contraband into the prisons. For example, back when they allowed us to receive winter coats from friends and family, men of influence would arrange to have a down coat sent to young, naïve prisoner too weak to defend himself. Then a gang would wait for that young prisoner's name to be called over the speaker system, and as the naïve prey walked back to his cell from picking up his new coat that he mistakenly thought was sent by a loved one who had had a change of heart, the predators would ambush the youngster and take his coat. What they were really after was the quarter pound of marijuana pressed down flat and hidden inside well enough to make it past the security checkpoints. This combination of drugs and money, testosterone, anger, frustration, lack of educational stimuli, and a culture that embraces "a war on everything" motto is a cocktail of sorts for a prison yard. It is no surprise that prison is a volatile place.

Every prison in the Michigan Department of Corrections does not fit this description but many do. Now in 2017, the trafficking "commodity" of choice is tobacco. Staff and officers are more open to smuggling a pack of cigarettes and charging the prisoner a $100 as opposed to smuggling an illegal substance like drugs. They all, however, still fall short in offering the educational and emotional support needed for true transformation.

Most of my trouble came by way of "entrepreneurial" endeavors. As a result of the banning of tobacco, one of my ventures entailed packs of Newport 100s for $125 via Western Union, which included a pack of rolling papers for each one. I broke down each cigarette into 10 smaller cigarettes, totaling 200 cigarettes per pack. At any time, a cigarette could be sold for $4 to $5 each. Instead of selling them myself, I would hand them off to someone that I knew and trusted through time and experience for $3 each for a total of $600, He would sell each for $4 to $5 depending on the market at the time. Sometimes he would wait until the other sellers ran out so he could drive up the prices. He would sell out within seventy-two hours because more people smoke cigarettes than weed, and they were more economical. I soon began purchasing five packs at a time.

Drugs like weed were expensive, and only the hustlers could usually partake. Yet in some prisons like in Jackson and Detroit, there were so many packages of drugs being smuggled in that the market was saturated, thus dropping prices to affordable rates. Affordable enough to where eighty percent or more of the population would drop dirty for drug use at random, three-in-the-morning lockdowns where drug testing was the objective.

I am a living testimony that the system *does not* provide for transformation or habilitation. The fact that I have succeeded and excelled is *in spite of* a system designed to strip a man of his autonomy, his sense of individuality as a creator. The system was Bitter on holding me in an overcrowded, under-fed, under-stimulated population whose educational level was that of fifth graders. A population warehoused and made to be dependent financially, mentally, and emotionally. This population is pacified with cable, a card room, a yard to go "play" in, and a basketball court to continue one's "chase-your-own-tail" dream. I chastised both administration and prisoners alike in this matrix, this illusion called "corrections." In the "legalized days of slavery" (I add quotations marks because some forms of slavery are still legal today), people could form a corporation, or a "separate entity," and house people who had committed crimes (felons) and put them to work at $.17 cents per hour. The government has always done it. After the abolition of slavery, slaves were simply disguised as felons under the Thirteenth Amendment.

I experienced a lot of adjustment issues in the early part of my imprisonment. Later, the correctional staff acknowledged that because of my age such "adjustment" is to be expected. One of my early "adjustment" episodes at the age of eighteen resulted in me being sent back to level four after beating a guy in the head with a combination lock. I was playing poker when one of the players I routinely played with started losing money and complaining about it. He was known for verbally antagonizing other players to get in their heads, so I returned the favor. Eventually, he lost his cool, and the guy started to say things like, "You think you tough, don't you? I'll beat yo' mothafuckin' bitch ass, you young punk." Once he took that course of verbal exchange, to my mind he had pushed my back to the proverbial wall.

At the time, I reasoned that I had no out to salvage my ego and my reputation but to harm him in front of every man in that room, every man who heard him call me a "bitch ass punk." Just as he disrespected me in public... he had to answer for that disrespect in public. *That* is how it went in prison. In that environment, if you allow someone to strip you of your self-respect, then what customarily follows is a subsequent violation of person, property, and...eventually, soul.

At the age of eighteen, in a level-two prison where men were getting their necks sliced open, I could not allow those labels to be attached to my character. So, I intentionally determined to make an example of that man right there at that same poker table amongst all of his lifer comrades, so that he would be reminded of the time that "young punk" slapped him in the head with a combination lock. Only then, I reasoned, will those men respect me.

I walked back to my cell, tied my shoes tightly, and grabbed my combination lock. As I waited for the third-shift officers to enter the unit to begin their shift, I sat quietly about ninety feet away from the shit talker. I listened to a guy vent about his wife as I stalked my prey. I figured I could get to him during the shift change of the guards. I sent the guy that was complaining about his wife up to the desk as a distraction.

"Look, as soon as the third shift officer begins his round, go up to the desk and ask for some stationary, kites, disbursements, anything you can think of. Make sure you walk up to the desk at an angle so he doesn't look behind him—"

"Mario, please, I beg you, don't do it! Whatever you're planning, please, brother, it's not worth it," he pleaded. *He lacks my prism, my frame of reference, my perception,* I thought. And as I've mentioned before, perception is reality. I had been conditioned by the streets and two years of confinement to seek an immediate resolution. I'd been conditioned to seek finality, now, not later, for my life depended on it. This is the reality for a youth behind bars.

As he distracted the officer at the desk, I took one last deep breath and exhaled. I had a hoody on with my back facing the entire prison day room, so my identity was not evident. Hoodies and hats of all kind were normal back in the 1997 era of Michigan prisons. Now most are state issued, manufactured by Michigan State Industries (MSI), a for-profit company that uses cheap prison labor in the manufacturing of diverse products. They then sell those products back to the prisons and jails at a 1,000 percent profit because of the slave labor. This was an inside scheme crafted during the former Governor's prison boom tenure.

I stood up and turned around. I saw my target, the loud mouth who said he was going to fuck me up. He was engrossed in his poker game, laughing and joking with the likes of "Money Mike," "Kool-Aid," and "Moore-Bey," all killers in their own right. There was also "Cuban Mario" as he was called, the head of the Latin Counts. I walked straight back to their table and without hesitation, I swung the lock hitting the loud mouth in the side of his head, knocking him out, as all the men except "Cuban Mario" jumped from the table with shouts and screams.

My victim slowly fell over into Cuban Mario's lap, as Mario simply lifted up his hands still holding his cards. My victim woke up with another blow, as I just kept beating him over ... and over ... and over. "You gonna fuck me up, huh, bitch? Come on, come fuck me up, you bitch," I growled. I turned to his three friends who were yelling, "Come on, man, stop. He don't want no more trouble."

"You want some?" I yelled and made motion toward all three of them as they backed up to the walls. The table was located at the back of the day room; thus, I was blocking the only path toward the exit. I continued to hit him with the lock, until finally, one of my boys yelled out, "Mario! That's it. Round is over!" in reference to the correction officer finishing his round. I immediately walked toward the exit and slid the blood-drenched lock to my boy who took care of washing and discarding it. I looked back and snapped, "I got your punk bitch," in disgust.

The next day the staff and officers came and got me. Turns out, Cuban Mario and the rest of the gang banging Latinos told him that he better not touch a hair on my head. As he tried to make his case to retaliate, the Latinos became hostile and told him that if he didn't lock up (ask to be put in protective custody which is synonymous to solitary) that they were going to finish the job. He locked up that morning and told the warden everything that happened. What was my version of events to authorities? Hey, when in Rome, do as the Romans: "He tried to assault me. He had a razor, so I had to defend myself." I played the little white-boy role, and it landed me with just a fighting ticket, instead of the assault and battery felony they wanted to give me. The way I looked at it, the system put me in an environment that required violence and aggression to resolve conflict and, guess what? I was going to raise that standard just a couple of notches. I did almost ninety days in solitary for this incident, and it got me kicked out of the first of many prisons.

October 4, 1999, Brooks Correctional Facility, Level Two

In January of 1998, I was moved once again to Brooks Correctional Facility in Muskegon. I had been in Brooks for nearly two years, still angry, still stirring up trouble, when I was sent to solitary once again. Let's just say I had a really bad day.

"Mario. Mario!" said a deep, husky voice. I looked up to see my cellmate, "Big Dubb," as he had eloquently named himself, a large, African-American man whose kind heart outweighed his looks, standing about three feet away. He'd moved in for a quick tap and then hopped back fast enough to not get punched in the event that I was startled out of my sleep.

"What?" I mumbled, one eye open. It was the middle of the night.

"They callin' you on the PA system, man," he said as he pulled his "big boned" 275-pound body back up to the top bunk. He hated that I had a bottom-bunk detail, but he loved me as a "bunk-mate," or cellmate, for many reasons. First, I was now in a level two, and up to this point I had spent most of my time in level four where you are allowed out of your cell only two hours a day. I stayed out of the cell most of the day. For someone who must live in a six-by-nine-foot cell with another person, having the cell to you all day is a luxury, so Big Dubb loved that I stayed outside of the cell. Second, I filled the room with prison money. In this world, they called it "penitentiary rich." I hustled at the poker table and took what my family sent me in terms of money and invested in large quantities of marijuana, which turned my $300 into $1,200, so Big Dubb never went hungry. And trust me, Big Dubb was hungry a lot.

After coming to my senses, I could hear what Big Dubb had been telling me. The PA was calling my name. Again. I jumped out of my bunk and hurried down the hall towards the officer's desk. "Yes, ma'am, I am Bueno #165821," I replied, addressing the officer using the proper etiquette.

"You need to put your blues on and go to control center. I don't know what for," she responded stoically. Prisoner's had to wear a uniform called "prisoner blues" or "blues" for short.

"Yes, ma'am," I said robotically as my mind delved into the possibilities of what I was being investigated for this time. With all my get-rich-quick schemes, I never knew what angle the inspector was coming from. And, yet, I hoped that it was an investigation. Otherwise, it could only be one other thing: someone in my family passed away.

I quickly made my way back to my cell and got dressed. By then, surrounding prisoners were waking up to figure out why the third-shift officers had yelled on the PA system at 4 a.m., which is completely against operating procedures. I walked over to my friend Ali's cell and cracked his cell door open, but I couldn't tell if he was awake or asleep. It was summertime, and our cells were upstairs.

The heat was unbearable. We were permitted to sleep with our doors open, but the catch was that there were killers all around. Ali was a light sleeper, a seasoned veteran in the concrete jungle called prison.

"Wassup?" he mumbled sleepily.

"Hold this. It's just weed; it's about half an ounce. They just called me to Control Center. If I don't come back, make sure Hec gets all those packs of cigs and the weed. You get the food, ok?" He simply nodded as I walked off quickly without awaiting a response. Hec was like an uncle to me. He'd been imprisoned for life since age seventeen for being present when his friend shot a guy. By then, he was in his forties. I knew that he and the rest of the Latinos would make sure my property was not stolen in the event I was placed in solitary. Latinos are feared and respected by staff and prisoners alike in prisons across the state of Michigan, for when they unite, they are unstoppable. You never know. One minute you're here, and the next you are gone, off to another prison.

That is how prison is. You are measured by your word, your character. I didn't have to worry about whether this guy "liked" me or not. His character told me that he would follow through. In the higher levels where men play for keeps, and there is no place to run and hide, your word is your bond. It may be likened to your credit score out here. Without good credit, you will run into a myriad of obstacles, whether in society or in prison.

As I made my way to the control center, I reasoned that it must have been a family emergency of some sort and suddenly became extremely afraid. I had never experienced someone close to me dying, and I feared that something might have happened to my mom or my dad so I walked faster. Breathing heavily, I pulled open the door to the heavily secured Control Center as I was buzzed through.

"Good morning, I am Bueno #165821," I said as I passed my

prisoner identification card through the slot, reminiscent of liquor stores all over urban, downtrodden areas.

"Hold on a second. The sergeant wants to speak with you," said the short, attractive black female behind the glass. Soon a large, black sergeant appeared.

"You Bueno #165821?" he said with a bit of an attitude, as if I were a bother.

"Yeah, I am he," I replied with the same dryness.

"Yo' grand-daddy died. Call yo' people," he said with a grin.

My grandfather, "Papa Mango," was a second father to me. He visited me often. I had just seen him on my twenty-first birthday a couple of weeks earlier along with my mom, dad, older sister, and her husband. I was only allowed up to five visitors, so there were always family and friends who could not come per department policy. It was during that visit that I realized he was ready to die.

"*Papa, que pasó? Que esta mal?* What happened? What's wrong?"

"*Justo ahora estaba en la pesca de Cuba como en los viejos tiempos.* Just now I was in Cuba, fishing as in the old days," he said, pointing to a painting on the visiting room wall of a simple man in a simple wooden boat who was fishing off the shore of a beautiful island. My grandfather was born and raised in Cuba, and he loved it. He fought against Castro and lost. What was his consolation prize? A bullet that penetrated his skull and became forever lodged in his back and, eventually, all of his assets (store, house, etc.) that were seized by the Castro regime. He immigrated to the United States with absolutely nothing to his name, forever barred from returning to the only place he called home. Before he left Cuba, he fished often with friends. They fished simply using fish wire, gloves, and their hands. These men of men hunted baby sharks barehanded to feed their families.

With tears in his eyes, he simply wished that I, too, would be blessed with the opportunity to live a long, peaceful, and abundant life as he had. At that moment, I did not understand what Papa was trying to tell me. Only after he had died did I understand that he was gently saying goodbye.

After the bad news, I walked back to my cell in shambles. A tear dropped from my eye, the first in a long time. It rolled down my cheek, which was cold and dry, both from the cool October chill and from a heart that had not cried in many years. I had buried my emotional pain until my heart had become calloused, until I'd become numb to the world around me. I looked back toward the Control Center, staring at the sergeant through the bar-filled windows, spat, shook my head in disgust and uttered aloud, "I got bigger problems than this guy."

I stared at the far off sunrise and I thought of Papa once again. Another tear rolled down my cheek as I walked faster. In my hand was the paper that the sergeant had slid through the bulletproof glass. It read that my "relative" called the facility to inform me that my "relative" passed away. I crumbled the paper up as I walked into the unit towards the prison payphones; it was time to console the family from long distance. This is one of the worse aspects of prison: the inability to console your love ones during times such as these.

Later that Same Day, Dallas and the Pool Balls

That day went from bad to worse. "Here, I'm done smoking," I muttered as I threw my pack of cigarettes across the poker table toward my beloved friend, mentor, and brother Joe "Hector Macho Camacho" Chavez. Hec, as he was called, had pulled me under his wing when I was twenty-one, a time when I couldn't see the pro-verbial light at the end of the tunnel. I couldn't see tomorrow, let alone my release date. They say that the two most dangerous men to avoid are the ones who have everything to lose and those who have nothing to lose. I felt like the latter. I was tired of smoking, cards, corrections officers, tired of being told when to eat, when to sleep, when to shit, when to hug my mom, when to call my dad, just tired of life.

I walked through the prison yard and went to the housing unit community bathroom. As I was using the toilet area, partitioned by a three-foot wall, I heard a *bang!!!* Then another. Then, I heard a lot of commotion as if people were running and yelling.

"What's going on?" I ask Big Moe. Moe's name represented his status as a member of the Moorish Science Temple of America, an Islamic Group recognized by the MDOC, and "Big" representing his 300-plus-pound frame.

"Cowboy done went c-r-a-a-a-zy!!! He chasin' the officers around the desk trying to hit them white bitches with pool balls," he said with laughter and excitement. I rushed to wash up and walked over to the railings. My cell was upstairs, so there were railings that looked down upon the officer's station called the base. What I witnessed was sad. I saw an old, tired, worn-out convict who simply wished to be left alone. Old Man "Dallas," as he was called, was a seventy-eight-year-old Black man who at that time in 1999 had been incarcerated twenty-eight consecutive years and was never going home. Dallas was serving four natural life sentences for multiple murders. Of course, we all have our limits, and, on that day, we found out what Dallas' were. I never knew the Dallas of old. I only knew the Dallas who was quiet unless he shared some words of guidance and wisdom. I knew a Dallas who was tired of fighting, or so I thought. Most days he just wanted to be left alone with his Little Debbie Honey Buns, Maxwell House coffee, and the housing unit pool table.

"So what the hell is going on, Big Moe?" Big Moe and I stood at the top of the stairs with a bird's eye view. What we saw unravel was not pretty. In the three large rooms that allow for common areas in the form of television, games (chess, cards, pool, etc.), and cooking, prisoners left what they were doing to pay attention to what was transpiring. Brooks was already ripe for a riot because the MDOC had taken away most of our property (clothing) to make way for Michigan State Industries to land a multimillion-dollar contract using prison slave labor to manufacture the clothes, shoes, cleaning products, food, and more. Michigan State Industries then sells these items at a huge markup from per unit cost to prisons and county jails throughout Michigan. This was some remarkable business engineering by the former Governor Engler before he fulfilled his third and final term.

When comparing staff to prison population in terms of race and ethnicity, prisons are obviously disproportionate. Governor Engler made it a point under his watch to ensure that thousands of rural residents in Michigan profit from the federal funding available for those states during the 80s and 90s. Passing stiffer, lengthier sentences brought more money to both house and build these facilities. Is it any wonder that a "prison boom" occurred? Guess where the population came to fill these rural warehouses? Yup, inner cities. Now we have prisons scattered in remote, rural areas of Michigan, areas that were part of the agricultural boom . . . and inevitable bust. The racial inequalities that are inherent in the very fabric of the criminal justice system are evident. As I watched Dallas hurl pool ball after pool ball at the staff, I realized another facet of the bitter fruit of a poisonous tree: the new plantation.

Other prisoners gathered, circling Dallas and the staff. The worse part was the throws were nowhere near effective because Dallas was so old and worn out from life's incessant battles. It was sad, almost pitiful. Dallas eventually ran out of ammunition, symbolic of him running out of time.

The "Goon Squad," as the Emergency Response Team had dubbed itself, tackled Dallas as if he really were a threat. The officers were extremely aggressive, one bending his arms behind his back while another officer had his knee on Dallas' neck. As Dallas struggled to breathe, the tension in the air could be cut with a knife. The prisoners began to chant, "Let him go. Let him go. Let him go." About seven officers were surrounding and pinning down this seventy-five-year-old man. As the Goon Squad became more aggressive, the prisoners, approximately 75 to 100 in total, became more aggressive and threatening. Big Moe and I walked down the steps as prisoners followed in droves. I looked at him as he said, "Stay right behind me. I got you," in reference to the recent surgery on my hand. I had received a hand injury from the assault that I had committed at Carson City where I beat the prisoner with a master pad lock for threatening me. Hec asked Big Moe, his long-time friend, to "watch over me" as I healed. In prison, a man's word is his bond. No more, no less.

As we crowded in, the staff eased up on Dallas. The large, white officer who had his knee on Dallas' neck looked up at Big Moe, who was now standing directly over him. "Get off him. Now," said Big Moe with an air of calm forcefulness. The officer stood up slowly, stuck out his chest and smirked.

"Stand down!" snapped a large African-American sergeant to the white officer. No response. Again, harsher now, staring down the white officer, he repeated, "Stand down, officer!" The white officer lifted his chin and took one step back. The sergeant, glaring into his eyes without blinking, dared the officer to disobey. The white officer took another step back, still grinning. All of the officers slowly backed up to the wall as the sergeant stayed in the forefront. "Okay, gentlemen, we are going to slowly walk out of here. I am personally taking responsibility for Dallas, and I assure you that he will not be harmed." The quietness of the standoff was deafening as Big Moe stared into the very soul of this black sergeant, these two giants of men, both natural born leaders with a gift of influence. Big Moe then took a slow step aside as he gestured for the sergeant to make his way. The sergeant gave Big Moe a look of appreciation and understanding. Big Moe was essentially saving these officers' lives.

"C-Unit lock down now!" blasted out repeatedly over the PA system as we made our way back to our cells in awe of all that had just happened. As I heard the men around me talk, it turned out that this entire debacle happened simply because the staff had confiscated Dallas' entire life: his Little Debbie Honey Buns and Maxwell House Coffee. Turns out that Dallas had over $100 worth, and lo-and-behold, the rules stated that we were only allowed $75 worth in our possessions at any given time. Instead of leaving Dallas with the allowed $75 and taking the remainder "contraband," they took all of it.

The officers turned the confiscated goods into the counselor for a hearing. The counselor had told Dallas, in so many words, "I got fourteen days to give you a hearing, so get the hell away from my door." If officers and counselors wanted to harass a prisoner who was, for example, exercising the grievance (formal complaint) system, this is what they would do; that is, confiscate all personal belongings, then wait out the 14 days to give the items back. All to simply discourage and instigate prisoners into a more downward spiral.

In case you're wondering, Dallas went after her first. She barricaded herself in her office and peaked out the tiny window as Dallas vented his frustration with every throw. It was sad. All of it could have been avoided if he had simply been listened to, empathized with, and validated.

Approximately Three Hours Later

A few hours later, eight large correctional officers, fully dressed in combat/riot gear, and one lady officer who was video recording the process, approached my cell. "Are you Prisoner Webb?" yelled the Goon Squad sergeant through the small glass window that allowed staff to look into our cells.

"No," I respond. Prisoner Webb (aka, Big Dubb) was my cellmate. With nametags on the door, I realized the sergeant was merely using the process of elimination to determine who I was.

"Turn around, get on your knees with your hands behind your head. NOW!" he shouted in a commando, hoorah kind of yell. I was taken aback, as I had no idea what I had done. I complied. The cell door opened and the riot-gear officers ran in and cuffed me from behind. I already knew where I was headed: solitary confinement. Again. I didn't ask why because I understood the process: nothing is ever explained until you are secured in a cell. I shook my head and thought, *What now, God?* As I was guided down the housing unit stairs with officers surrounding my exit, I looked over at the housing unit staff. Officer Max, a housing unit correctional officer, winked at me. That wink told me most everything I needed to know. My only thought was *What kind of lie did Max tell this time?*

Officer Max was known for fabricating information on black and brown prisoners. Earlier that month, I'd had a fourteen-day "time-out" as a result of this officer's lie. At that age, my arrogance and pride, augmented by an unforgiving environment that rewarded aggression and violence, brought on continuous harassment from staff. I was an anomaly: a light skinned, Latino youth with no facial hair who didn't fear any man and was respected by all, or there was always a repercussion. Most of the white youths were being taken advantage of monetarily, physically, or emotionally. Such taunting in that predatory environment leaves an imprint resulting in PTSD.

Since I walked to the beat of my own drum, the staff theorized that I was part of a gang or that the Latinos were extorting me. They had yet to realize that I was a lion, not a sheep to be slaughtered.

Since most prisons are built in rural, post-agricultural communities that are predominantly white, I was compelled to defend myself not only from the adult prisoners, but also from the mind games the staff played, both for entertainment . . . and for keeps.

Officer Max was an example of the numerous Michigan Department of Corrections staff that utilized the mightiness of the pen and the power of their position to oppress black and brown men. "According to Officer Maxwell, 'Prisoner Bueno stood at the top of the stairs and yelled, let's get these bitches! Come on, guys. Fuck these bitches up.'" Officer Maxwell continues to assert that, "Prisoner Bueno then stepped onto the base and began yelling for all the prisoners to attack the staff." The sergeant read the misconduct through the cell food slot. He then asked,

"Any comments or requests for witnesses?" I looked up at him and laughed.

"Yeah, I want as witnesses all twenty staff who were on base at the time. In addition, I want the video feed from all the cameras in the unit." Of course, none of my requests were fulfilled. Two hearings (both adjourned pending more evidence) and nine days later, not one officer of the twenty who were present corroborated Officer Max's story. The video showed nothing of the sort. Yet on day ten, the hearing ended when two officers, both close friends of Officer Max, stepped up to corroborate his story . . . verbatim. I was devastated. Losing my grandfather, ten days in solitary, and a guilty finding of one of the most serious misconducts in prison, was too much. I had failed my family one too many times. I theorized that I would cause them no more pain . . . no more heartache. I was tired of living.

Shackled and escorted back to solitary confinement, I resolved to end this miserable life of mine. A tear flowed down my cheek as I stepped into my cell. As they removed my shackles by reaching their arm through the food slot carved into the heavy, iron cell door, I thought, *they will win no longer.* I had learned in quarantine to always inspect my cell for contraband upon entering because I would be held responsible for whatever was found once I accepted that cell as mine. On the first day of being in solitary, I had inspected my cell, found a small, sharp piece of glass and tucked it away just in case I would need it. I waited for the officer to perform his routine round performed every thirty minutes. As I sat there, I thought about how wonderful it was that this world as I knew it would soon be over. No more suffering, pain, or heartache. I would win, and they would lose.

The officer opened my window cover, peeked in, and kept it moving as I sat on my bed staring at the wall, glass cuffed. I looked down at my wrist and began cutting. The shock from the guilty finding, the hopelessness of facing long-term solitary confinement once again, and the anguish of losing my grandfather kept me numb from the pain that I would have otherwise felt. I was numb to any vision of a better tomorrow.

The blood trickled down my arm and a drop fell to the ground. This fueled me further as I pressed and cut harder. Only about three minutes passed from the time I started cutting when I heard, "Open cell six, now! We have a suicide!" I heard the cell door open as the staff ran in one after the other to restrain me. There was no more fight left in me. I was done fighting to exist, to live, to be at peace. I was done.

I laid back on the bed, and a nurse whispered, "It's okay, my dear, we are here to help you." My tears were flowing now as I sobbed for what I had thought was to be freedom, the end of my suffering. I went in and out of consciousness as the emotions of it all overtook me. I vaguely heard an officer explaining how he had stumbled upon me.

"Yeah, so if I hadn't come to give him his copy of the ticket, who knows what we would had found thirty minutes from then?" *A free man. A free man is what you would have found,* I thought bitterly.

For the next seventy-two hours, I was placed on suicide watch while in solitary. Everything was taken from my cell, and a guard was assigned outside my door in shifts of eight hours. They watched me as I sat in reflection. I hated life. I was angry with God, and I lacked any vision for a better future. I was going lower and lower. *Now what's your excuse?* I thought. *Whose fault is it now? Even in here, I am a failure.* My spirit was perishing. My faith was at its weakest point, and when faith escapes you, so does hope. Without hope, one ceases to have meaning and purpose. As I sat there thinking about where my life had "ended," my eyes welled up with tears. From somewhere deep inside, I heard a still, small voice ask, "Are you listening now?" I slid from my concrete bed and fell to my knees.

"Yes, Lord. I am listening." Now for the third time in solitary in five years, I recognized that I always exited solitary spiritually stronger then I entered. On my knees, in silent recognition of this omniscient, omnipotent being, I smiled. I realized that faith does not require a clear vision. In fact, true faith requires a blurred vision as you are trained to hear what the Spirit is saying as you navigate through the pitfalls towards your purpose.

CHAPTER 9

NELSON MANDELA COMES TO "VISIT" ME

November, 1999, Eight More Months of Solitary
in the Upper Regional Facility

AFTER APPROXIMATELY SIXTY DAYS in Brooks Correctional Facility's solitary confinement, I was placed in shackles and belly chains and put on the "Snowbird," a doctored up (much less comfortable) Greyhound bus that transfers prisoners for a drop-off up north to Upper Regional Facility (URF). Being shackled on a bus for over fifteen hours really makes you wonder, *Is this hell?* Between the evil nature of the guards and the bitterness and indignation of the prisoners, such confined spaces for long periods of time can be daunting. Men are chained and shackled as beasts then made to sit in caged areas for hours on end with no bathroom facilities. It requires an inner strength and a consciousness that many don't possess. What is the trauma from such conditions on the psyche of young impressionable minds? This is a question worth answering, for the long-term implications must be assessed if we are to adequately safeguard of our communities, neighborhoods, and resources. Remember, most of these same prisoners will return to our community at some point as returned citizens (Uggen, 2010).

Having done over two months in solitary without shaving makes one realize how luxurious the simple things in life truly are, like being able to walk to a shower without cuffs or without being watched by staff; or a longer than three-and-a-half-minute shower because they counted the one-and-a-half minutes it took to walk you to the shower with a leash hooked to the cuffs that are behind your back. As I exited the Snowbird, I anticipated a long, hot shower, a fresh shave, and a bowl of hot ramen noodles.

"Prisoner Bueno #165821!" a small sergeant shouted. Three huge guys who could have been linemen in the NFL Super Bowl that year surrounded the Napoleon-like figure. They wore leather gloves and looked like they were hoping to try some new strangleholds.

"I am he," I replied, looking up at the sergeant. I knew this couldn't be good. Yet, the past sixty days in solitary resulted in a reminder of my inner strength . . . that rests upon Divine Kingdom Principles, thus, I was internally unmoved.

"Stand up and turn around!" he ordered. I complied. Once again, I knew that they were procedurally barred from telling me what was going on until I had been cuffed and secured into a cell. As we walked out of the control center to what I assumed was the segregation unit, I wondered once again, *where are you leading me, Lord?* Funny thing about God is that He is not big into giving too many details.

The group of officers laughed and poked fun at me as they pushed me forward, cuffed and connected by a leash. I thought about how Jesus was tortured, spat upon, and ridiculed, and I whispered, "You did not deserve this, Lord. Yet I do."

"What the fuck did you just say?" said one of the officers says as he yanked my arm back.

"Back the fuck down. *Now!*" snapped the small sergeant. It was clear that this young, humongous guy had a temper problem. At that moment, I was praying that I would never be alone with him for many had come to the URF never to leave again. When I arrived in 1999, this prison had a reputation that preceded itself throughout the state of Michigan as being a place for the incorrigible. I am still uncertain as to whether that reputation was for the prisoners or the corrections officers.

As the sergeant led the way down a path that seemed to never end, we finally approached a building. Another gigantic white male kicked open the door. "Welcome, my friend, to, 'You are Fucked,'" an overplayed joke on the acronym URF that resounded around Michigan by residents and staff alike. The Upper Regional Facility was known to be the most dangerously corrupt prison within the Department of Corrections at the time that housed the "incorrigible." Many prisoners were committing "suicide" while on suicide watch. Many other prisoner homicides were swept under the rug as suicides. Thus, I carefully measured and calculated my response to each and every one of their comments.

Solitaries differ in terms of comfort or the lack thereof, but they are all similar in one way: a prisoner leaves a scholar or a schizophrenic. Forced solitary confinement can destroy an individual's mind unless approached from a spiritual mindset. I witnessed many youths lose their minds while in solitary, from covering their walls with feces to placing their private part inside a locker door and slamming it until it until he is severely harmed.

I am saddened by memories of this apathetic environment in which I was "raised," as it is a system foundationally built upon punishment and torture instead of compassion. It is a system devoid of education that seeks to maintain the status quo through an inflated recidivism rate. This stems from systematic illiteracy and highly populated police states in minority-rich neighborhoods all the while giving agricultural ghost towns metropolitan status through the building of the industrial prison complex. The Upper Regional Facility was literally like being in the south during the 1800s, only the prisoners were the slaves and the politicians, local contractors, business owners, and prison administrators were the plantation owner, with officers as the cruel overseers.

December 23, 1999, Nelson Mandela Comes to URF

Up to this point in my life, at twenty-one years of age, I had no post-secondary education, and I was full of, ironically, righteous anger. I blamed everyone and everything outside of me for my circumstances, my pain, and my failure. I blamed my father for taking a three-year "time-out" from my life during a time that a boy needs a positive male role model. I blamed my mother for choosing to numb her pain through drugs, alcohol, and gambling, instead of easing my pain. I blamed my grandfather for showing favoritism toward my cousin, treating me as inferior instead of breathing life into me. I blamed Tone, my cousin who was like my brother, for betraying me. Just as I had yelled at my grandmother one night before slamming down the phone, I believed that "The *only* mistake I made was that I didn't kill three people that night! Samuel, Jay, and Tone!" I blamed a system that showed preferential treatment to white youths by sending them to the juvenile system ten times more frequently than brown and black youths for the same crime. I blamed my uncles for not being there for me when I needed them the most. I blamed the staff for not allowing me the graph paper for my calculus course, which 'made' me quit. And, most of all, I blamed God for dealing me a losing hand and then punishing me for losing. I blamed everyone and everything except myself. I was in a prison *within* a prison.

I remember as if it were yesterday, sitting in solitary, watching a

Christmas Carol, as tears rolled down my cheeks. Christmas had always been my favorite time of the year, but in prison, it was the worst. Then suddenly, the television blew out. I shook my head and mumbled, "Great. Merry *fucking* Christmas to me." Now I wouldn't have television for the holidays, for it takes over a month to receive such an order. I stared at the busted television and the graffiti on the walls for what seemed hours, just feeling sorry for myself. Then suddenly, the slot in the door where food trays are slid through opened and a voice said, "Bueno #165821, you got some property." I snapped to my feet in child-like giddiness, ran the whole three steps to the slot, signed the paper receipt, and was handed two gems: a Panasonic radio that I had ordered several weeks earlier and an artifact that has forever changed the trajectory of my life, the autobiography of Nelson Mandela.

I stared at the book in disbelief. My mom had said she was sending me a good book. I looked at those large words on that thick book, *A Long Walk to Freedom*. I fell to my knees, lowered my head in submission and whispered, "Thank you, Lord." Then I sobbed like a child as I realized the depths of my failure as a child of God, as a man, and as a son. Regardless of the challenges, my mom and dad loved me, and . . . now . . . I *felt* both their love and my loss for *just* realizing it.

I was tired of being a leaf in the wind, of being a victim of my circumstances. Just tired. I pulled myself to my feet, walked to my bed, turned on my new radio as I gave thanks and praise to God for such timing and flipped open the first page of a book that forever changed my paradigm, my belief system.

Nelson Mandela was the president of South Africa from 1994 to 1999 and is most well known for being an anti-apartheid activist, politician, writer, and philanthropist. Mandela had a passion to free his South African people from the long history of repressive apartheid, the country's institutionalized racial segregation and discrimination based on race that was in place from 1948 to 1991, when it was abolished. He approached his passion, his purpose, through the study of law. He learned his captors' ways and means, rules and laws, so he could use these against them in their oppressive ways. After studying law in the 1930s, Mandela began to work as an attorney in Johannesburg in the early 1940s where the political climate was heating up. Mandela became involved in anti-colonial and African nationalist politics, joining the African National Congress (ANC) in 1943 and co-founding its youth league in 1944. In 1948, the National Party's white-only government established apartheid. From that point on, Mandela committed himself to overthrowing this oppressive government body. He was repeatedly arrested for seditious activities and was finally sentenced to life in prison. This was where he started his autobiography and continued to act as an inspirational leader through his writings. After serving twenty-seven years in prison, the president of South Africa finally released him in 1990 because of the growing international pressure and fear of a racial civil war. Mandela then became the country's first democratically-elected president and went on to be a winner of the Nobel Peace Prize. He is still revered today as one of the most influential leaders in the fight for human rights and racial equality.

In his autobiography, I read about a man who worked in coal mines fifteen hours a day in order to educate himself. This only gave him enough money for his law books, schooling, and one meal a day. I, on the other hand, lay there in prison for taking a man's life during a drug deal turned armed robbery. I felt disgusted with myself as I read about a man who fought for an education not for himself, not for personal gain, but for a greater ideal: to fight the injustices of an oppressed people. I read about a man who embraced education as a means to an end, not the end itself. I read of man who faced an enemy, first internally then externally, and conquered both through a disciplined, loving spirit. I read of a man who found purpose in his pain, who lived for an ideal greater than himself, and in so doing, he got through any *what* because his *why* was greater than his circumstances. Because he had a vision, he never gave up.

I read that book voraciously over the holidays, and I was amazed. At the age of sixteen, I could not comprehend a twenty-two to forty-year prison sentence. Yet now, going on twenty-two years of age, I realized that my life was not over, and most important, I had the epiphany that how I would spend those years was up to me. This fact, this truth, that it had always been up to me, was mind-boggling. It was a paradigm shift from victim to victor. Up to that point, I had mistakenly believed that I had no power, no control, over how my circumstances were unfolding. I didn't understand the interplay between action and response. I didn't understand the inherited power of the observer to respond any way they choose. I didn't understand how I had relinquished my personal power when I shifted responsibility from myself and imposed it on anyone or anything outside of myself.

During that eight-month stay in solitary confinement, I was blessed with the greatest gift that God could ever bless me with: the understanding that it is not what happens to you that matters most but what you *do* with what happens, how you respond. This was the gift of empowerment. Blaming *anyone* or *anything* for my shortcomings was the relinquishment of the god-potential inherent in me. I learned that discomfort was my provision to stir me to act, to put an end to the confinement that had its origins in my thoughts and beliefs. My pain was simply a message . . . not a condition; it was a reminder that who I *think* I am . . . I am not. It moved me to uncover that which I AM destined to become . . . it moved me closer towards my *purpose*.

One of the greatest facets of love a parent can give a child is a sense of safety and security. My parents separated after that fight when my father pushed my mom through the bedroom window. I had become afraid of my father, of the aggression and violence. I hid in my closet facing the darkness alone, just as I faced it several years later as I watched my mom destroy herself. I faced the darkness of a fatherless home alone when my father turned his back on me. I was alone when God ignored my pleas for help. I was alone when I hit the streets to hustle, to rob and kill drug dealers, and, eventually, I was alone when I walked through the razor wire gates with shackles and belly chains. Alone. It was safer and easier because I no longer had to deal with the disappointment of being let down. That single attribute was the cornerstone of the foundation that kept me strong within the prison system because only the strong can walk a prison yard alone. The drive to find safety and security had shaped a victim story that infiltrated my paradigms, shaping my self-defeating behavior.

Nelson Mandela's *A Long Walk to Freedom* was the living embodiment of the concept that personal development and the fight for an ideal greater than self *is possible,* even in prison. Mandela served twenty-seven years in prison. He understood isolation and feeling unsafe. Despite his captivity, he lived in a state of gratitude. His attitude, that manner in which he perceived his situation, was heavenly, while his reality was that of hell. He inspired me to be great and great I determined to become. This concept, coupled with belief, gave me the roadmap for achievement. I promised myself that I would spend the rest of my life in pursuit of self-discovery and personal development for an ideal greater than myself. I committed to the improvement of a corrupt system that has literally thrown millions of young lives away. I had found my *why*, my reason for living within this hell. I found meaning, and this produced hope.

I often think about the effect Nelson Mandela's autobiography had on me. It challenged my beliefs and made me truly look at my life in an entirely different light. New information will do that to you. This is why education, and reading in particular, is the building block to self-discovery, for learning is the development of a relationship between something you do know and something you do not. I often wonder whether it was the solitary confinement that readied my mind and opened my ear to the whisper of enlightenment or simply maturation.

Now approaching twenty-two, thirty-six did not seem so far off. My sentence had been lengthened somewhat by then due to infractions and misbehavior. At the time, the law incorporated a 15% reduction of your time upon entry into the Michigan Department of Corrections. Every misconduct report would result in the forfeiture of good time ("good time *forfeitures*") that was given upon entry into the system, thereby, delaying or extending the prisoners captivity. But there was a mechanism in place to gain back the forfeiture through good behavior. That bit of light, that small glimpse into what *could be,* provided vision, and vision combined with faith produced hope. Hope for a better tomorrow got me through the heaviness of prison and its concentration camp-like effect.

Solitary provided me with such opportunities, though for many, solitary is a fertile ground for delusion, mental illness, and suicidal behavior, for it gives prisoners the misguided belief that they are not a part of the whole, that they are not loved or loveable. If people are not worthy of humanity, then inhumane treatment is to be expected by both prison staff and society. Solitary confinement is a dismembering of sorts, a banishment that reinforces indignation and anger rooted long ago in sadness and trauma. Most men walk out of solitary worse than they went in, for they didn't like what they saw. In an attempt to avoid such examination, they dig deeper into the burrows of an unconscious mind that is not stimulated, not open to education or evolution, and a mind that continuously focuses on the pains of life, the onslaught of insult and injury. This translates into a victim story that is disempowering and self-perpetuating. What you *believe* . . . you invariably *conceive*.

Solitary, for me, was a smelting process of heat and pressure likened unto the process used to purify gold. Like any metal that appears naturally in the earth, there are impurities that must be removed, ore must be separated from the gold, which is done so by crushing the gold ore and then placing it in a furnace that reaches temperatures in excess of 1,064 degrees Celsius in order to elevate the gold above its melting pot.

Imprisonment alone crushes the spirit and mind of the imprisoned, and solitary may be likened to that furnace. Yet the process of removing impurities from gold still requires another step that is not resolved through fire. Chemicals such as cyanide solution or mercury are introduced to the gold to remove the remaining traces of other metals. My "chemicals" came in the form of books. I have often heard, "Knowledge is power." Yet, I believe that it is the *application* of knowledge that makes it powerful.

The men and women in solitary are, for the most part, those who lack the functional coping skills to respond to the everyday stresses of life within prison, let alone society. Most of these individuals lack basic interpersonal skills that can only be found through an *adding* and *multiplying*, not *dividing* and *subtracting*, like solitary does. Solitary confinement completely divides the individual, forever harming the whole. What we must quickly embrace is that nearly ninety percent of all violent offenders will receive parole (Uggen, 2010). This begs the question: What quality of returning citizen would you like as a neighbor? For what we give to the imprisoned, "Shall be given unto us pressed down, shaken up, seven times seven."

After my internal paradigm shift from reading Mr. Mandela's book, I pursued wisdom with all of my heart. I embraced life,

specifically *my life*, as a purpose-driven life. I refused to main
a slave mentality, so I read. I recalled something Viktor Fran⌐
expressed in his book *Man's Search for Meaning*: "When we are
no longer able to change a situation, we are challenged to change
ourselves" (Frankl, 2006). My message of pain was that of dissatis-
faction with where I was and, since I could not change *where* I was,
Frankyl's insight challenged me to change *who* I was.

Another book sent to me by my father, *Man's Search for Meaning*
raised a mirror in my face as, forcing me to take a look at the
root . . . instead of the fruit . . . in my life. Up until this point, I was
angry at all the results ("fruit") in my life; and, yet, I was ignoring the cause ("root"): my own perception of things that guided
my response. It was a painful reality, the fact that *I was where I
was because of who I was*. I was an arrogant, angry teen that was
hurting everyone I came across. I now stood naked, to the world,
humbled by life's divine correction, for a father chastises the child
he loves.

I now recalled the agreement that I made with God while con-
testing my case: *If you save me, then I will spend the rest of my life
helping young men like me.* I was beginning to understand that
although my heart had been purified and now corrected onto a
path towards purpose, my skills to fulfill that purpose were only
undiscovered gifts. God was uncovering my gifts through the purifying process of suffering. In time, I vowed, these gifts would be
made into a skill.

I read more books of substance than I can count, over a thousand. In that, I was different than most men around me. Most staff
and prisoners alike despised me because of it. I disobeyed the law
enforced long ago on a slave population: Thou shall teach a slave
anything *but to read*. Today's slave, the imprisoned citizens, don't
even want to read. I used to chastise the men around me who were
sloths to an unstructured system that demanded nothing of them

but that they not rebel. "You want the world, but what do you give?" I would say. "You expect sugar, but you give shit. In that is your dysfunction because you don't understand the universal law of harvest . . . or reciprocity. You think you can pray five or ten times a day, yet your actions do not mirror your words. God shall not be mocked. You shall reap what you sow. If you sow nothing, you reap nothing."

CHAPTER 10

EDUCATION: A PRIVILEGE
NOT A RIGHT WITHIN
THE NEW JIM CROW

WHEN MY FATHER offered structured learning through correspondence school, I found my purpose, my meaning, my *why* while imprisoned: education, education, education with a final goal of using that education to help other young men avoid the pitfalls of the path to prison. While still in solitary and before finishing Mandela's autobiography, I sent a request to the "school principal" (GED schooling) expressing my desire to pursue a post-secondary education, that I had the funds to do so, and, hence, needed an application.

After about a week, I received the application and filled it out with great excitement. I was going to college. When I committed myself to inner expansion, this led me to another great secret: happiness is found only through progress. And in the world of tangibles, progress is the antonym of prison. For in sentencing individuals to a "time-out" for years on end, prisoners believe the illusion that the experience is a waste. The belief that there is no progress in prison is augmented and reinforced by the culture of both staff and prisoner alike, compounded by the administration that embraces the status quo as its mission. When there is no redemption, no personal development, it becomes easy to give up. Thus, it's not what you get, but who you become that matters.

About three weeks later, I received my application back rubber-stamped in big bold letters, "DENIED," with the Deputy Warden noting: "College correspondence classes are a privilege afforded those in general population. You are in solitary. You are denied." I have never been one to let things go so easily, so I slapped that deputy warden with two grievances.

The officers had mentioned on more than one occasion that they had recommended my release, yet the deputy warden had denied it. They told me to write to him, which I did twice. On both occasions, he responded with, "Give me three more months of good behavior in solitary, and I will grant your release." What was the purpose of a bi-monthly assessment conducted by a "committee" if the deputy warden had already decided that I must complete an additional three months?

So, the first grievance was for fraudulently filling out an "Assessment of Behavior" form that was supposed to be done bi-monthly to determine whether or not I should be released from segregation. Thus, my first grievance was for "Corruption, Collusion, and Abuse of Authority." I asserted that the process of earning one's way out of solitary—a "committee" —was a sham; that the deputy warden was illegally pre-determining release or continued isolation. That was really just to get their attention. My true focus was on my education; hence, the second grievance was for a violation of (1) the MDOC mission statement that is aimed at the rehabilitation of prisoners and (2) the violation of my civil rights in discriminating against me in comparison to similarly situated individuals. You see, the MDOC allows for GED continued study and engagement while in solitary. You are allowed to minimally educate yourself. Just don't try to get too smart. Sound familiar? Good old slave days. I was now determined to get "too smart."

I was released from solitary approximately two weeks after writing the grievances. The administration approached me with the response: "Grievant has been released from solitary confinement. Grievant is now approved to study through correspondence. Grievance resolved." The slave owners were correct. Teaching a slave how to read is a threat.

Approximately five years earlier when I was seventeen years facing twenty-two to forty years of imprisonment, I had enrolled in two college classes that my dad paid for and supported my taking, saying that he would pay for my education but not my attorney. I struggled with a *why*, a reason to fight through the petty obstacles inherent within a system designed for enslavement of body and mind. Thus, the Thirteenth Amendment that allows for slavery to be legal only if the person is brandished a felon. Back then, the slave was not allowed to read, thus, the mind was strategically enslaved as well as the body. The slave master knew that reading expands vision, imagination, and the ability to achieve. At seventeen, I, too, was enslaved mentally and physically. My mind was enslaved to the aggressive and violent ways of expressing pain and heartache. When the college sent me my materials list, it included graph paper for my pre-calculus class. During the hearing to determine whether or not I could receive the graph paper, a female sergeant said with a smirk, "Really? You're educating yourself, huh? Aren't you doing like twenty years or something, kid? Paper is supplied in the prisoner store, so this is deemed contraband." The graph paper was denied. She didn't care that it was graph paper for a pre-calculus class.

After that, I threw the pre-calculus and English textbooks in the garbage out of frustration and a lack of hope. Coupled with the lack of physical, emotional, and social maturation to understand the complexities of the new world around me, let alone my physiological development, I gave up. I gave into my present conditions that were screaming, "Your life is over!" Remember, if you will, back to when you were sixteen-years young, the inner struggles with self-knowledge or, better put, self-ignorance. Remember the struggles with puberty and rebellion and all of the major challenges that high-school kids face. Now imagine stepping inside an adult prison at that impressionable age and not leaving once for the next nineteen years. I gave up when I threw those books in the garbage. A piece of you dies each time you give up on your dreams and goals. Worse yet, each time you give up, it gets easier and easier to do so. As the great Vince Lombardi said, "The harder you work... the harder it is to surrender."

Later, I yelled at my father on the phone as a tear of frustration and defeat slid down my cheek. "What will a degree do for me, Pops? I'm a convict now. I'll be the best convict that I can be. Why does it matter if I have a degree... if I'm a convicted murderer?" I silently cried in frustration to my father who was now listening to his boy.

But now, five years later, I was consciously choosing to grow. My stay in solitary had ignited within me a burning desire to educate myself at all costs, for the root word of education is *educo*, meaning, "To lead, draw, or take out. To raise up or erect." Now, I was an arrow in motion destined for an intended target. I was determined to lead with character and to only follow others wisely, to draw out of me my god-potential, to remove any impurities bestowed upon me by my environment, to raise up from the ashes of my failures and defeats and to erect within me a shining spirit to help lead all those similarly situated to a better tomorrow.

With approval from the administration to study in hand, my father made me an offer I could not refuse: "Son, I told you years ago that I support your education. I will pay for it. However, I will only pay for one class this time, and you must send me every grade. If you do this, then I will pay for two classes and so on. I will not put up with you quitting on this. This is the most important thing that you could possibly do for yourself while in *here*," he said emphatically as he tapped on the non-contact window.

Solitary always strengthened our relationship. We were able to sit across from each other and *listen,* not just talk. I agreed. I informed him of my desire to re-enroll in Ohio University's College Correspondence Program for the Incarcerated. The program was a complete package aimed at the prisoner population; therefore, it included everything one needed to complete the course, down to the addressed stamped envelopes, included in the price, for assignments to be returned to the professors. Michigan Department of Corrections' school staff proctored the exams.

A few weeks later, I heard a heavy slap and something slide under my cell door. I jumped off my bed, grabbed my mail, and eagerly combed through Ohio University's Catalog of courses for the incarcerated, the accredited one-stop-shop. As I reviewed the degrees offered, I made a checklist that became my plan, my map, to self-liberation, self-discovery, and purpose in this otherwise meaningless existence. "Meaningless existence" is the essence of the prison mindset. It strips you of your individuality, autonomy, and self-discovery through love, compassion, and understanding. Prison also attempts to strip you of the knowledge and truth that you are created in God's image and likeness and are, therefore, not in need of change but of simply forgetting the dysfunction the world has imparted upon you and remembering the greatness that is inherent in every cell, every hair, every breath. You are a phenomenal part of a glorious whole. We are but to forget, and then remember.

First, I chose Principles of Logic because it sounded interesting and because it satisfied a math requirement. It taught me how to form sound, rational arguments in proof form and how to analyze and breakdown unsound arguments. I. Loved. It. It was literally the first thing I had ever completed in my life from start to finish. I got an A on every assignment, which I quickly rushed off to the mailroom to send to my father. It gave me a sense of accomplishment and purpose, feelings rarely found in prison.

Seven Years to an Associate's Degree

It was challenging being a college student within an environment that was more like a war zone than a college dorm. Taking college classes was a status of wealth within the prison culture, for a prisoner could only take college classes if he had the funds within his account to pay for them. In 2003, Ohio University was charging about $400 per class. Most prisoners never saw $400 in their accounts in a given year. That status was dangerous within the confines of prison, especially for a youth. I fought the onslaught of loneliness inherent with taking a path less travelled and pursued education with a fury.

After my initial success, my father gave me the go-ahead to enroll in two more classes and the precedence followed: I sent him every grade for approximately seven years until I earned my associate's degree. The classes were heavily weighted in business and psychology. I loved school because it gave me a measureable way to experience progress, and progress equals success, regardless of geographic location.

This newly found meaning and purpose pushed me further toward rebellion: they could take my liberty through solitary, but they could not take away who I was becoming. I was determined to liberate my mind, knowing that eventually my body would follow. This kind of liberation called for transformation of mind and spirit.

It compelled me to look not out the window but into the mirror. This was a powerful shift in perspective, for it was the discovery of Self. As the Apollo of Delphi's entrance so eloquently states: "Know Thyself." The discovery of what really matters allowed me to be in the moment, leaving behind a past of pain, and to forget about an uncertain, dark future. Ironically, the realization that meaning could be found in my books, in my mind, and in my thoughts created some turbulence at first because it lead me to not care where the system sent me or what it did to me as long as I could study and have my books.

October 2001, Jackson State Prison

At twenty-two, I had been imprisoned for over six years with almost three of those years being in solitary. I had been in three different solitaries in 1999 alone. I was now in my sixth prison. I had adapted to the subculture around me, an easy transition from the street life where violence and aggression are the tools by which conflict is resolved. I had matured to a place of solace with the understanding that I could protect myself, no matter the prison I was sent to. Now I was at a place in my life where my basic need for safety and security had finally been met. Silly, huh? In prison, in solitary confinement, at the age of twenty-one with the voice of Nelson Mandela breathing life in my spirit, I finally felt safe, and this made a space and a spark for the pursuit of self-actualization. I wrote my vision down: "I am a scholar, an educator, a thinker." I wrote my goal down: "Bachelor's Degree." Lastly, I wrote down the plan: "I will educate myself every day for the rest of my life to better the world . . . as Mandela did."

The next seven years in pursuit of my associate's degree involved seven more prisons, each filled with challenges and triumphs. I requested a transfer for four of them. If you go without a major misconduct for twelve months or longer, most prisons will allow you to request a transfer. I had found that moving from prison to prison actually made the time go faster, delusionary as it may sound. I was kicked out of the other three prisons for legitimate reasons. Although I pursued education and personal development, I still rationalized and justified my criminal behavior and way of thinking. I figured that if the prison industrial complex was going to hustle, then so would I. If they were going to charge me $15 for a 15-minute phone call, then I would traffic drugs within their institutions. My transformational process was just that . . . a process. While my heart had been healed to a significant extent in terms of the hurt little boy who sought violence, aggression, and the illusion of power to numb the emotional turmoil that he was experiencing, I still saw myself as "convict," which carries the connotation of a gangster or hard-nose criminal, instead of an "inmate," which carries the negative connotation of a rat or snitch. I ran poker tables to pass time and earn an income, something that I had witnessed as a teenager, so I saw no harm in it. Of course, in prison, running gambling tables is probably not the safest pastime one could choose.

The structured learning that I performed as self-study gave me a vision that pulled me out of my bed most every day at 3:00 am. I was hungry for goal accomplishment. I tagged a vision board on my wall in my cell next to my bed where I would have to look at it every morning when I woke up, every count time, and every night when I lay down to sleep. Count time is an internal control measure conducted by the prison every few hours during the course of a day that takes a snap shot of the number and location of all prisoners in that prison. The goals I wrote on my vision board worked as targets that kept me aiming to be the best me. I wrote down simple yet life-changing goals, for when you change your thoughts, you change your life. It read like this:

Without Vision the People Will Perish

1. "Seek ye above all else the Kingdom of Heaven and its Righteousness, and all things shall be given unto thee." [I defined the "kingdom of heaven" as being in alignment with one's purpose, with what one is created to *become*.]

2. Take four classes every semester.

3. Obtain at least a 3.0 in all classes.

4. Read one book a week.

5. Complete bachelor's degree.

I aimed at a double major in business and psychology; thus, those were the classes that I enrolled in. The more that I developed Self, the more I had to give others. My natural leadership qualities were being sharpened and polished. The prisoners around me began to seek me for counsel, for leadership. This did not go unnoticed by prison administrators. Such influence could pose a potential problem for administrators of a prison. This is another reason I was routinely transferred. My books kept me busy. My vision had never been clearer. I loved checking off my goals as they were accomplished, and I regurgitated the wisdom that I absorbed from the works of Deepak Chopra, Plato, Buddha, Jesus, Nietzsche, Neal Donald Walsh, Thomas Mann, Ralph Waldo Emerson, Viktor Frankl, St. Paul, Job, Proverbs, James Allen, Napoleon Hill, Dr. Dwayne Dyer, Eckhart Tolle, and the list goes on.

My path toward higher learning came in the form of more solitary, ironic as this may sound. It was self-teaching and self-study. I immersed myself into my books. The feeling of progress inherently woven into our souls is what pushes us past the other five million sperm to win the ultimate prize: a life of progress through struggle. If not that, we have an unfulfilled life. The immersion kept me out of trouble and out of the spotlight. This only added fuel to the fire in relation to the administration's perspective of me. "Now we've got a smart slave that can read, huh?" type mentality. Thus, I hid my pursuit of enlightenment, awareness, and my desire for freedom.

I was returned to the Carson City Facility in July of 2007, and on one occasion, I was called to the desk and told by the corrections officer, "The principal said she got a test for you to take, boy." Carson City was a very pro-Trump type of crowd if you get my drift. "You got a 165 number and your dumb ass still hasn't passed the GED?" he said as the other officer behind him chuckled, one combat boot up on the desk and a toothpick in his mouth. My prisoner number was 165821, indicating that it was issued in the 80s. I looked at both with a grin, "No boss, this will be the third time that I try, but I think I got it this time." I was playing dumb. Of course, I am a smart-ass, but also, I had learned that it was always best, as *The 48 Laws of Power's* First Law mandates: never outshine the master. Had I said that I was taking college classes, it would have offended his intelligence, or at least threatened it. I knew from experience that it was better to appear *less* intelligent then the ones that hold you captive. Funny thing is, I was on my way to take an accounting midterm.

Over the next several years, as I accumulated more college credits, and I met the thirty-credit threshold, this meant that I was now able to get better pay in clerk positions and even get pushed to the top in the job pool. My goal was to get the sixty credit (or associate's) mark, because then I could earn $3.56 a day, which meant over $60 a month and a guaranteed push to the top of any clerk job pool unless a fellow prisoner had a Bachelor's, which was pretty unusual. Even within this slave plantation, an education created different socioeconomic statuses. This was simply a reminder that I was on the right path.

The jobs I got as I reached for that threshold of credits provided a space for me to develop close relationships with staff, which helped me destroy the "us versus them" mentality. I was growing structurally and socially. My safety and security within, after so many years of seeking such a state, provided a foundation upon which I could build my life toward self-actualization. The darkness of this subculture of solitary, of prison, had become the dark, fertile ground in which I was buried. Yet, what I discovered in the depths of that darkness was the realization that I was a seed indeed capable of growth. When you change the way you look at things, the things you look at change. I was beginning to understand that every adversity brings with it the seed of an equivalent advantage. Prison was hell on earth . . . and, yet, Jesus only made it to Heaven by going through Hell first.

We live in a world of polarities. One cannot have friends without having enemies, just as one cannot know success without knowing failure. I lived a delicate balance. Some staff and prisoners greatly disliked me, but there were more who conveyed words and deeds that supported me. This taught me not to care what others thought, so long as I am in alignment with who I am . . . and, with the vision and goals that are molding me into who I am destined to be.

I studied accounting, economics, criminal justice, real estate law, business law, psychology, and the list went on. The funny thing is that these were topics that I read as my "free-reading" material. On a few occasions, my father sent me the likes of *The Lord of the Rings* or other fiction books. "Father," I had to explain to him, "Your reality is my fiction. I seek to escape to *your* reality, as you attempt to escape from it." Business and accounting fascinated me. I wanted to prepare myself for the opportunity that was coming. I considered success to be ninety percent *preparation* and only ten percent *opportunity. If I just focus on gaining as many tools and skills as I can, then I will be prepared,* I would remind myself every morning that I pulled myself out of bed to study.

I took classes that challenged me, such as pre-calculus and statistics, and others that expanded my vision of who I could become,
such as philosophy and business. I ran across challenges every
day, but I embraced the stress as *eustress* (good stress) instead of
distress (bad stress). When I would run into an academic challenge, I would reach out to the professors via correspondence. I
didn't really know my professors. I just received graded papers
and notes. Or I would find a staff member in the GED Prisoner
School building, or have my family send me a book on the topic. I
did not stop. I was no longer that seventeen-year-old boy looking
for an excuse to quit, to give up. The harder I worked . . . the harder
it was to surrender.

The more I refined myself, the more I had to offer those around
me. My inner growth began to impact my outer environment. Just
as I had been an influence for the bad, I was beginning to have
significant influence for the good. This did not go unnoticed by
my captors. I had to balance this influence, though, for although
my intent was pure, the culture of corrections trains the staff to not
trust the enemy . . . the prisoner.

For the first time in my eleven years of imprisonment I was recognized for my transformational behavior when asked to facilitate
an anger management class to the younger population of prisoners
that were creating problems on the prison yard. This lasted only a
short time, though. Soon a letter from the administration advising,
"Prisoner Bueno shall not facilitate any classes now or in the future
effective immediately" was placed in the prisoner file that travelled
with me to every prison. This was a bundle of information to "better house and secure" the prisoner. Influence, whether good or bad,
is not acceptable on a slave plantation unless that influence comes
from the master.

Summer, 2008, Carson City Correctional Facility,
Don't Let the Enemy Know What You Value

Prison is volatile. Not only from the perspective of your peers as it relates to the prisoner population. You know what to expect from them, whether it's a set-up, a shank, a squeeze play, or extortion. The list goes on. I was well versed with the streets and prison life, but the volatility is exponentially heightened in terms of the correctional staff, for they are given free reign over a forgotten world. This is similar to the famous Stanford experiment (1973) in which Professor Zimbardo was interested in finding out whether the reported abuse among guards in American prisons was due to the sadistic personalities of the guards or had more to do with the prison environment. The two-week experiment had to be aborted after only six days due to the trauma experienced by the student prisoners at the hand of the student guards who took on a persona of punisher. The most concerning aspect is the fact that, "the behavior of prison guards in our simulated environment bore a remarkable similarity to patterns found in actual prisons" (Haney, 1998), which tended to be negative, hostile, confrontational, and dehumanizing.

One such incident I personally experienced of this type of mistreatment was when they brandished me a gang member. An inspector and his lieutenant crony barricaded the office door and threatened to classify me as a gang member if I refused to sign a "Renunciation Agreement" stating that I renounced a prison gang, the Latin Counts. If the Lansing's Security Threat Group (STG) director believed the inspector, then I would be classified as being part of a security threat group and prohibited from continuing my college classes, one such idiotic rule for gang members. God forbid a gangbanger wants to enroll in college and pay for his own schooling. Then he might be transformed. "Inspector, last week you called me in here and asked if I was a Spanish Cobra. To my knowledge, sir, they are enemies, aren't they?" I responded. I knew they were. I was being facetious. I also knew that the administration disliked Latinos getting along, especially factions from different sides. You see, "the haves" win by "the have-nots" embracing the concept that we (minorities versus whites) are enemies. Thus, the administration feared the Latino population congregating, fraternizing, and socializing with their own. But because I was never blessed into any gang, I had the privilege, the character, and the charisma to bring all the leaders together, and this was a "no-no" in prison.

Divide and conquer has been an age-old motto that continues to prove effective today. When imprisoned men are showing signs that contradict division, the administration begins to crackdown. No wonder men are returning from prison disconnected from the whole. They are thrust into a system that mirrors and magnifies the code of the streets: only care about yourself, but whatever you do, don't express your individuality or God-given potential. After decades of imprisonment, men are released into an environment in which one's very success hinges upon interpersonal skills that facilitate relationships, the essence of life. They have been conditioned to be separate, though they want, no, yearn, to be a part of a whole that they now wish to protect and guide, but they are told, no, you are not wanted or needed. You are not a good person. You are on parole. You are a felon and you must stay away from all felons. Yet, most, if not all, of their acquaintances, friends, and family are felons. Divide and conquer, just like the slave days.

As the inspector went on and on about sending the "informational packet" to Lansing's STG director to confirm my classification as a gang member, I thought about all the work, the sweat equity, that I had poured into my studies. I was taking five classes.

Prior to the start of that semester, my father visited me with tears in his eyes. "These must be the last classes for a while, son," he said. He had always wanted to provide me with an education while inside these walls, but now he was going on his third divorce, which forced him to move back into his mother's house to regroup, so to speak. It broke my heart to see him hurt over my schooling. "I have this last $5,000 so that you can take the five classes to complete your associate's degree." I put my hand on his shoulder.

"Thank you, Pops. You are leaving an inheritance to your children's children." Now six months later, I sat there months into the five classes at risk of losing it all. The lieutenant looked smug. I was now thirty years old. I had read many books, but the content of my material had refined. I went from studying books like *The Art of War* to digesting and craving books like *The Power of Now* that offered intangible food to feed my mind and spirit. In the old days when I saw no light at the end of the tunnel, I would have spit right in his face and baited him into a fight. But by then, I had learned, through both word and deed, that you become that which you hate. Thus, I hated no more. I learned that when you are quick to fight, life is quick to fight back. I was tired of fighting. My only reservation in signing the document was that I was not a gang member. But I understood how the system works. It's not what you know. It's what you can prove. "Hand me the paper," I said with venom in my voice. The inspector grinned.

"Aw, it's not all that bad, Mario." Below my signature, I wrote, "I have never been in a gang." I stood up and looked toward the door that had been blockaded with a chair.

"Now open the door."

"Sit down. Relax," said the overweight inspector in a low voice. I was standing between the two of them. "Now, tell me who gave you the confidential information about your transfer." My head snapped up, and my eyes narrowed. The week prior I had been notified by someone (prisoner or staff) that I would be transferred the next week to a prison in the Upper Peninsula. This was confidential information that I was not supposed to know in advance. Going back to the U.P. was the last thing I wanted to do at that time, so I called my family and had them call the prison administration immediately and make a big deal. Once they did that, there had been a clear breach of security, which caused the transfer to be cancelled. The residual effect was that an inspector had to figure out who his security breach was. I told the inspector, "If I tell you it was a prisoner, then my life will be in danger. If I tell you it was an officer, my life will be in even more danger."

I stood up squarely face-to-face with the slim, muscular lieutenant. "Open the fucking door. *Now*," I said with ice in my eyes. He stepped aside, removed the chair, and opened the door.

While this was one of many such experiences with corrections' staff, it did not take the wind out of my sails. They feared my intellect that afforded me autonomy. Again, what is the greatest danger for the slave owner? It is the slave who knows how to read . . . and, think.

Another incident involved an officer accusing me of being uncooperative. The lie came in the form of a ticket an officer wrote up on me, which stemmed from a misunderstanding my father had with an officer during a visit. The ticket asserted that he gave me a direct order and that I had refused to comply. The danger in this accusation was that because it happened on a visit, my visitation rights were supposed to be terminated. Thus, I was compelled to call my father and get him involved to prevent this. The assertion that I did not comply with an order during a visit where civilians come to visit their love ones said that I was a possible threat.

The next day, when I read the ticket to my father, he was quiet at first. Then he responded with, "You're just kidding around, right?" He was in pure disbelief because the ticket was a blatant lie, yet it had been written in a form that I could not contest. It was not until my father experienced the correctional staff lying on him that he began to understand the underpinnings and dangers of a criminal justice system that takes an officer's word at face value over anyone else, especially when we take into account the purposes for which such a system was developed.

My father called the warden's office the next day and then the central office in Lansing. It was simply a safety measure. When the administration saw that I had support outside the razor wire fences, they responded differently. I was found guilty of the ticket, but they dared not restrict my visits. Still, I lost good time, and my parole was pushed further away once again.

Each experience taught me that your vision tends to become cloudiest when blessings are right around the corner. When it seems as if there is no hope, no remedy to your pain, the clouds peel back, and the sun peeks forth in its brightness. I finished the five classes to complete my associate's degree from Ohio University. The staff continued to harass me, and I continued to minister to the brothers around me. I considered myself a disciple of Christ; a student, rather than a follower (apostle). While I am Catholic-centered, my teachings are curbed to the audience before me. Thus, my teachings are more Kingdom-centered, meaning that your kingdom is found in your purpose, and your purpose is found in following facts over feelings, principle over pain. "No excuses" was the message of my ministry, for the mantra of the prisoner is, "Woe is me." My reference point was Jesus . . . "Pick up your cross and follow me . . . " With such a reference how may one complain about the pain and suffering in one's life? Such a mantra reminded me that there must be struggle in order to obtain strength. It also fueled my resolution to finish the race, to not give up, because at the end of every persecution . . . is a prize.

CHAPTER 11

PURPOSE REVEALED AND A
PROPHECY FULFILLED

2008-2012, The Odyssey Continues

T HE ODYSSEY ENTAILED five more prisons within a four-year period. I landed at Jackson Cooper Street Correctional Facility (JCS) in the early months of 2012 after being kicked out of Muskegon Temporary Facility (MTF). Though I was a dedicated student, I was still the hustler, still the "Gotta make a dollar out of $.15 cents" type of guy. I had found some measure of safety within prison, but I still had the mindset that I had to make my own way. At that time, there existed an opportunity for prisoners to conduct legitimate (and illegitimate) businesses if they possessed the means to do so. Barbwire, from what history has shown, has never stopped a determined mind. Although we were no longer allowed to receive goods from our family and friends, we were allowed to purchase goods through funds placed in our own account from approved state vendors. In order to sustain oneself physically, it was imperative that a prisoner purchase additional food items to make up for the lack of calories provided by the state. As I grew into more of a man, I felt an inner burning to achieve through self-sustaining measures. I no longer wanted to be dependent upon others for resources. I wanted my own.

Shortly after a visit with my father revealed his soon-to-be third divorce and impending financial calamity, I came up with the idea of purchasing a vending machine that could be located in my mom's office, but I needed "seed" money to purchase the vending machine. My dad had been holding onto a classic Corvette for me to have when I was released, but that wasn't going to be for another six years. I decided that selling the Corvette now would do me more good than having my dad hold on to it for six more years. My father moved it to my sister's house once his third marriage began to go down hill. "This is all I have for you, son. I need for you to have this," he said as he embraced me on one of his many visits. I spent as much one-on-one time with both of my parents as I could throughout those two decades.

Once I sold the car and had the money, I would need my mom to purchase the vending machine for me, so I begged her, "Mom, please, just Google vending machines and print out everything you have. I will get the money, and then have you order it so I can put it in your place of business," I would tell her in phone call after phone call. Poor mother. I was always moving from one project to another, and they all involved making money.

"And, who is going to fill it?" she snapped.

"Aly will, Ma," I replied in reference to my younger sister, Alexis, who was attending the University of Michigan. I had an answer for every question. I was determined. I even ordered and studied a book on vending machines by *Entrepreneur* magazine. But step one was to sell the Corvette as soon as possible.

For the first couple of months, I tried to bribe my sister and her husband, Nick, to assist with selling the car. "Please, I will give you a $1,000 if you can just get $6,000 dollars for it," I explained to Nick.

"Man, I wish I would have known. Just before the market crashed, a guy came by offering $7,000 dollars but the battery was dead. I never did get back in contact with him because I didn't know you were looking to sell it," Nick explained. But our conversations didn't lead to any action. Little did I know, Nick was battling a cocaine addiction while my sister Sandra was killing herself trying to support them and their two children. I found out much later that Nick was simply an anchor around my sister's neck, stealing money from her whenever possible. I decided that I could not wait, so I took that matter into my own hands.

I had been sitting at a poker table playing high-level poker by prison economic standards when I whispered to my long-time friend and leader of the Latin Counts, Romero "Rome" Silva, "I got a nice-ass Corvette for sale." At the time, I knew that he was calling the shots from the inside involving drug trafficking and enforcement issues. Rome was one of the original gang leaders who literally lived, ate, and breathed the gang life. I handed him a picture that I'd had my father send in. "The Blue Book values it between $5,500 and $7,500. Check it out. I'll give it to you for $6,000," I said as he stared at the picture. *I got him thinking.*

"My brother-in-law is looking for a car," Rome replied.

"Take the pic and talk to your *familia*, bro," I said, as we continued to play cards. I was desperate, having tried to sell the Corvette through my sister and her now husband, Nick, over the past year.

I let about a week go by, but I knew that the longer that I waited to buy the vending machine, the more potential revenue I lost. The sooner I put that vending machine in my family's medical clinic waiting area, the sooner I could make some money. I peeked down the hall toward the officers' desk. No officer in sight. I slipped down the hallway to Rome's cell and tapped on the door. "*Hola, hermano*," I said.

"Wassup, bro'?" replied Rome, lying there watching his personal television. In prison, if you have people to put money into your prisoner account, then you can purchase such luxuries. Most prisoners, however, suffer economic woes that transcend the razor wire to their families who lack the resources to survive themselves let alone to send their family member money in prison. Rome and I were two exceptions to the rule; we didn't worry about money or meeting our most basic of needs as most unfortunate prisoners did. We were, "penitentiary rich," as the label goes within the subculture of prison.

"Alright, $4,000. Today is Tuesday. If you can get me $4,000 by Friday, then you can have the 'vette," I said.

"Deal," he snapped back in a less than a second. His brother in-law had test driven it the week before, so I knew he was really just waiting for me to cut the price. It was okay, though. Within a week, I had my vending machine, and the revenues began to roll in.

I used the profits to purchase packs of tobacco from corrections officers and fund the operation of smuggling marijuana. I looked at the product as commodities and the money invested as stockholder's equity. I had "stores" where I sold prisoner store goods to prisoners at a usury tax, usually being "Two for one" type trade. We were only allowed to order from the prisoner store every two weeks; thus, loan sharking was a good business in prison, however volatile. The sale of the Corvette to Rome (Rome, the leader of the Latin Counts who sold more drugs from a level-five prison than most hustlers in the street) positioned me to have a cash flow each month. This was my start-up money, as the skills and tools of studying business were teaching me.

I rationalized my illegal behavior that sowed seeds of discord within our prison community until I had a conversation with a friend and mentor, Dwight Henley. It was in 2009, and I was at a Carson City Correctional Facility. It was my second time there. The first time was 1996 when I got transferred to another prison for beating another prisoner with a combination lock. Dwight was serving a double Natural Life Sentence for first-degree murder and for the distribution of more than 650 grams of cocaine.

On one occasion as we walked the prison yard, Dwight tried to convince me that my running of poker tables, stores, and selling weed within the prison system was that of the criminal mind. "If you don't change now, Mario, you will become a sociopath who rationalizes every criminal act. That our crimes aren't worse than that of the rapists and pedophiles is not rational." See even in prison, there is an ethical code: rapists and pedophiles are considered the lowest of the low. But that day, Dwight challenged this and helped me understand that what I had done was even lower. In short, I came to understand that I had no right to judge . . . anyone.

We were both studying through Ohio University's Correspondence Program for the incarcerated, so we often conversed about philosophical and sociological topics. He handed me a book that forever changed the way I looked at my crimes and the criminal mindset, my *falling short*. The title of the book is *Inside the Criminal Mind*, by Stanton Samenow. In answering the ethical questions of crime and criminality, Samenow poses the scenario of having to choose between the lesser of two evils: if you had to choose between the allowance of your child being raped or murdered, which would you choose? (Samuel Yockelson, 2004) Dwight said, "Think about it deeply, but don't answer now. Go back to your cell and allow it to marinate for some days. Think about having a child, a little girl. Then answer that question." Dwight squinted his eyes, the sun shining down upon two murderers on a prison yard debating the rationality of the very culture in which they must live, eat, and breathe.

Here I sat in judgment of ones who have harmed others, just like me. But at least their victims lived to have a *chance* of survival, despite the quality. My victim, Samuel, on the other hand, was afforded no such opportunity. Samuel was only twenty-seven years old when I shot him. I reflected on how angry and volatile my behavior was at that age and how, shortly thereafter, a transformational process began to be evident in my actions, not just my words. What if Samuel had had the opportunity to transform, as well? I robbed Samuel, his children, his mother, his brothers, and all who would have loved him of the opportunity for him to *become* as ordered by God to Adam. I felt like a complete failure and a hypocrite for judging another's sin when my falling short was the gravest of them all.

I walked away from that experience with one reality: *I am a menace to the very community that I wish to protect.* I was tired of who I was, but even that tiresome "feeling" is a part of a process that leads to transformation if coupled with the right synergy. I was ready for change. And, as it is often said, "When the student is ready, the teacher shall appear."

I arrived at JCS at a time that some call opportune while others deem it providence. They had a transformational program called "Under-25" that focused on critical thinking, effective communication, and conflict resolution as a means for creating paradigm shifts and changes in the internal locus of control in its participants. What was the vehicle of choice to deliver the program? Ironically, it was transformed, influential prisoners. For those who truly embraced the aforementioned disciplines, they were offered the opportunity to continue their development through mediation training. Upon my arrival, they were launching a pilot program aimed at the male population aged twenty-five and under; thus, essentially, sixteen to twenty-five-year-old male prisoners. I had been with the early founders of the program, a group of imprisoned lifers who wanted to learn the skills to influence positive change within the prison environment by changing the way men resolved conflict, communicated, and thought. The notion of the problem becoming the solution was at the foundation of using transformed prisoners to teach other prisoners. I had never been in one prison long enough to benefit from taking the program. To say that I was excited to take the program is to put it mildly. Again, the student was ready.

"Bro', what did you do to get kicked out of Muskegon Temporary Facility?" asked Richard Speck, one of my best friends of ten years. I met Rick at St. Louis Correctional Facility level four when I was there from 2001 to 2002, and now here we both were at JCS ten years later in 2012. We were completely different men back then. It was a violent prison, and we raised our aggression to meet the needs and demands of the environment. We played for keeps.

"That's a loaded question," I smirked.

"I explained to Deputy Warden Riley how I needed you as a mentor in the Under-25 pilot program," he said.

"And?"

"He said for you not to unpack because you ain't staying here at JCS. He said this prison ain't built for you," Rick said, looking deep into my eyes, weighing my every word, trying to read my body language. What I had learned over the course of the few days at JCS was that Rick had put his heart, soul, and everything into this program I will call "A Chance to Live," and he protected it with his very life. I considered it a divine move on the part of the Creator to place me now, with my friend Rick, when he was on a path toward righteousness. I knew, at that moment, that he was measuring my words to see whether he should invest in my transformation, or whether I'd be a threat to what he *now* valued. "So, what did you do?" he asked with a smirk.

"Ahhh, well, there was a half a joint stuck down deep in the corner of my jacket, and during a pat-down this Nazi sergeant actually dug his fingers deep in my pockets and found it. It was a half joint from New Year's Eve of some good kush," I reminisced, shaking my head over the unnecessary trauma of it all. "The sergeant put the joint on the officer's podium as another officer padded me down. He called for backup because of the joint, so I had to act quickly. I saw two prisoners exiting the library door, so I yelled out at them as loud as I could, 'Hey! You two! Stop right there!' and then I ran as fast as I possibly could at them. By the time the sergeant and the large officer realized what was going on, I had grabbed the joint and run out the door, swallowing it in the process."

"Damn, what the hell is wrong with you?" Rick asked. "You ain't doing a big bit anymore, bro'. You only have a couple of years left." He was right. The problem was that I was programmed to live as if I was never going home. I literally had to keep reminding myself that I only had a couple of years left. It was mindboggling to believe that I could actually go home. I didn't even know what home meant anymore.

A long conversation with Rick ensued. He had been working with the deputy in a collaborative effort to bring transformational change to the community around him. Because the culture of prison was reliant upon aggression to resolve conflict, it was the deputy's mission to train these young thugs into being critical thinking mediators. An outside program offered the critical thinking, and the deputy brought in the mediation certification through the Jackson Resolution Center. It was a perfect fit: prisoners who were once the most violent would be transformed into instructors who train and mentor the rest of the prison population in principles of critical thinking, effectively communicating, and peacemaking. An almost Jesus-like approach to cultural transformation: start with the worst. Rick had been made chairman of the program.

When the deputy warden said that I did not belong at that prison, Rick spoke to the deputy's heart on my behalf. He called on his humanity and sense of justice. He explained how he needed my experience in that classroom. He needed a chance to influence my transformation because he knew I had the potential to influence many others. Though Rick had worked with the deputy for several years, he had never asked him for a personal favor. He vouched for me at a time when I had no credit with the administration, except bad credit. Yet, here I was, sent to a prison, to the same housing unit, even to the same hallway, as a close friend from the past who was the chairman of a program that I had always wanted to be a part of. The deputy agreed to my stay on a probationary basis.

"Okay, okay, I will give him six months, but if I get *one* problem, even just one complaint, he's gone. You let him know that he has one foot on a banana peel and the other one out the door!" Rick definitely relayed the message many times over. And so we were off to change the world! At least, the world we lived in . . . the world as I knew it.

Rick was a friend whose influence stretched beyond those walls. I allowed him past the layer upon layer of "insulation" that I had built around my heart, which protected me from the staff and the other prisoners. My entire life seemed to be one huge wandering until now, until this program. Now I had a reason for having read over 1,000 books, for spending over three years in solitary, for suffering for nearly two decades in prison. This punishment will forever fall short for taking a man's life, but I have to believe that there was a purpose in it all. This is exactly what has brought me thus far: faith that all this suffering I have imparted upon others . . . and upon self . . . is for a *purpose*. Viktor Frankl described his ability to overcome the atrocities of the Holocaust concentration camp was that he found true meaning and purpose in the midst of the suffering. Frankl asserted that life has meaning under all circumstances, even in the most miserable ones. He called this Logo therapy, which focuses on the search for meaning in human existence. In his book *Man's Search for Meaning*, Frankl taught me "the lack of meaning is the chief source of stress as well as anxiety" (Frankl, 2006).

Over the next six months I trained with the under twenty-five class, even though I was thirty-three-years old. In addition, I trained in the program's other areas of discipline with the over 25 adult prisoners in order to complete my training as quickly as possible so that I could begin teaching. Because of my aptitude and hunger for progress and growth, I was pushed through the curriculum all at once, as opposed to completing the program in separate stages. I quickly drove up the ranks, and my gift for ministry was transforming into a skill for reaching an otherwise unreachable crowd.

We worked with Deputy Riley and the administration at Jackson Prison to transform a housing unit into an environment that embraced learning. We taught effective communication and critical thinking as a prerequisite to teaching them how to resolve conflict peacefully. We created an abode that promoted the resolution of conflict through peaceful dialogue, the objective being to gain an understanding of another's view by using effective paraphrasing. We guided the men in the ability to empathize, the stumbling block for every criminal. Empathy is the cornerstone of his reformation, his rebuilding of self into that of a citizen, giving to those around him more than he takes. A true lion awakens for the hunt to bring it back to feed the pack. This is what we were becoming. Invariably, one learns what one teaches, and we were reproducing ourselves in droves. Rick assisted the captain of the prison, Captain Wiborn, in quantifying our work. We trained and mentored over 1,500 prisoners that the captain described with empirical data as saving virtually millions of dollars.

We called ourselves the Peacemakers. Doubted and not trusted by staff and prisoners alike, we were an anomaly. After all, we were former armed robbers, drug dealers, gang bangers, and murderers turned teachers and mentors to the most hardened of the prisoner population. We were the first housing unit in the history of the state of Michigan to tout no critical incidents for an entire year. We accomplished this two years in a row, not because there was no conflict, no assaults, no theft, no fights, because there were. The difference was in how everyone around responded to the situation. Offenses happen, but how one responds determines one's quality of life. Between every stimulus and response exists a moment, regardless of how fractional. In that moment laid their power, to respond as they wished, not just to react. So first we taught them that they have a choice in how they respond. In this, we challenged their core values in resolving conflict with violence. Then we gave them tools and skills in how to respond peacefully. Then we gave them the opportunity to practice and teach that which they had been taught in a space that was safe to do so. As I explained to the Deputy Warden, "We teach them the skills to resolve conflict in the classroom, but then they must live in an environment that does not honor such pro-social responses to aggression." He gave us our own housing unit. It was brilliant. Literally, the problem became the solution.

The Peacemakers transformed the very culture of our housing units. After one unit, the administration wanted us to transform another and we did. We raised the standards above and beyond that of the institutions in what were agreed upon as expectations. The participants willingly gave us their signatures, demonstrating their agreement to use what they'd been taught. Within six months of a two-year program, Rick pushed me through the ranks because of my education, my abilities, and my passion. I was made Lead Program Facilitator, and I raised the standards of the curriculum by creating midterms and finals to accompany the ninety-day tiers. The program was broken up into three tiers, or *phases*. The first tier consisted of the learning and mastery of critical thinking and conflict resolution. The second tier consisted of anger management, conflict resolution, and leadership training. And the third tier consisted of mediation training. My associate's degree in the social sciences positioned me to already know most of the curriculum.

I understood that it was the stress, stretching, and struggle of preparing to perform and to be tested that better prepared the men. I learned of the essential component to success, the one variable without which one would not "shine bright like a diamond." I had been through college correspondence courses and been trained by my beloved brother and mentor, Brian, to learn that one essential component: *pressure*. Webster's Dictionary defines pressure as, "The continuous physical force exerted on or against an object by something in contact with it." As trainers and teachers of this at-risk prison population, we were given permission to challenge, mold, correct, inspire, and, yes, *press*ure them into that which we had become: Peacemakers.

We became their mentors, trusted teachers, and counselors, pillars that every young man should have. In this pressure was a rite of passage so needed by every young male by an elder male with whom an organic, mentoring relationship had been nurtured. It is inherent in the nature of a young boy to be pulled by purpose to leave his secure abode and venture off into the unknown, to become the *hunter*, to become that which he was created to be. But he needs that push from a father figure who says, "Go and find your purpose, for you are ready now." They need that look of reassurance, the nod that reminds them to be still and know that they are enough. They need that unshakable strength that only a father figure can give. We provided this to the young men who were tossed into an unforgiving environment and told to become forgiving.

We had such an impact on this prisoner population and staff that we got the go ahead from Deputy Riley to paint "Blessed are the Peacemakers" in our housing unit dayroom. He said that the law would not allow us to put in the second part, "For they shall be called the children of God." It was worth a try. We painted positive affirmations on every wall as a reminder of who we were. Lus Ybarra, my beloved brother and friend, was the artist that painted portraits that resonated with the curriculum: the thinking man, six pillars of character, and quotes from the John C. Maxwell Leadership book that we trained from. Lus was the epitome of sinner turned saint in having committed a murder at the age of seventeen, committing three violent felonies in prison as he was the leader of the Latin Kings, serving five years in super maximum security, and now, one of the most effective mediation trainers we had. He was my friend . . . and mentor. Lus also trained me in the disciplines that we taught.

The first cohort of Under-25 Men began with the deputy choosing twenty-five of his prison's most at-risk seventeen to twenty-five year olds . . . and, me, a thirty-three-year-old man who had yet to put childish things away. The program was twelve months with a measureable outcome of twenty-six certified mediators who could then facilitate what they had learned to the rest of the prisoner population. I developed bonds of mentorship in that program that exist still today. I did not last the entire six months with the young men because Rick had a larger vision for me. Rick did not see me as one of the mentees. He saw me as a mentor, a trainer, as an influencer for the good. We need that in our lives, especially during times that all our eyes are seeing is failure. Rick saw in me what I couldn't see for myself at that time.

After a few months, I was pulled into higher classes with the

adults, though Rick's entire plan was to push me through the curriculum training that I was already familiar with so that I could be
boots on the ground in terms of mentoring the at-risk populations.
After the twelve months, only twelve of us remained who were
completely trained. Those twelve youths who remained became
assistant facilitators for the following cohorts. We literally transformed the problem into the solution.

It became routine for the deputy warden to refer the most challenging of prisoners. Over time, it became a culture with his staff
following suit. I developed a reputation for being one of the most
challenging trainers of the Peacemakers. Bottom line: I don't take
any bullshit. I would often say, "You can't bullshit a bullshitter, my
man," toward those slick, at-risk prisoners in need of mentoring, in
need of a relationship that entailed a sincere desire to add and mul-
tiply, not subtract and divide, as this population was accustomed to.

There were youths of all colors, all backgrounds, referred to us,
the Peacemakers. We had a team of men that had turned a gift
into a skill in the connecting and training of the most hardened
men. In time, the hardest of cases were referred to me. They would
end up either as my bunkmate or in my cubicle, where a total
of eight prisoners (four bunk beds) would reside. It was a level
one with a pole-barn setting, which increased the volatility of the
environment if the prisoners decided to be unreasonable. There
were no cells doors or any enclosures to isolate you from the rest
of the 129 other prisoners who occupied the building. Thus, to
empower the men with the skills and tools to respond effectively
in an overcrowded environment that empirically makes even rats
behave dysfunctional was beyond a miracle. The referrals slowly,
and at times, forcefully, adapted to the expectations and culture
that permeated the Peacemakers' premises. We promoted education and resolving conflict peacefully while mediating the conflicts
that naturally arise in any confined space with hurt men . . . for hurt
people, hurt people (Senghor, 2016).

I grew close in particular to the men who lived around me: Ryan, a beast of a young man who was imprisoned for robbing businesses with his own father, and Beano, who had been locked up since the age of sixteen who was Latino and Black. Beans, as we called him, was the leader of the bloods on that compound and was referred to me by the deputy. Upon hearing that he would be my new bunk-mate, therefore, living on the top bunk above me, I heard that Beano's response was, "Hell, no. I don't want to be *Mario's* bunkmate. I'd rather ride out to another prison than be *his* bunk-mate!"

"If that is how you feel, then that's *exactly* where you are going to go," the deputy replied. I was called out by the staff and told the story before Beano actually moved. I laughed. When Beano was told that the "other prison" would be located in the Upper Peninsula, he relented.

"I can't wait for him to be my bunk-mate," I said, smiling ear-to-ear. Beano was more like a little brother to me than anything. I protected Beano from himself, and yet, I still loved to beat on him like a bothersome little brother. He was a tough kid, no doubt. I grew to love him, and the rest of these phenomenal youths who were being put under immense pressure.

God positioned me in places of influence in these last few years as I ministered and did his work. I shared control of the Prisoner Benefit Fund, made up of the revenues (or losses on some projects) of the prisoners' ventures such as fundraisers and, the main source of revenues, the prisoner store. The prisoner population voted me in because I didn't take shit from prisoners or prison guards. These funds paid for everything from the weights in the weight rooms to the scissors in the barbershops to cable TV for all prisoners. The time came to renew the $60,000 cable contract for the entire 1,500 prisoners. Though the contract required my signature, I knew that they would just ride me out and pull into my position whoever I beat out in the "block representative election." Despite this, I decided to try and make a point. "I think that it's in the best interest of the prisoners if we don't buy cable, and we pay the local college to come and teach us instead," I said to the business manager (CFO) and the deputy warden as two secretaries took notes on either side of them. As I uttered the words, both secretaries pulled their pens up from the pad and looked up in shock.

"Well, u-m-m-m-m, well, Mr. Bueno," stuttered the white business manager with gold nugget rings on each pinky, slicked back salt and pepper hair, and a belly that hung over the seat. "You should really reconsider, ya know," he said as he looked over at the deputy for help but received none. In his arrogance, he was against providing any comfort for the prisoner unless it was in the best interest of the facility, just as my job was the inverse. I looked at all of them one by one and noted their detached, aloof, cold expressions, including the stoic deputy, forever the politician. Although he was a great ally and supporter, in public he had to stay neutral. I allowed for the long pause to settle in before I facetiously whispered, "Why? What might happen? Might the slaves begin to read?" My eyes bulged as I leaned forward. There was always a white prisoner representative and a black prisoner representative on each committee, so I had a partner (fellow prisoner) who represented the black population sitting next to me. The administration was furious that I ran for the white block rep position, being that I am Latino. But when they tried to remove me, other staff warned of a possible civil rights infringement, so they backed off. Thus, the blacks and the browns had the political positions locked down, no pun intended. The business manager's face turn beet red.

"URF is gonna get really cold in the next couple of months," he grunted while grinning, peering down his pointy, pink nose as if to threaten me with a transfer to URF, but I was no push over. I looked down at my notes for the meeting as I reminisced about the days at URF more than a decade before. "Yes, I know this. I was there, in solitary, for six months during the coldest part of the year. That was a difficult time," I said as I looked up from my notepad. "But, sir, I have already died. I cannot die again. There is nothing you can do to me to harm me anymore. I don't care where you send me. Just know this. Neither you nor anyone else can stop *that* right there," I said and pointed at the clock that hung above us on the wall. I looked at him, and then over at the stoic deputy warden. There was silence until the deputy warden spoke out.

"Mario, we would never wish to harm you. But don't you think a lot of the men would be upset if they did not get cable?" he asked, forever the mediator, focused on the issue. I looked over at him as I snapped out of "URF combat mode."

"Yes, sir, I believe there would be a significant amount of push back," I said before I surrendered the fight and conceded to signing the contract. I was going to sign it anyway. I just enjoyed ruffling the pompous business manager's feathers.

July 2012

Back in 2007, my mom went to a funeral in Miami, and on the way back, she had lunch with a friend at the airport, some guy who had a gift of prophecy. He told her that close to the time of my release he saw me in a classroom teaching the prisoners around me. At the time, I scoffed. Now five years later, I had news for her.

Sometimes when I called home, she was grouchy. I am laughing as I write this because I called my mom more than anyone else during my nineteen years of imprisonment, so I understand that sometimes (she may say a lot more than sometimes) I would bother her.

"Ma, do you remember when you talked to your friend at the airport after the funeral and he told you about what I would be doing when it gets close to my release?"

"Yes," she replied dryly.

"Ma, are you paying attention to me?"

"Yes, *coño*," she snapped back with her Cuban accent and attitude. "No, *coño*." Then, a pause. "Teaching? Didn't he say that you would be teaching? He said God was using you for something big but that you had to have a change of heart first because you were still angry and involved in things you shouldn't be." She snapped back into "mom mode" with a tone of critical conviction.

"Yes, Ma, he said that I would be teaching. Focus on that for a second. Guess what they are training me for?" I said with a huge smile.

"What?" she said as if she was doing something else. I understand that women, especially mothers, often multitask.

"Teaching," I said with a huge grin. "They are training me to teach young men ages sixteen to twenty-five."

"I *told* you that is what he saw, and you said it was impossible that you would be teaching in there!" she said laughing.

Having experienced the prophecy that described my imprisonment, I had spent years trying to hear a prophecy of my release. Each prophecy was similar. "God is using Mario to do something great, but he must have a change of heart first." Suffice it to say that I did not buy into any of them. And, yet, they were all correct: *I needed a change of heart*, a rebirth, for you chase what you value, what you love. I discovered *peace* in teaching these young men. For the first time in my life, I felt *true peace*. I discovered that God couldn't lie. The Covenant was not "null and void," as I had thought, but, rather, it was being fulfilled.

As time passed, I bonded with these men, these Peacemakers, through both wins and losses, on a mission to nurture and enrich the environment around us. I began to discover my gift and my purpose: teaching the most lost, the most disconnected, the angriest of young men, for I had been exactly like them. Before I lacked a vision for my future. The Bible says, "Without vision the people will perish." Any vision that entails a path not in alignment with purpose is destined to fail. It was through my fellowship with these men that I found what I was created for: to give more to those around me than I took. I can truly say through experience, "It is in giving that we receive."

CHAPTER 12

GOING HOME

October 2013: Do you Waive Your Thirty-day Notice?

I T WAS MY RELATIONSHIP with the deputy that shifted my paradigm as to how I viewed the system as parts of a whole instead of simply "us versus them." I learned that not everyone who is working for the system is supporting the demise of the black and brown man, but the policies, by and large, set in place by congress and enforced by the executive branch and its justice system are. If we are to reach any progress toward social change in areas that have resulted in the disenfranchisement of entire populations, and subsequent generational dysfunction, then we must begin to judge a tree by the fruit that it bears. This society looks at the children and protests, "What animals! What barbarians!" Are they not the fruit of a bitter tree? Are they not the effect of a cause?

Mrs. Grant, the Assistant Unit Residential Supervisor always used to call me "Prisoner Bueno," even though she knew I hated that word "prisoner." We called her Mrs. G.

"I am Mario, disciple of Christ and child of God," I would respond in jest, as this was another relationship with staff that assisted in my transformation into citizenship.

"Yeah, whatever, you weirdo," she would usually respond with a grin.

Mrs. G called me into her office one morning. "Prisoner Bueno, report to the Assistant Residential Unit Supervisor (ARUS) office immediately!" I heard her yell over the PA system. I smirked and shook my head.

Another previous time, upon entering her office, she asked me to sit down and said softly, "Mario, no one is going to hurt you anymore. I mean to say the threat is no longer there. I try to imagine how it must have been as an adolescent within this environment, but you must let down the wall. You are okay now." As she finished that last sentence, a tear fell from my cheek as I lowered my head to let out eighteen years of sorrow. She continued, "I know that you had to be stronger, more aggressive than everyone else in order to survive. Now you have to learn that wall is no longer necessary." We bonded through that conversation. But now there was no telling why she was calling me into her office.

"Good morning Mr. Bueno!" Mrs. G said with an unusual smile.

"Good morning, Mrs. G. What's with all the smiles?" She was somewhat of a smart ass, especially since I was the representative for the prisoner population and the housing unit. I represented "issues" to her on behalf of my "constituents." This did not always go over well between us, but my charm usually won out. I saw my good friends Rick Speck and Cam'ron Colts seated beside her in the office. Rick was the still the chairman of the program, and Cam was the board secretary, so he was always with Rick. Part of the duties of chairman required Rick to meet and communicate with the administration on behalf of the program and its participants.

"Sit down. I need to speak with you," she said in a grave tone.

"Come on, stop playin'. Wassup?" I said with a grin.

"I have been ordered to ask you, officially, 'Do you waive your thirty-day notice in order to receive a parole hearing in accordance with your new out date, which has been moved ahead per the warden's restoration of all your good time credits?'" she said with a huge smile. Rick and Cam grinned right along with her. I had waited nineteen years to see the parole board, so to ask whether I was okay to see them before the legal thirty-day notice offered by law was more of a joke than a serious question.

"You're bullshittin' me, aren't you?" I said, too shocked, too timid to actually believe that I was to see the parole board after so many years and to possibly go home.

For so long, I had found solace and comfort in *not* thinking about home and all that it entailed. Even now, I was afraid to dream.

November 6, 2013, "Come with Me"

Again, my name rang out over the prison PA system. "Bueno 165821, report to your housing unit immediately," ordered the officer.

"Bro, they called you on the PA system," my workout partner said, tapping me on the shoulder to get my attention.

"I heard them," I replied and kept doing my sets. For the most part, any time your name is called in the prison system, it is not for anything good, so I always got my work out done. It had been thirteen days since I had seen the parole board, and I was nervous to find out their decision. Every time my name was called during those thirteen days, my adrenaline rushed.

About fifteen minutes later, I heard, "Yo, Bueno, let me holler at you," my boss, Mr. Chad Guthrie yelled out. Eight months earlier, he had been assigned as acting "special activities director," since my boss was on medical leave. I trained him in his job duties, and he mentored me toward deinstitutionalization.

The first day I worked for him and we were left alone in the office, he broke the ice with, "I expect you to hustle. I know your barbershop agreements, photo hustle, and the like. But I expect to not be fronted off. Don't embarrass me. You hear me, bitch?" he snapped. My body stiffened, and I choked on my saliva. Such insults required immediate redress. They were cause for spilling blood to assure such offenses never happened again. Yet this was staff, a correctional officer, and I was thirty-five years old and a couple of years away from freedom. Thus, I was compelled to measure my response heavily. I stared long and hard. He grinned. "You don't like that, huh? Well, guess what? That's exactly how some will treat you... like a bitch. Get used to it. You can't kill everyone, Bueno," staring me in the eye, letting me know that he was well aware of my criminal past. I learned right then that there was power in *not* responding with aggression. I grew a lot from working under Mr. Guthrie.

Eight months later as I followed him to the school building, I knew my parole decision had been made. He looked me in the eyes and said, "Come with me." I put my head down. *It must be a negative decision for parole. He must want to tell me in private so he can encourage me while making sure I don't do anything irrational.* My heart sank. *I don't deserve it, anyways.* I brushed a tear away as Mr. Guthrie walked in front of me. He always did that, walked in front of me. It was policy for staff to always walk behind prisoners. Small gestures like that made me feel human. Mr. Guthrie treated me as a friend, as a human being.

"Mr. Guthrie, I don't have state blues on," I said sheepishly. Prisoners were required to be in Prisoner State Issues Uniforms in most areas of the prison and the school building was one of them. I was afraid now, and I hated it. I never dreamed about going home until I saw the parole board, but now I had grown attached to the idea, and I knew that attachment to anything impermanent created suffering. *It's okay, I shall not want, for thou art with me.*

"Don't worry about your clothes. Come on, I need to speak

with you. It's important," said Mr. Guthrie, not changing his poker face. I walked behind him into the office belonging to Mr. Porter, the hearings investigator. I had grown close to him and several other staff during my time at JCS. There were five staff members all standing around Mr. Porter's desk. Mr. Porter directed me to sit down.

"Wassup?" I asked. I wanted to hide my nervousness by being nonchalant.

"We are here to give you some bad news," Mr. Porter began. I immediately cut him off.

"Get the hell outta here. I got my parole, didn't I?" I almost shouted. I knew that he wouldn't have called me in that room with all those people to give me bad news. At least, I hoped. He grinned from ear-to-ear.

"You are going home, Mario. Finally." The words fell on numb ears. It was unbelievable. I had blocked out the thought of going home for years. They all smiled and patted my shoulder. I shook everyone's hands and embraced Mr. Guthrie and Mr. Porter.

"Finally, it's over," I mumbled. I ran back to the unit and begin calling everyone, mom, dad, and sisters, but no one answered. I call my lifelong friend, Theresa. Adrian, her husband, had begun to visit me the last year of my imprisonment. He wanted to get to know this "friend" his wife had spoken about all these years. At the time, Adrian had been pouring all of his extra energy into the campaign of Mayor Mike Duggan of Detroit. It just so happened that early that morning, just hours before I was given my parole decision for release, Mike Duggan had been named the official winner of the Detroit Mayoral Race of 2013. Adrian answered the phone, assuming correctly that I was calling to congratulate him on his hard run marathon that entailed campaigning and helping manage Café Cortina, his family-owned Italian restaurant in Farmington Hills, Michigan. This guy spends his days running the streets of

Detroit trying to convey a new vision for the city and working all night to maintain his father's dream turned legacy.

"Mario-o-o-o!! We won!!!!" he blasted. I could see Adrian's huge Italian smile shining through the phone.

"Congratulations, my beloved brother. I told you, resilience is the key. I am extremely proud of you," I poured into him, just as I had been doing since we met. We had built a very special co-mentoring relationship.

"Yes, resilience. I spoke of you last night," he continued. "People are waiting for you out here. There are high expectations for you, for your help with the city of Detroit. Mrs. Duggan, the mayor's mom, said that her greatest wish is to leave a lasting legacy for Detroit's returning citizens. I told her I have the perfect man to lead the charge. I told her all about you."

"I am humbled, my friend. My only desire is to both serve and bring glory to God," I said sincerely. "I did call to inform you that I, too, have blessed news to share." I lowered my voice. It cracked a bit as tears ran down my cheeks. "I got my parole. I'm coming home." I heard him try to speak. He, too, was crying.

"I am so happy right now. These are tears of joy," I heard him say as the phone was snatched from him.

"What did you do to my husband?" yelled Theresa in jest.

"I told him I got my parole," I said, grinning ear-to-ear. She started screaming in joy.

When I was finally able to reach my family, all of them were overjoyed too. When I called my mom, I could not resist teasing her a little.

"I got my parole decision back, mom," I said in a monotone voice. "I have bad news."

"Oh, *mijo*, please don't be sad. God is with us. Do not worry. He will find a way," she said, as always, one of us soothing the other.

"Ma, you're going to have to buy a lot more food now, 'cuz I'm coming home, and I eat a lot," I said with an enormous smile that I swear could be seen through the phone. She paused.

"*Qué? Qué?* What?" Then another long pause as I listened to my mother crying, silently, as she had all those years alone, envisioning, praying, supplicating the Lord for my protection and my release. Her prayers did not go unanswered.

December, 2013, Afraid to Go Home

I had developed many close relationships with the young men we were mentoring. One of them was a young man named Ryan who lost his college football scholarship as he drank his way into alcoholism and began a robbing spree of over 200 businesses with his *own* father. He was my bunkmate, assigned to me to mentor. Rick and I resided within the same cube that held a total of eight prisoners. It was Rick, myself, and six other prisoners that yet to reach the age of twenty-one. "You afraid to go home, big bro'?" asked my mentee, lil' *big* brother, Ryan, all 300 pounds of him. He was standing over my bunk as he and the rest of the youths were waiting for the lunch bell.

I knew why he'd asked. For the past two months since being told that I'd be seeing the parole board, I'd been internalizing what I did nineteen years ago. I had accepted responsibility long ago, and, yet, it was the first time in my life that I had been called to explain, verbally articulate, why I took Samuel's life. A thirty-five-year old man was called to explain why a disconnected, angry, sixteen-year old boy shot a man during a drug deal turned armed robbery and murder almost twenty years earlier. I had struggled with taking Samuel's life internally for many, many years. But now, I was being called to answer for it. This internal struggle was rooted in the "fear of going home syndrome" as many men who serve decades in prison face. I thought about Ryan's question and reflected on how

I felt about the impending release. I saw all the men around me, including Rick, waiting for my response.

"No, lil' bro', I'm not afraid to go home. But I am afraid of losing what I've found," I said softly.

"What's that, bro'? What did you find?" Ryan asked genuinely.

"Contentment, my brother. I'm afraid of losing the inner peace with *what is*," I said as I lowered my head down in self-reflection.

January 21, 2014, The Night Before my Release

Nineteen years in prison, sixteen different prisons, and dozens of housing units later, I had many close bonds with the men around me. This thing called *prison* had, unfortunately, become my home, my abode, and my comfort zone. It had tested me using an immense amount of pressure, to the point of wishing for death, but by the grace and guidance of God's Holy Spirit, I was able to use that pressure to form an internal diamond that was a spark for many of the men that I was leaving behind.

I spent literally *all* day saying goodbyes to staff and prisoners alike. I spent hours in the deputy's office, reminiscing about the good ole' times when I had "one foot on a banana peel and the other foot out the door" as my beloved mentor so eloquently warned me. I spent time with staff members who saw in me a man that I had yet to see in myself. I spent time with friends who had become family. Young men who, initially assigned to me for disciplinary purposes, now followed me, watched my every word, every deed, in admiration of a boy-become-man within the same concrete jungle that they had to face. I was a boy-become-man who was now their respected elder, leader, mentor (trusted teacher and counselor), one they were never afforded, to lead them through their *rite of passage*, a necessity inherent to all males.

I refused to say goodbye. I would only say, "See ya'll later, 'cuz

I'm comin' back, like Moses." That was my mantra for all the imprisoned lifer youths. I was determined to get out and influence the system in a manner that safeguards our communities while bettering the men that I left behind in the process. Thus, that statement applied to all the imprisoned. *Education* was the great equalizer, and I knew it. I *was* it. Education was crucial to this remedy for the disconnected, criminal mind. I was on to something, and those closest to me were prodding me into defining those terms and serving the community by providing these services. Yet, all that would come in due time. For now, I look around at those young men; "youngsters" as I referred to them, and in the depths of my soul, I knew there was *purpose in my pain*. There are moments in your life when you feel, think, and spiritually understand your connectedness to the *whole*. These are those rare moments that you just *know* that you are in alignment with *all that is*. Walking down those last hours the night before, I *knew*.

"Hey, bro', can I please speak with you in the dayroom after they close the unit for lights out?" asked Ryan, my lil' big mentee, politely. I had grown to love this kid who never had a chance to be one. A co-conspirator with his biological father, at the age of twenty, football scholarship in hand, his father deemed it more profitable to groom his son into crime and alcoholism as they burglarized over 200 businesses. This was Ryan's "mentor." The kids are the problem, huh? What a joke. "I wanted to say my goodbye now, not in front of the fellas." With one teardrop rolling down his cheek, Ryan continued. "You and Rick are the most positive men that has ever been in my life." He paused as more tears flowed. "I am so happy that you are going home, that you finally . . . get to go home. But I want you to know that you have forever changed my life for the better. I am going to miss you, and I love you." I embraced him as my lil' big brother picked me up off my feet. I walked back to my "cell" for my last "lock down and lights out" and thought, *this is my why. I love you, my God. I praise you for your correction, your chastisement. Thank you for never forsaking me even when I didn't deserve your love.*

January 22, 2014: Day of Release

Sitting on the bench in control center as I waited for the security gates to open, I reminisced over the two voices that, for the first time in my life, had spoken directly to me. The first voice came as I was taking a shower. I literally heard a thunderous voice boom out, "You cannot fathom the blessings I have in store for you!" I quickly yanked back the shower curtain to the single-man shower. Nobody. From the shower, I was able to see under the bathroom stalls that the bathroom was empty. Heart pounding, adrenaline rushing, I quickly rinsed off, grabbed my towel, and got out of that bathroom as quickly as I could. I made it back to the cubicle in which I was living with my friend Rick and the six at-risk mentees assigned to us by Deputy Riley. I walked up to him clearly startled.

"You won't believe what just happened," I said breathing heavily. After all I'd been through, I didn't scare easily, and Rick knew it.

"What bro'? What's up?" he asked in earnest.

"God just spoke to me as I was in the shower," I said as I saw his doubt in his eyes. "I am not crazy Rick," I emphatically said as we both knew that I was experiencing a lot of stress since I was told that I was going home.

"I know he did, bro. God speaks to all of us," Rick said as he patted my shoulder.

"I'm for real, Rick, I am not crazy!" I said with anger and frustration, more for myself than at him. "I *can't* be going crazy now!"

Rick paused and looked at me intently. I could tell that I now his attention. "What did He say?" Rick genuinely asked.

"He said, 'You cannot fathom the blessings that I have in store for you,'" I stated, looking into his eyes for a reassurance that I was not losing my mind.

Rick looked deep into my eyes and said, "Okay. I believe you, my brother," and embraced me.

The second voice came from a warden who was known for his hardness toward prisoners and for having an old-school correctional school of thought that relied heavily upon punitive strategies, solitary, and imprisonment as the best means toward behavior modification. Thus, it was challenging for me to find a middle ground, a similarity as is taught in mediation, from which I could approach and build a relationship. Considering, however, that he was the man responsible for me being released early, I felt an urge to genuinely thank him.

"Excuse me, Warden. Do you have a second?" I asked as he was writing in the logbook. He was doing his routine rounds through each housing unit. I continued to speak after he gave me a nod of permission to continue. "I just wish to say that I am sincerely grateful for this opportunity to go home early. My grandmother's ninety-first birthday is in two weeks, and because of you, I can attend." Closing the logbook, he looked up at me. He was a big man, tall and wide, quarterback size.

"You did this. Thank yourself." He leaned in. "You have a gift. Don't waste it." The Warden, who had never said a word to me, spoke life into my heart, soul, and mind. A warden. A *Deputy* warden. A counselor. Officers. All of them were now a part of my fellowship, just as were the prisoners. "And the lion shall lay down with the lamb." God is good.

CHAPTER 13

IN PURSUIT OF PURPOSE

February, 2014, It's Not what I Dreamed it Would Be

I WALKED OUT of prison with an Associate's Degree in the Arts and Social Sciences with a 3.67 overall GPA and the Dean's List for 2008. My area of concentration was business and psychology. The entire time in prison, from the beginning of my college education, I was being groomed to come home and put those skills to use in my family's pediatrics business that was now thriving. I voraciously read every business book and studied accounting, finance, marketing, and organizational management. I was excited to come home to work and contribute to a family who had been there to support me my entire nineteen years of imprisonment.

The first few months of working at the office was turbulent at best. Hindsight being 20/20, placing me as the receptionist of a pediatrics office just three weeks after being released from a nineteen-year prison sentence may not have been the best idea. This was the vision my little sister, who was now my boss, had for me: a receptionist. Filing paper work and "making my bones" at $500 a week, before taxes, for 40 hours a week was a blessing considering the fact that most "felons" don't stand a chance to get a job, let alone a clerical one. Trying to work through my PTSD, I locked myself in the employee bathroom as I cried in pain for the wanting of purpose. No matter how miserable prison was, *that* is where I discovered my purpose, thus, in a sense, I was in mourning. I had lost the only meaning I had ever experienced: teaching and training other lost men such as myself.

My stepfather felt it and on one occasion said, "Mario, people like you have purpose, an inner desire to achieve and progress. I do not like to have employees like you. This is only temporary. Know that. This is not where you will stay." His words penetrated my heart as I choked back the tears, for I simply wished to fit into the family's business, friends, and routine, but I didn't fit in anywhere. The tears that flowed were in part the pain of the past coupled with the horrific reality that a newly released man must face: I was helpless in a world I did not know. The taking of Samuel's life was felt just as much out here, twenty years later, as it did while in bondage.

Determined to attend the University of Michigan in pursuit of a social work degree, I confidently walked into the admissions office at the University of Michigan Dearborn with my associate's degree and certificate for being on the Dean's List in hand to fill out my application. "The computer is right over there, honey," said the receptionist, pointing toward the far wall. I looked at the computer and then looked back at her. My confidence vanished. I walked over to the computer and stared at it for several minutes. I didn't know how to turn it on. I walked back to the front desk and politely whispered, "I am deeply sorry. I am a returned citizen. I just served nineteen years, and computers were just coming out when I went in. I'm sorry," I mumbled, putting my head down. She graciously helped me with a hard copy of the application. While some prisons provided the opportunity to learn computer basics, you are allowed to choose only one "skill trade." Since I chose to take carpentry level-one training, I could not take the computer basics course. I had a tiny bit of experience with Windows '98, but it wasn't the programming that had me confused. In this situation, I didn't even know how to turn the computer on!

About a month later, I received a denial letter from the University of Michigan. Paraphrased, it said something like, "We are greatly concerned about your education and would like for you to re-apply in twenty-four months after you have completed parole."

I later received a phone call by an administrator to assess how I felt about the letter. It was one of the strangest conversations I had ever experienced. I told her that I was resilient and determined to get my bachelor's and that it was too bad for them that they missed out on a diamond in the rough. Inwardly, however, I was devastated. The rejection from the University of Michigan was a reminder that I could never run from my past, from what I did, regardless of how much I have reformed.

This rejection was followed by a denial from Wayne State University's School of Social Work. I wanted to help others and I thought that the platform to do it would have been in social work, but they shunned me as well. The denial at the University of Michigan and the school of social work was a trigger of a past pain: prison is the epitome of stagnation, death and decay of the body, mind, and soul through a deprivation of positive stimuli. To be denied only reminded me of my captors, of a system resistant to the nurturing of its fallen youth. I failed at sixteen, and that failure would be an anchor around my neck for years to come.

Lastly, I applied to Just Leadership USA (JLUSA), an organization founded and run by the formerly incarcerated whose aim is to cut the prisoner population in half by the year 2030 through policy change. Just Leadership USA is a program that pours some of the best leadership training that the nation has to offer into returned citizens who demonstrate leadership talent, so that they can return to their leadership positions within their communities as stronger, more effective voices of change and positive influence. They take the good and make them better. But just like U of M, I was denied for being on parole. The catch was that you had to be released from prison for at least three years in order to apply to the program. I had only been out less than a year. To be denied from my "own" was the most hurtful rejection. Coupled with the sense of rejection at work from a path that I thought was to be mine, I sank into a deep depression. All I wanted to do was help people, but I couldn't even help myself.

I was compelled, therefore, to create a new vision for myself. I applied to the School of Business at Wayne State University (WSU) and the "shark tank" accepted me. Go figure, like attracts like. Turns out that God had a plan all along. I enrolled in that spring/summer semester with four classes. The WSU advisor said, "I'm worried about your course load. You spent a lot of time away, and if you fail... I'm afraid you may quit," she said with sincere concern and compassion. I laughed.

"Quit? Ma'am, I don't know that word means, *quit.* I am resilient. You will see," I replied, reassuring her that four classes would not give me trouble. That semester, I achieved a 3.3 without even understanding how to use a computer. What you believe within wholeheartedly, invariably, you will achieve without. Then it came time to decide my major.

"Which is the most challenging?" I asked the advisor.

"Accounting and finance degrees are our Bachelor of Science business degrees. They are the most challenging," she replied hesitantly, as if she would recommend something easier. I raised my chin up.

"Accounting it is!" I replied. A newfound chip on my shoulder had developed. I'd been rejected time and time again from those institutions that claimed to be open for all those seeking an education, a human right, or so I thought.

As I walked the college campus of Wayne State University, I giggled inside and quietly whispered, "Thank you, my God, for I am undeserving." I was in awe, for I had only dreamed of attending college, and after so many years, it felt as if that was all it would ever be . . . a dream.

I engrossed myself in my studies. I took at least four classes for the following eight semesters while working two and sometimes three jobs in pursuit of purpose. My mom and dad were concerned about my health. "You cannot continue like this Mario. You will burn out," my mother would say. But they didn't understand how powerful purpose can be. It was the whispers of Samuel's restless spirit that stirred the nest. I had to succeed in order fulfill the covenant of helping other youths like me. Unless I personally succeeded, I would never gain the credibility to have access to these youths.

Those first few months of my release involved a lot of emotional release that had been building up over decades of suffering. I cried often, and, at the time, I didn't understand why. My brothers from prison, the Peacekeepers, would call me in joy and hope for a better tomorrow only to hear me break down emotionally at the sound of their voices. I would lock myself in the closest empty room when we spoke so that no one would see my vulnerability, everything that I could not show within the confines of an environment that would shred you to pieces if you displayed such "weakness."

"Bro! Bro,' you okay? Bro, what's wrong? Please, you're scaring me. Tell me, why are you crying?" My close friends and mentors that were a strong influence to my transformative process would ask. I would whisper through the cries. It is dangerous for a man to lose his *work*.

Truth is, I chose that major just to prove a point to myself: I must choose the path less travelled if I am to be great, driven by the internal loathing of self as a result of taking Samuel's life. Some things, no matter how much you desire, can never be erased.

Every day I woke up trying to make up for lost time, running toward my destiny with cinderblocks tied around my ankles. Regardless of work responsibilities, class deadlines, or family expectations, one thing, and one thing only, came above all else: my purpose, that, a broken young man in need of guidance. I took every possible opportunity that presented itself to minister in the hopes that I might save a life in return for the one I'd taken.

March, 2014, Mrs. Joan Duggan

Theresa's husband Adrian helped make one of the most important introductions of my life to Mrs. Joan Duggan, the mother of Detroit's current mayor, Mike Duggan. "Mario, I want you to meet with Mrs. Duggan, the mayor's mom," said Adrian, now in an official position as the mayor's Director of Customer Service. "She wants to pick your brain in her pursuit to help returning citizens. We need to keep this hush-hush because the mayor doesn't really want her to be so active, but her passion pushes her down this path so it's hard to tell her no," he said with a protective demeanor as he gave me her number. Overwhelmed, yet open to Spirit, I allowed myself to be led and called her.

"Mrs. Duggan, this is Mario, ma'am, Adrian's friend."

"Yes, dear. Do you have time for lunch sometime this week?" said Mrs. Duggan, her voice soft, yet firm. We made plans to meet at a Lebanese restaurant in Dearborn. I eagerly waited in the parking lot hoping to hear a message, a sign from a God who had grown silent once again.

"Hello, son," said Mrs. Duggan with a smile ear-to-ear. Her energy and aura was that of an angel. We talked, laughed, and cried for over three hours. I was a phenomenon to her and with sincerity in her every fiber, she helped me feel normal, human, and deserving of love. When prisoners serve a significant number of years in confinement, we adopt an unconscious belief that we don't deserve to be treated humanely with love or compassion. I had become conditioned to expect, and prepare, for the worst from humanity, especially authority. We bonded over the next few months as she got to know me, and as *I* got to know me. I knew who I was in prison. Now I was getting to know who "Mario" was in society.

Mrs. Duggan and I began there, at that Lebanese restaurant in Dearborn, Michigan what would be one of the most powerful mentoring relationships I would ever experience. She loved my gift, and me for she is love, and one may only give what one has. She guided me to other people who would assist in the manifestation of a legacy that would safeguard the community by helping to heal broken men.

April, 2014, Meeting in Greek Town

Mentors like Mrs. Duggan and Adrian encouraged me to be active in the pursuit of mentoring at-risk populations. I knew that I needed help to get this idea off the ground, so I reached out to Cam'ron Colts, my close friend and fellow Peacemaker from Jackson Cooper Street prison, now a returned citizen. "Cam, Mrs. Duggan said we need to meet with a guy named Vaughn Arrington," I explained to him. "She said we may want to include him within our vision." Up to that I point, I had never heard of the guy. I came to discover that Vaughn had been raised on the East Side of Detroit and had served about seven years in prison for armed robbery he committed as a teenager. Upon his release, Vaughn went to Marygrove College where he earned a Bachelor's of Social Work (B.S.W.). Since then, he has been working to help mentor at-risk youth in the area that he once ravaged with violence and criminal acts, the East Side of Detroit.

"You talk to James and Tanya yet?" Cam asked. I had not. People I will call James and Tanya were the mentors who had come into the prisons as representatives of a prison-created program that aimed to train the most influential men on the prison yard in leadership training focused on conflict resolution and mediation. Many promises were made during our imprisonment as we served as peacemakers for that prison. We trained over 1,500 men in critical thinking and effective communication, and the cream of the crop went on to be servant leaders trained in mediation and equipped to facilitate the curriculum they had learned. Though the program was a multiplier of servant leaders, little support was given to us men upon our release, let alone a platform to exercise the skills and tools earned in one of the harshest, most aggressive, violent environments that a peacemaker could be trained in. This was disappointing to say the least. I appreciated all that James and Tanya had done for us, but I knew it wasn't enough.

Cam and I met with Vaughn at Five Guys burger place in Greek Town, Detroit in April of 2014, but it soon became clear that although we had had similar experiences, our visions were significantly different. Vaughn had served seven years in prison and was college-educated. Vaughn could not grasp the benefits of training and mentoring prisoners or at-risk youth in mediation training. He had a vision of helping the criminally-charged youth with the legal process from start to finish by giving advice and mentoring because we had gone through that frightening process of not knowing or understanding what was happening . . . or was going to happen. Most lay adults are not savvy at navigating the legal system. How much less so is a sixteen-year-old youth? He had a great idea, and we were open to it, though it was not necessarily our field of expertise.

The fact that Vaughn could not embrace our vision made sense, for what the men had done within the confines of Jackson Prison was impossible to believe … unless you *had seen it*. Our experiences shape our vision. When I explained our position to Vaughn in terms of our current loyalty to an organization that appeared to no longer be concerned about its members, he said something that motivated, pushed, and prodded us to move to action. "Mario, sometimes we sow and sow and sow in one field only to reap in another." Vaughn walked away with a little cutie by his side as they hopped on his motorcycle. Cam and I remained seated inside Five Guys.

I looked at him and asked, "So, what do you think?"

"I say we wait for Rick," said Cam in reference to the same Rick who had fought for me to participate in the training and mentoring program in Jackson Cooper Street prison. He was good brother and mentor of ours who was due to be released within a few weeks.

"Do you realize what it's going to take to become successful at this?" Cam stayed quiet like the gentle soul he is. His mere presence balances my fighting energy that is more like Aaron, the right hand of Moses from the Bible, who demanded of God of God, "Do you stand with us or against us?"

"We're going to have to *give* and *give* and *give*, just like we did inside until our credibility has been restored," I continued. "Only then, will we become successful." I looked deep into Cam's eyes to measure his response.

"Then you and Rick must have a sit down with James," he said with a smile. Cam and I knew what we, by the Grace of God, had manifested within those walls in Jackson. We also knew that there were important people who wanted us to exercise that skill set. The subculture of prison is the antithesis of peace. It is the inverse of pro-social. Gaining the skill set that positioned us to obtain permission to lead a disconnected population toward a different mindset was to not be understated. Literally, *the problem had been transformed into the solution*. The conflict was that we *yearned* to do it with the group we had been a part of while inside. That was the vision that James and Tanya had imparted to us, and anything that deviated from that created cognitive dissonance within us. But thus far, James had displayed some signs of being self-serving that concerned us, so we had not shared some of the opportunities that were surfacing for us. We decided to wait for Rick.

Around this same time, I ran across an old acquaintance from long, long ago—Brenda, the same young Puerto Rican and Spanish girl who was having dinner at my mother's house the night of my crime, only now she was a grown woman. Brenda had been one of my alibi witnesses back in 1995. One Saturday night we serendipitously ran into each other at a salsa club for the first time in nearly twenty years. "Mario?" she said, as she covered her mouth in shock.

"Yes," I said with a huge smile. She was still beautiful. She was there to celebrate her sister's birthday, and we danced most of the night. We talked a lot and exchanged phone numbers. She had never been married, no children, and was running a successful medical practice. She was a medical assistant and an all-around player on her family's business team. She had a thousand questions, as did I. It turned out that we had memberships to the same gym, so she invited me to my first yoga class. Over the next six months, we simply got to know each other as friends.

Spring 2014, A Chip Off the Old Block

Right after my release from prison, I lived with my mom and stepdad. One evening as I was returning home late from one of my five college night classes, my mom and stepdad's neighbor, Mr. Darvin Lewis, Sr., a man I call "Unc," short for "uncle," approached me.

Unc and his wife attended my homecoming party where we met for the first time. They had been doing global prayer services in my name and for my salvation for five years ever since my mom had confessed to them that she *did*, in fact, have a son who had committed a horrible crime at a young age. I was kept secret most of the time—a stain on my family's name. The day of my party, Unc whispered, "We prayed for you Mario," as he embraced me tearfully. He was large black man with the energy and heart of a man who has experienced pain but who continues to raise his hands in praise. "As soon as your mom told us about you, my wife and I dropped to our knees and begged God for your protection. We begged God to anoint you in the blood of Christ," he said as he continued to embrace me like a father. Unc had come from a demographic that could *identify* with my experience. He had grown up in hard times while lacking a positive male role model. He fell to the temptations of easy money and began hustling drugs until turning legit after his brother received a life sentence.

I ended up working a little side business hustling Obama phones for Unc, and we bonded. His wisdom and insight into life assisted me during dark times. He had learned the hustle of amortized mortgages and was entrenched in the market when the housing bubble crashed. They moved from New York to Michigan, right next door to my mother and stepfather. Then he hustled unregulated energy and government phones. Unc also purchased a route of vending machines for his son, DeQuincy, to own and manage. Thus, DeQuincy always had money, which impressed the ladies at the high school. What Unc did not understand was that while you may teach what you know, you could only reproduce what you are.

That night as I exited my car, Unc said, "I need you to talk to my son, DeQuincy. Mario, I'm afraid he may be making some wrong decisions. He just got suspended from school."

"For what?"

"Some BS. Some kid came up to DeQuincy while he was in the hallway and handed him a bag full of pills," Unc said. "Then the security guard approached DeQuincy and caught him with the pills in his hand. They suspended him for two weeks. I don't know what will happen."

"Okay, I'll meet up with you and DeQuincy at the clinic later this week," I said, in reference to my stepfather's medical practice. As it turned out, DeQuincy was scheduled to go in for his football physical, anyway. I looked at his Facebook page the day before our meeting and saw that was his nickname was "Q." Q was six-foot-three-inches with a muscular frame that was touted as a varsity football star, though he was only in eleventh grade.

A few days later, now in my stepfather's office, He slouched in the chair with his sagging pants, big diamond earring, gold necklace and gold watch. Q had it made. But he was just a little too "into himself."

"So, Q, that's what they call you, correct?" I asked him already knowing the answer. This was a means of gauging his body language and response pattern when answering questions and to make the kid feel comfortable.

"Yeah," he responded with his cool self. I introduced myself to this youngster who had heard of me for years but had never met me.

"Q, as they call you, do you know who I am? Who I really am and where I come from?" Q shook his head no. "Q, when I was your age, my parents struggled, ya know? They struggled to love themselves," I paused, staring into his eyes. The tone, once jovial and light, was now tense and serious. "When I was around twelve," I continued, "I started to sack up ounces of weed and sell dime bags. By ninth grade, I was selling ounces and quarter pounds. And by tenth grade, I just started taking people's shit," I said as I kept staring into his eyes. Q looked down, and I continued. "In eleventh grade, at the age of sixteen, your age, I robbed and killed a man for his money and his dope. He was a real big guy, like you, but even bigger." I continued to stare into his eyes when he would periodically raise his head. "I did a year in solitary as I fought my case. I had two trials. The first was a hung jury. After the first trial, they offered me a deal to tell on the guys who had ratted on me, but I manned up and took it on the chin like a soldier. You know what that did for me, Q?" He looked up and shook his head. "It empowered me to tap into my god potential . . . it brought me through the hell that led me to my purpose," I whispered to him, using church lingo knowing that this young man comes from a Christ centered home.

Then in a normal tone, I explained to him, "I ended up doing nineteen years in sixteen different adult prisons. I never set foot in a juvenile facility," I continued to look intently into his eyes. Q no longer lowered his head, for I had captured his attention away from himself. "So, tell me what happened, Q?" Then Unc stepped in.

"Well, Mario, I already told you what happened—"

"Excuse me, sir, with all due respect, *you* asked me to speak to your *son*, correct?" Unc nodded his head and quieted down, understanding where I was going with this. "Then, please, allow me to do my job," I said, in affirmation of what *was to be* one day, for at the time I merely emptied trash bins, mopped floors, and answered phones. I looked back to the youngster. "So, Q, tell me exactly what happened." I leaned back, examining *every* gesture, *every* body movement, for almost 70% of our communication is through body language.

"Well, you see, what happened was some kid—"

"What was he, a Black kid?"

"No, he's Chaldean," he responded looking at me strangely as if to ask does it matter? "He came up to me in the hallway, between classes . . . and he handed me this bag that was wrapped in white tissue, and I didn't know what it was. Before I could look at it, a security guard came up to me—"

"Which security guard?" I asked

"Jessica," he said, again with a strange look. What he didn't know was that I knew Jasmine very well. She happened to be the sister-in-law of my little sister Alexis. We had spoken at family get-togethers about the delinquency in West Bloomfield High School and her passion to help the youth. I asked her about this situation later.

"So, Jessica grabbed it out of my hand, and it turned out to be a hundred pills of some narcotics," he finished, meekly putting his head down. *He's good, but not that good.*

"So where do you think this Chaldean kid got these narcos from?" I asked, though I already knew the answer.

"I *guess* his family owns a pharmacy," he replied. *He guesses.* I chuckled inside.

"So, what you are telling me is that this Chaldean kid..." I started and then paused, taking a different tactic. "How big is this kid?"

"He's about your size," he replied.

"Okay, so what you are telling me is that this Chaldean kid who is half your size just walked up to you and shoved a bag full of pills in your hand, and you have no clue why?" He nodded yes.

"Hmmm, that's real interesting to me. You know, I've been doing this shit for a long time, Q. I'm thirty-six years old, and I've literally been hustling one way or another for twenty-five straight years, and this shit just doesn't sound right." I chuckled and paused, allowing more silence to rattle the youngster. "You know what was one of my gravest mistakes at your age, Q?" I changed the tone and lightened it up, just to get him back to being comfortable. "I messed up by not trusting my father. I mistakenly thought that it was better to protect his *feelings* by hiding the facts. But this man, *this* man before you... Pick your head up and *look* at him!" I snapped, and the youngster complied immediately. "*This* man is the *only* man on this *earth* who will literally die for you." As I said these words, a teardrop rolled down Q's cheek. Then another. "*This* man, Q, is the *only* man you must *always* be completely honest with regardless of how ugly the truth may be. You owe him this much." As the tears began to flow, he lowered his head. His father watched in amazement as I continued. "You know, Q, I am just putting myself in your shoes and thinking what I would have done. Well, shit, I tell you what I did do when my buddy owned a pharmacy. I bought a bunch of wholesale, and I sold it retail. I think you were gonna get these pills at two dollars a piece, which is only two hundred dollars, and then sell them for about ten dollars a piece." I paused to see a response. More crying. I looked at Unc who was sitting across from us in my stepfather's chair behind his desk. I nodded my head as a gesture for the father to come and console his son. Unc complied. As I made my way out of the office and shut the door behind me, I looked behind to see a father and son, now weeping, embrace one another.

Late one night, months later, Q was shooting baskets when I pulled up. "Mario," said Q. I looked over. It was dark, but I could see him smiling ear to ear.

"Waddup doe?" I said, using the signature greeting in Detroit.

"I went over to your house, and your mom said you would be coming home late tonight 'cuz you had class," he said, in a genuinely meek tone. Q was a good kid with a good heart whose parents were people after God's own heart. "I wanted to ask you a question, Mario. We had a guess speaker in school today, and he had been addicted to heroin for over twenty years. He even went to prison for hurting someone, and he said that every day he lives in regret. That is when I thought about you. Mario," Q paused, as the clear sky allowed for the full moon and all the stars to lay light upon our gaze. "Do you regret what you did? Do you regret killing that man?" he finally got it off his chest.

I dropped my bag of books on the ground and lowered my head. Tears welled up in my eyes as I raised my head back up. "Q, I am now thirty-seven years old, and I live with my mom. I have nothing. I own nothing. I am nothing. Everyone around me who I knew has accomplished something while all I have done is destroy. The only friends that I have, I left behind in prison. I don't understand this world that I live in, and I cry every day, for *everything* that I experience reminds me of my sin," I said as tears rolled down my cheeks. "But this was a *just* sentence for what I did." I paused. "To answer your question, Q, every waking breath I mourn Samuel. Every waking second, I wish that I could give my life in exchange for his." I lowered my head and brushed the tears off my face. I looked back up. "This is why I do what I do, Q. I am only here to help people like you. This is the cross that leads to my peace." I picked up my bag and slowly walked into my house.

These were the moments I lived for. These were the moments that got me through my long, exhausting days and sleepless nights. As I continued to pursue my purpose, I encountered angels . . . and devils. One of my first angels came in the form of a woman who happened to be the mother of our mayor.

May, 2015, Rick's Homecoming

I couldn't wait to be back in action with Rick, our friend, mentor, and potential business partner. Things were getting worse with the program that we had once lived for. The month before Rick's release had involved more prodding and pushing by my angels, my mentors, Adrian and Mrs. Duggan. Adrian took me to lunch at the Mayor Coleman Young Building and said in a serious tone, "I'm unsettled that you have not been helped by the people who are supposed to be helping returning citizens. You *must* have a sit down with this James and ask him what their plans are." I assured him I would once Rick was released. I had already explained Rick's relevance along with the rest of the men from the Jackson Prison yard who were soon to follow.

On the day of Rick's release, Cam and I were waiting for him at his sister's house where his entire family congregated in anticipation. After fifteen long years, Rick was finally home. I will never forget seeing him holding his grandson, smiling ear-to-ear, basking in his newly found freedom.

Later, he approached me as I sat by myself in a lawn chair in his sister's back yard watching the setting sun on that beautiful May evening. "You good, bro'?" he asked. I was overjoyed that Rick was home, yet, saddened to break the news to him that "A Chance to Live" was a sham.

"Rick, we have to have a sit down with James and Tanya. So far, they have done nothing for any of us who have come home. They expect us to meet every two weeks, feed us $5 Hot-n-Ready's from Little Caesars, ask us how we feel as if we were in an AA or something, and make sure they capture our signatures on a sign-in sheet. Something isn't right. Adrian said we need confront them, respectfully, about what's going on and, especially, about how we desire to help the community."

"Okay," replied Rick with a slow nod. "I guess we are going to have to gain an understanding." On his first day out, Rick was disheartened to hear the possible reality that our mentors were merely wolves in sheep's clothing. I was excited and relieved to know that his commitment to purpose was still as high as Cam's and mine.

July, 2014, Pulling off the Mask

In time, Rick experienced first hand the empty promises of James and Tanya. That prompted him to arrange a meeting with James. By then, I recently began an internship at an accounting firm. The day of our meeting with James, Rick was sitting in James's office and I was on speakerphone on my lunch break. "So, Rick said ya'll got some questions," I heard James's voice say on the other end of the phone.

"Yes, sir," I said. I had always respected James . . . until James disrespected us by mistakenly thinking that we were vulnerable and weak, mentally and emotionally. The poverty pimps in Detroit prey upon the vulnerable populations that are the children (Detroit Public Schools) and returning citizens (felons on parole). At times when I was still in Jackson Cooper Street, I had noticed James being arrogant and dominating in his speech, a trigger to a long-term imprisoned man such as myself.

I went ahead and asked the question, though I already knew the answer. "When you get the funding for 'A Chance to Live' (ACL) reentry proposal, what do you plan to do with it?" Crickets. After about ten seconds, James went on a three-minute tangent explaining to me *what* ACL was, as if I had never heard of it. "Does that answer your question?" he replied with an implication of finality.

"Actually, it *doesn't*," I said with venom. "Allow me to dumb it down. Once you get the money, are you going to hire the men from JCS to be mediators in the worst parts of Detroit as you promised?" I demanded.

"Why do I hear aggression in your voice, Mario?" James asked. Rick intervened.

"Well, James, I think Mario is just under a little stress right now." James cut back in.

"It was never the plan to hire any of you. I don't care if I *ever* see an ACL man again once he's released, as long as he doesn't re-offend." I sat there in shock, but that was all I needed to hear. Rick continued to mediate the situation.

Though we ended the phone call with tension, I still went to the next ACL meeting. It was in my best interest to stay connected because I had worked on an assessment of the Latino population of Detroit. I had specifically targeted their needs and wants in terms of getting them to assimilate by working with the community and not staying isolated from their families at the expense of their safety or because they were undocumented and afraid of being sent back. This fear had created a population of sheep upon which the documented wolves would prey. I worked on the assessment and gained much of the data from face to face interviews. That assessment led to a luncheon meeting with the governor and the most "influential Latino leaders of Detroit." James asked me to attend, in representation of ACL, and I gladly accepted. The lunch took place at an upscale restaurant in Southwest Detroit.

Over the next six months or so, James and Tanya called upon me to participate in other events. They took me into Muskegon Correctional Facility to speaker to the prisoner population. The administration and James and Tanya were having challenges connecting with the prisoners in order to start an ACL program at that facility. Thus, the mission at hand was to recruit men. As soon as I walked onto the prisoner yard, prisoners that I knew from the old days began yelling, "Mario! Mario! We see you!" with smiles.

The feeling of speaking in front of 300 prisoners and pouring my lifeblood into their souls, to be an image, a light in the darkness . . . was absolutely phenomenal. "To the measure in which you give shall it be given unto you pressed down, shaken up, seven times seven," I shouted from the podium into the hearts and souls of the men. "Become that which you wish to possess. You do not get what you *want* out of life. *You get what you are!* You wish for freedom, yet you remained imprisoned within your own minds by turning against your brother, by lacking the understanding that what you do to another, you invariably do to yourself. It was when I stopped trying to beat the doors down that they opened. It was when I focused on *becoming* that which I was created to be that the doors opened." The men were in awe at hearing this from a fellow brother who had once walked the prison yard in a blue uniform with an orange stripe who now stood in front of them with a tailored suit and cufflinks: *I was a mess turned into a message.* "The truth is you have failed to utilize your resources, the greatest of them being *time*. Much of your time has been taken away to never to be regained; but what you do in this *very moment*, what you do in the darkness of the night as the world passes you by, will create and determine your destiny. At this very moment, you have been blessed with the opportunity to recreate yourself in the image and in the likeness of who you were destined to be: God." The men jumped to their feet and gave me a boisterous standing ovation.

When I finished and jumped down from the stage, the prisoners rushed around me, hugging me, whispering how they were going to try and contact me. They were stunned by who they saw before them. They were in a level-two facility that housed mostly lifers, but most of them knew me because I had done most of my time in higher levels. They wanted to know how I did what I did. How did I succeed? I told them about the training that I had received at Jackson Cooper Street a few years before my release. I described the training and the teaching that we were doing outside. "Brothers, when I was at JCS, we were training and mentoring the seventeen to twenty-five-year-old population that was wreaking havoc on the prison yard. We transformed an entire housing unit that embraced *our* expectations that superseded that of the MDOC's rules and policies. We stood on integrity, for a house divided cannot stand. *And* we came together as the apostles did. 'When two or more come in my name, so shall I be there.' Come together, pray together, and transform every man around you. Be a light unto the darkness until the darkness can hold you no longer." I loved being amongst the men.

I glanced up at the corrections officers and the warden who was sitting with James and Tanya. She was giving me a mean look, so I walked over to them. "Who are *you*?" she asked with disdain. Though this was a planned event, the warden thought that James and Tanya would only bring the customary ACL members who were not so inciting or motivating. As I reflect, the last thing a warden wants is a prisoner population that is motivated for change, because the status quo is safe and comfortable from their perspective. I had noticed her in the stands giving me dirty looks as I energized and motivated the "slaves," for a prisoner, by constitutional law, is a slave. Period. Forget political correctness for the sake of society's feelings. Remember, *facts over feelings.*

"Great question and one that pulls me through this thing we call *life*," I said with an equal tone. I felt my heart rate increasing and my breathing becoming shallow. My PTSD was kicking in.

"Really?" she said as she rolled her eyes and looked at Tanya.

"Mario is one of our motivational speakers," Tanya said smiling. I could tell she was trying to repair some damage.

"My name is Mario Bueno, and I used to be slave on these plantations," I replied as I reached over and shook her hand. I then walked away, leaving her mouth hanging open. I have never really cared how my captors feel about the realities of institutional racism that continues to oppress targeted have-nots.

James and Tanya continued to offer me experiences and exposure like this as a result of my gift (definitely not because of my affable personality), so I continued to attend ACL meetings for a few more months. I walked in, suited and booted, as James would request, every two weeks like clockwork over this time period. Even after our blowup on the phone, I walked into the next meeting with a smile on my face and embraced him. "I apologize for my disrespect," I said with humility. I learned long ago that it was better to grow better than bitter. He smiled and embraced me. During this meeting, James planted a seed in the minds of the men in relation to a vision he must have had.

"Fellas, Mario is the kind of guy who they might offer a hundred thousand dollars to work for them and the question is would he turn his back on ACL for the money?" I never did get to ask him who "they" were, nor did I get to ask him why making a hundred thousand dollars and being a part of ACL were not compatible, since he was doing that, and then some.

From that day of our phone call when he confessed that he never intended to use any of us from Jackson Cooper Street to do his work on the outside, the energy to manifest LUCK, Inc. was set in motion. Before that, it had been mere potential, that is, stored energy. James' offensiveness ignited the process of transforming that stored energy into kinetic energy, that is, energy in motion, all rooted from powerful e-motion, no different from the fear that empowers a mother to lift a car that is crushing her child. "Be angry, but do not sin," says the Lord. We were angry...and we were moved to begin the process.

July, 2014, My Accounting Internship

While my passion was to help others, I still needed to put food on my table. A returned citizen has few paths open to pursue that lead to a livable wage job. My resiliency and tell me that our suffering was simply the purification of false layers of our true selves imparting pain in place of purpose. The American criminal justice system offers two paths for the imprisoned: the first is a path of continued and perpetuated delusions of grandeur, narcissistic ways, for the criminal who does not learn or change and continues to harm all those in his or her wake. With each prison experience, this individual becomes more refined in his or her self-serving critical thinking skills, schemes, and strategies.

The second choice is to look oneself in the proverbial mirror and say, "I die to *that* layer of self to be closer to the God in me, the God that is a solution to the plethora of problems around me." Those who have walked the steps of crucifixion of self while imprisoned have an advantage: they are closer to *who they were intended to become* through the pain and fire of purification. The Buddha taught that to be enlightened, we must become detached to all that is non-permanent. Attachment to *anything* impermanent leads to suffering. So, when Wayne State's School of Social Work denied me of my "dream" of being a social worker, I didn't suffer long, for such titles are impermanent. Instead, *I became,* as is the man-date by God, and decided to pursue the accounting with vigor and ambition. I decided that I would create my own accounting firm, understanding that the major accounting firms had twenty-year-old kids that didn't have a murder case on their record, so why in the world would they hire me.

I've read somewhere that having two options is not equivalent to having a "choice." In this situation, I was running out of options. Mama always said, "A bird in the hand is better than two in the bush," so when I read Wayne State's School of Business acceptance letter I had no hesitation in pursuing that which I once chased: business.

Since accounting was my major, I sought out a mentor, a model, so to speak, from which I could learn. Manuel, my mom and step-father's longtime accountant and friend, thus, likened to my uncle, was my first thought.

"Mom, can you call Manuel and ask if he'd let me work there for free for the summer so I can learn how to run my own account-ing firm?" I asked, interrupting her from her paperwork for her business. Mom was completely different in terms of substance abuse and dysfunction. Of course, we didn't see eye to eye on a lot of things; however, the days of old were no more. Looking at my mother with pride, I continued, "I have to learn how to actually *do* accounting in the real world."

"Call him," she said, annoyed because I tended to interrupt her during her work.

"*Mom,*" I said in frustration, "Influence goes a long way. If you ask, then I am sure he will concede much easier than if I asked."

She called him right then and he agreed to an interview with the opportunity for a $10 an hour internship. "Mom," I said with excitement, "What did he say?"

"He asked if you were serious about accounting, and I told him that was what you were studying at the university," she said, focused back on her work.

I was excited. Getting denied in social work made me shift my target. Having a target, a *why* is crucial just to find the energy to get out of bed, let alone face the onslaught of life's challenges.

"Buy a bottle of wine for the interview," she said as she adjusted my dress shirt and put a hundred-dollar bill in the front pocket. "I will text you what wine to buy him," she said with a smile. She and my father had really struggled in trying to meet my emotional and mental needs since coming home. She loved me even though I had failed so many times.

Family reunification is a process of pain and pleasure for the ill-equipped juvenile lifer who finds his way out of the maze called the criminal justice system. Neither family nor felon is given the skills and tools to adjust and assimilate to the new roles that each will now play. We understood the process of prison visits maybe too well. For, now we struggled to get to know our real selves out here unrestrained. It saddened me that I didn't know how to console or comfort my mom beyond those prison gates where I had grown comfortable. I simply did not know how.

Now I needed that comfort and the convincing that "all was not lost" and that life would get better. But I was conditioned to not ask for anything, including help.

"Thank you, mom," I said, uncomfortably. The trauma of imprisonment had created within me, as in most of the released juveniles, an unreasonable fear that, sadly, was once reasonable. I had never experienced a job interview, and "not knowing" is the root of all fear.

Later that week, I did as my mom said and I showed up to Manuel's accounting office with a bottle of his favorite wine in hand.

"So why do you want to be an accountant?" Manuel asked, in his Cuban accent with his James Dean look. Manuel was a handsome ladies' man but having been divorced five times, coupled with a party lifestyle, his body was wearing down.

"I always studied the language of business, even while in prison. Now, I am an accounting major at Wayne State University and set to graduate in two years," I said, eager to learn *this* hustle. I sat at his dining room table as he made us Cuban coffee.

"You know, I am looking for someone to buy me out," he said. "I want to retire in about four to five years, which gives you enough time to both finish your degree and build viable relationships with the clients so that they stay with you throughout the transition of ownership," he said. He stirred sugar into the coffee and watched me for a response. I was in shock. *This* is my opportunity, my shot, I thought.

"I own seventy-five percent of the firm. The way I see it, you finish your degree as you work here developing the relationships with the clients," he said with a grin as he sipped his coffee.

So, just like that, I was hired. I started that week at his office on Junction and Vernor, in the heart of Southwest Detroit. I worked two days a week as I continued to work at the medical office answering phones and filing paperwork. When my mom told me that I was due for a raise, I asked to work fewer hours so that I could devote more time to the accounting firm. That way, my earning per hour was increasing. I began at the medical office working 40 hours per week at $500. By the end, I had increased my earning power at the medical office by taking over the cleaning of the entire clinic during the midnight hours. To clean the entire office took just over two hours of hard work, so the way I figured I was now making $50 an hour (10 hours a week at the same $500).

My mom and stepfather provided the opportunity for me to attend the university and be flexible in my working hours at the same time. Without this single opportunity in the form of shelter, clothing, food, job, and transportation, I would *never* have been able to experience the amount of success to date. Employment is crucial to a parolee's reentry into the community, for it brings the tangibles like money for food, shelter, and clothing, but also the intangibles like meaning, purpose, and a positive self-image. How we view ourselves is crucial to how we interact with the world around us. Parolees who are ingrained with a belief that they are separate from the world around them will find it easier to harm that world.

In addition, the lack of employment and basic needs perpetuates the scarcity mindset of the criminal, furthering the cycle of incarceration, release, and re-offense. "As many scholars have noted, employment is central to the reentry process, and evidence demonstrates that stable work can reduce the incentives that lead returning prisoners back to crime," (James B. Luther, 2011). The two greatest barriers for prisoner reentry are: 1) the internal barrier within the mind of the released that they have been dealt a bad "hand," that life is not fair and that they lack the power to change their present circumstances, and 2) the very real, tangible, systemically designed barriers of employment and housing. To be brandished a felon in America is to be stripped of a birthright that allows one to pursue the "American Dream" on a level playing field. Without access to a job because of the felony, and lacking the funds and credit to purchase a house, parolees are guided to small pockets within the metropolitan communities. Thus, they negatively affect the community by bringing with them paradigms of society that are saturated with cynicism for the law and authorities. This taints the attitudes of those in that designated community when it comes to "parolee refugees."

I did not suffer such struggles, not by my own doing, but by grace. Now, after all those years in prison, I was working toward the ownership of my own accounting firm. I smiled inside as I thought of those words *You cannot fathom the blessing that I have in store for you.* There were times that I was positive that God had spoken to me and other times I feared I was crazy. Working toward the accounting firm offered an opportunity for success and, in that superficial, non-permanent situation I felt secure. It was during such times that I felt God *did* speak to me.

August, 2014, The Birth of LUCK, Inc.

I consciously continued to build new relationships with people aligned to my purpose *and* who were people of integrity, like Mrs. Duggan. She operates on the highest energy level: *agape*, or unconditional love. When I am in the presence of such energy, I feel emotional, for I am in the presence of God's love, an energy that serves as the glue to my brokenness. She spoke life into me from the moment I met her. Her passion to help this population with a job as the "be all and end all" was tempered by my insight into the need for transformative education, training, and mentorship before getting a job. Otherwise, business owners would just get a high turnover rate. She got it. She understood how I had been transformed, and she got to know the organization that provided the platform for that transformation. "You need to start your own organization, Mario," she told me one day at lunch. "You and your men have a doctorate in how to transform the most hardened of men. Such resources must reach those in need. Those resources are meant to serve," she said. She spoke LUCK, Inc. into existence, and her faith was not without action. She was the first person to donate towards our cause. She planted that mustard seed and cultivated it over the months to follow.

So, Rick, Cam, and I created LUCK (Leaders Under Correct Knowledge), Inc., a name birthed in prayer early in the morning one day. "LUCK, Rick. It stands for Leaders Under Correct Knowledge. What do you think?" I asked excitedly.

"I love it," said Rick. We had business cards made, and we stayed in motion. "This is physics, not philosophy," has been my battle cry. I would say this in reference to people staying idle and talking about their woes as opposed to getting in motion.

We registered for our Employer Identification Number with the filing status of a "non-share" or non-profit status that fall of 2014 and created our Board of Directors beginning with Deputy Warden Riley who was retiring. As we pursued opportunities, he vouched for our work and integrity while under his guidance. Below is the transcribed letter:

Will Riley
Deputy Warden
Cooper Street Correctional Facility
3100 Cooper St.
Jackson, MI 49201

November 13, 2014

To Whom It May Concern:

I am happy to write this letter of support for L.U.C.K. Inc. Rick Speck, Mario Bueno and Cameron Colts were under my supervision for 4-5 years and consistently impressed me as young men who, if given a second chance, would become very valuable assets to society. I say this without hesitation because I observed them evolve into extremely influential and positive forces on the men incarcerated at the Cooper Street Correctional Facility.

These three men are among the most dedicated men I have observed in 30 years of correctional experience. They excelled as star pupils in the Michigan State University Inside\Out Class and other educational, cultural and social events sponsored at our facility. These men were always prepared to aid and support staff, volunteers and their peers in any internal or external endeavor the facility undertook. They have given impressive speeches to very large audiences and especially visiting dignitaries to our facility including Gov. Rick Snyder and former U.S. Ambassador Andrew Young.

Rick, Mario and Cam put forth great individual effort, time and personal sacrifice in learning how to reach and mentor incarcerated young men who needed understanding, guidance and positive role models in their lives. They were amongst the hardest working mentors who I chose to work with the most difficult mentees. We shared numerous discussions and they were provided with excellent training opportunities on how to effectively reach and change the lives of young men.

The founders of L.U.C.K. Inc. participated and subsequently rose to leadership positions in the Chance [to Live] program and benefited from this excellent program personally and from a leadership perspective. They each are committed to utilizing their knowledge and skills in helping others succeed. Countless young men have credited them with changing their outlook on life and helping them successfully return to society with a different and more positive attitude.

Rick, Mario and Cam's performance in successfully changing their own lives and working with and positively changing others during their period of incarceration demonstrates that they will be energetic and will unselfishly contribute to helping change the violent culture of our communities and will be positive influences on the people with whom they interact in society.

Although they are no longer incarcerated, the impact of their endeavors remains in effect at our facility yet today. I feel confident in saying that they will be effective and successful in deterring others from the following the pathway to prison.

Thank you for your consideration and please feel free to call me (517-780-6826) or email me at (rileyw@michigan.gov) if I can be more helpful.

Sincerely,

Our intention from the inception was to create the ultimate one-stop shop for transformational training that leads to a livable wage career and a path towards self-actualization. We wanted LUCK, Inc. to exist on its own in fulfillment of its mission and purpose, forever, even when Rick, Cam, and Mario were no longer around. That process to build the infrastructure and file all of the numerous documents it took to apply for the non-profit status recognized by the IRS took two years, the development of many relationships, and the cultivation of an accounting degree for me to be able to follow through with it.

With full-time college, two jobs, and a dream, I lived, ate, and breathed LUCK Inc. "God placed Adam in the Garden of Eden to *work* the garden." The true translation of the Garden of Eden simply refers to an "atmosphere" or an "environment" that is in the presence of God. And, if you notice, God's first command to Adam was not to worship or pray to Him, but rather, to work. The Hebrew translation of the word "work", in this context, means "to become". Thus, our only command of God is to remain in His presence so that we may *become.* I was slowly discovering that we are not an experiment, but rather an assignment, sent from the unseen to remedy a solution . . . to fulfill a purpose.

CHAPTER 14

ALL THOSE WHO WANDER
ARE NOT LOST

O VER THE NEXT EIGHT MONTHS, a lot happened. I soon began to realize that Brenda had every quality that I had written about in a letter to God back in 2007 after reading a great true story, *Left to Tell: Discovering God Amidst the Rwandan Holocaust*, by Immaculee Ilibagiza. In the book, she wrote a letter to God describing, in detail, the husband she wanted. I followed that model of faith by writing a clear description of the woman that I longed for: God-fearing Catholic, educated, sober (no vices), strong-spirited, loyal, brown-skinned, Latina, and, I hate to admit it, a gorgeous rump. She matched every detail. Knowing that she was special, I asked her father for his blessing before I popped the question on New Year's Eve of 2014. My alibi witness of 1995 had now become my fiancée of 2015. While this relationship was progressing, it seemed as if my other relationships were regressing.

Pursuing a bachelor's degree in accounting had to be one of the toughest challenges that I had ever faced. I now had to learn several foreign worlds: the streets, that sucked the life out of the youth; my family, who no longer knew the Mario who stood before them; this thing called college life, where deadlines are a norm; and, lastly, the foreign language of accounting. This was no longer the "comfort" of self-study, albeit I had done it from the discomfort of a prison cell. Perspective is funny like that. Prison, as I adapted and grew to know it, had become my comfort zone. Yet, the rules of engagement differ out here than in prison and, I was learning that at the expense of friends and family that had been there for me for all those years.

The struggle to stay committed to school came in the form of external (and internal) pressure that really had nothing to do with the academic challenges of school. Whether it was the stress of not fitting in with those classmates around me, or the inadequacy I felt from the lack of accomplishment in comparison to other men my age, at times it became unbearable, to the point of not wanting to live, a theme I am witnessing amongst us juveniles thrown into the adult prison system to die and, on a certain dimension we did.

As for LUCK, Rick, Cam, and I were struggling to reintegrate. In order to survive in prison, we had to become something that we were not created to be, the inverse of love. Thus, we now suffered from the reality that we did not know ourselves. Let alone our families and the world around us. This epiphany shook my foundation for now the sense of displacement was not simply theoretical or philosophical. It was real.

For decades, we had mastered the rules of the game, but now we wrestled with mundane activities like learning to work a TV remote. Tears that had been withheld for decades now found an outlet without cause, rhyme, or reason. Having endured the onslaught of depression and self-talk based in self-loathing, I was better equipped to counsel those coming after me. "You will cry for what appears to be no reason, but it's important for you to know that this is normal. This is part of the process, and it is healing." This is often how I broke the ice with those coming home after decades of imprisonment that still sought my counsel beyond the razor wire fences. My ministry continued with the same population but in a different geographic location. This was my calling, my reason, my why. And, yet, the tests did not stop, for God tests everyone He uses. When it was time for Jesus to begin his ministry, he was led by the Holy Spirit to the dessert to be tested. Yes, tested, so that he could be strengthened for the next level, which indeed was to bring new devils. The first encounter Jesus had as he stepped outside of the dessert from his 40 day fast was a demon-possessed man.

Sometimes we have the tendency to think that because we are in a storm, God must not be with us. Yet, I challenge that so common . . . so easily embraced belief. God will not appeal to your senses in your storm. He will not make you comfortable but this does not mean God is absent. On the contrary, the storm is strengthening you for the next level of devils (challenges). If God were to make us comfortable in the "storm", then we would not be moved to act . . . moved to a level of discomfort that re-shapes us . . . re-forms us . . . into *becoming* who we must be in order to go to the next dimension of both blessings . . . and burdens. At times, it did become unbearable, but I knew that if I screamed out in pain for being overburdened, then, the universe could not give me more. There is power in our words . . . thus, Jesus said, "Not my will but yours be done."

March, 2015, Tina Frank and Emmanuel Realty

This journey continued to unveil new insights into the mysteries of God's will for my life. While chasing after purpose through serving those most in need of my insight, counsel, and mentorship, I still struggled. Most of my struggles were internally rooted. I was but a boy when I knew this world, and now, twenty years later, in a lot ways I was still facing that little boy's challenges that existed pre-imprisonment. I failed to fit in with my family. As the sibling of the prodigal son, my sisters questioned the kindness and support that was poured into my life from my parents. I struggled with fitting in everywhere, whether it was in the line at Taco Bell where I suffered stress from the multitude of choices (prison provided three predetermined meals a day) or the college campus. Being twice the average student's age compounded my sense of inadequacy. It was stressful, to say the least.

Yet just like inside prison, I reminded myself that the stress was a mere stretching of my inner self towards a larger purpose. I constantly reminded myself that *discomfort is essential for success.* I didn't understand the rules of engagement within this world, and I continued to respond in a manner that was not fitting for society's standards.

Invariably, I lost most of my relationships with my immediate family as a result of a lack of understanding on both sides. I did not understand *what* I was feeling or *how* to express it in a way that was not threatening, and they, too, continued to engage in conflict with aggression. When I couldn't find comfort within the abode of my own family, I questioned my own self-worth.

The world outside was not a safe place, but neither was the world inside. Just as in prison, I found my solace and place of safety in my progress, my books, and my education. I have come to realize that the only facet of life that is forever fulfilling is *progress.* The progress that I was experiencing in school pushed me toward new heights. Regardless of the intangible progress that I was making, it was still a struggle to make ends meet. I embrace the belief that *failure* does not exist; only results. Thus, *failing forward* with new insight based on new results was my inner mantra. I failed forward.

Up to that time, LUCK was still just a vision that was being challenged both internally and externally. Us three co-founders of

LUCK were all full-time college students working two jobs while attempting to battle every institutional barrier that said, through both word and deed, "LUCK will never succeed." The stress of it all was becoming unbearable. I continued to build the LUCK Life-Map, which is now the LUCK curriculum. I continued to serve anywhere and everywhere I was asked. I gave and gave and gave all in pursuit of, as my dear friend Rick said, salvation of self. When a conscious man has taken a life, he forever lives with mindset that his life must be given in recompense and with equal measure. In my unending service to the community, I was dying to myself, thereby paying my debt. But the pressures began to choke a vision that was questionable at best. Why should they believe me? My own family didn't. Worst of all, I began to question my own sanity. Had God really spoken to me, or was I just delusional?

My next "failing forward," or misstep, came from of my past. It occurred during the dark times of not being around my brothers, Rick and Cam. Fellowship . . . who you place yourself around . . . will determine your outcomes in life, for you become like the ones that you are around the most. As the pressures and demands of life attacked us, we scattered, just as the apostles did.

Having run across my "old friends" from back in the day, several of them owned marijuana dispensaries. Having drinks one day with a friend, a possible business opportunity came up. "If you come up with the space for a dispensary, then we can talk about what type of money we will need. Don't worry about the equipment. I got that. I just need someone I can trust, someone that I can teach the trade to," said my friend. I was intrigued and determined not to fail. It seemed that everyone around me was making money off this thing. *You are different. I have a different purpose for you,* God said in my thoughts, but I pushed them out. *I refuse to keep suffering!* I yelled out to the heavens. *How much longer must I pay for my sin?* I demanded to know. I shut down my internal voice of wisdom again, searching for the right property amidst the ruins of Detroit. I was calculating the numbers, salivating at the possibility of not having to worry about money, about how I could stand on my own two feet. *Your destiny is to free minds, not enslave them,* Spirit continued.

Funny thing about the Holy Spirit: once you pray for the Spirit long enough, and once received, it will not only guide you into purpose, but it can also prevent you from detours. Those will be the times that you do not wish to hear what is being said, for it is contrary to your will. And yet, God wishes so much for us to simply believe in Him, to have faith in Him and His Word above all else. It's when you are at your lowest point, when you have succumbed to the reality that you cannot achieve your inner greatness without God that miracles happen. The storms that come to shake your foundation are merely the evidence of your weakness and the proof of God's greatness in your life. But I had to learn this lesson again and again. So, I met with a realtor to look at some property with the intention of opening my own marijuana grow house.

"Hi, Mr. Bueno, I'm Tina Frank, owner of Emmanuel Realty. We actually have a mutual friend in Toni," Tina said with a smile as the sun shone behind her. I squinted and thought to myself, *Damn, what a small world.* I scrambled to think of the pros and cons of working with her since she was Toni's friend.

Toni and I had had a crush on each other long ago. Upon my release, when Toni discovered that I was college-bound, she took me shopping and purchased a Macbook Pro for my education. "No, you must take it," she insisted. "Your family really helped me at one time, and I simply wish to help you," she said as we sat there in front of Best Buy with her daughter near the table. I was conditioned to not allow people to help me, a residue of long-term, early imprisonment as well as my early determination to be completely independent from my parents. After about an hour, I relented and humbled myself to allow for this gift to enter my life.

"Really, that is serendipitous," I said quietly in response to Tina being friends with Toni. I thought about something Mrs. Duggan had told me. "Serendipity is God quietly at work, Mario, and don't you ever forget that the Spirit is with you." We walked the property as we got to know each other. This property was deemed unfit for my needs, but I hesitated to tell Tina exactly what those needs were. Now on our fourth property within a few weeks, Tina was pressuring me to explain exactly what I needed 5,000-8,000 square footage of commercial space. Tina was adamant that she needed to know what the building was for, especially since I was seeking a land contract.

"I am willing to work with you," I started, "however, what we discuss, our business that is *must* stay between us. No gossiping with anyone, especially Toni. She wants the best for me, but right now, I don't really want to hear anyone's opinion."

Tina looked up at me, saddened, and said, "Mario, this is business. Just know that you guys are doing a lot of good in the community, and this is not the path you should take." I glared at her for a few seconds, knowing the Spirit was speaking.

"Tina, I don't want to hear that again," I said as I walked off into the rain.

As the days passed, I continued to be restless. I had stopped getting on my knees to pray in reverence and respect to the creator, to the One God. As Adam hid himself from God in the Garden of Eden, ashamed of his sinfulness, his falling short to that which he had been created, I, too, was ashamed, and this shame lead to avoidance. As if I could avoid God.

April, 2015, A Meeting to Remember

I was living on Wayne State University's campus directly across from the School of Business. I was a full-time college student and scrubbing toilets at night while finishing a thesis for the Ronald McNair Scholars program titled "Incarceration of Adolescents in Adult Prisons: Adult Recollections of Their Experiences and its Impact on Adult Adjustment." I was also doing my utmost to get LUCK, Inc. off the ground. At the time, LUCK still just consisted of Rick, and Cam me.

Up to this point, LUCK had been volunteering everywhere and anywhere there were at-risk populations with which we could identify, empathize with, and counsel, but we were struggling to get any paying contracts. LUCK was still building credibility and a reputation. When we approached established agencies, they were leery of a "murderer" and his crew of "ex-felons" who wanted to train and mentor youths and returning citizens. I explained to the Rick and Cam as we sat in my apartment in Midtown Detroit, "This is why our education is so important. We walked a mile in the shoes of the men that we left behind. Now it's time to walk a mile in the shoes of all those who are blocking us out of mainstream society, all those naysayers, all those educated people. After we walk a mile in *their* shoes, then what? What will they say then?" I vented as we strategized on reentry for returning citizens and how to make it better.

"All I know is that they treat people who come home from prison like they ain't shit," Cam said, as he leaned back on my futon. He was right. Two major colleges had denied me simply because of my parole status for a crime I committed twenty years earlier, at the age of sixteen. *If higher learning turns us away, then who will accept us?* I wondered. I became even more obsessed in the development of LUCK. "I will get my Ph.D. and then what? What will they say then?" I shouted. I was angry but motivated. "Be angry, but do not sin," says my Lord. I remained *e*-motional, in other words, *energy-in-motion.*

Again, through my blessed connection with Adrian Tonon, I

was invited to attend a high-level meeting in the mayor of Detroit's conference room. The room was fit for kings as Cam, Rick, and I walked around in awe before the meeting began. "This place is breathtaking," I remember mumbling, as Rick snapped one photo after the next.

"Bro', we are on the eleventh floor of the mayor's building," said Rick, in contrast to the dungeon that we once called home. It was there that I first met Representative Harvey Santana, the Vice-Chairman of Michigan's House Appropriations Committee. Adrian, Director of Customer Service for the City of Detroit, and Detroit's 6th District Manager, Rico Razo, were also in attendance. Representative Santana focused on disrupting the gang problem that permeates the inner-city streets of Detroit. These gangs are riddled with young, fatherless, adolescent males who are full of pain and who lack the knowledge of their purpose. That is a dangerous combination for an impoverished community.

Representative Santana and I soon became engrossed in conversation about the subculture that embraced aggression, violence, gang life, and an anti-social way of being. This is a familiar and not terribly stimulating topic to us at LUCK, but an intriguing topic to most lay people. We were accustomed to this as LUCK was trained within the snake pit. "You were fucking phenomenal in there," Rick said, as we made our way down the elevator. I chuckled.

"It's always easy when it's the truth."

"They have no clue how to resolve this conflict. They have no clue how to stop the violence," Rick said, looking us square in the eye.

"I know, and we can do it in our sleep," Cam said, grinning ear to ear.

"That's because we *are* them," I said. "You can't lead someone from somewhere you yourself have not travelled." We all grinned as we left the Mayor Coleman Young Municipal Building with this simple reminder: we are on the path of purpose.

A week after LUCK's introduction to Representative Santana, Rick and I were invited to attend the Raising the Age Conference in Lansing, an initiative led by several organizations, lobbyists, and political figures. Every state, local, and nonprofit agency that dealt with at-risk children and adjudicated youths, our target population, was in that room. At the time, Michigan remained one of the few states that still prosecuted all seventeen-year-olds as adults, whereas most state laws and national and international policies declare adulthood to begin at eighteen. This campaign was aimed at raising the age of the juvenile court jurisdiction from seventeen to eighteen. Now remember, I was a business major. Seventeen-year-olds are the bulk of youthful offenders in Michigan. That *doubled* the marketplace for many of the entities in the room. We accepted the invitation because I had been fighting to change the juvenile laws from within the prison system for over a decade, but anytime money was involved when it came to helping at-risk youth, I was wary. I knew all too well how easy it was for entities to exploit well-intentioned resources and leave the youth with little to nothing in the way of the concrete, life-changing skills they so desperately needed. But LUCK, Inc. needed to build relationships with the community, so we accepted the invitation with gratitude. In fact, that day opened the door to many of our future working relationships.

Rick and I were surprised to learn that Representative Harvey Santana was the keynote speaker and the author of the bills. We had no idea that he would be the keynote speaker when we drove the hour-and-a-half in support of the youthful offenders and the raising of the age. We did not yet understand that he was an authentic champion of the most at-risk youth. We did not yet know that he was a kindred spirit, a man who would help open the proverbial closed doors that every felon who has harmed the community must face. On the path toward your success, you can never connect the dots looking forward. It is in listening to your innermost spirit, which communes with the Spirit of the Lord. It is in pursuing those glimpses of destiny, that inner sixth sense; it is in following those "gut feelings" that we stumble toward our purpose.

In the midst of his keynote speech, Representative Santana began to speak about the heinous crimes these at-risk youths have committed, or are on the verge of committing. He talked about their need for mentors who have walked a mile in their shoes, who have transformed their lives in a way that could serve as a light for these youths. To our surprise, then Representative Santana introduced LUCK, Inc. to the room. "It is men like Mario Bueno and Rick Speck," said Representative Santana as he looked at Rick and me and motioned for us to stand, "who have fallen into the pit of despair only to pull themselves up and mentor those around them while still in that pit. If we are to turn these youths around, if we are to safeguard our communities from the atrocities that these lost youths commit, then we are going to have to let men like them into our schools and juvenile facilities to train and mentor these kids." This was the endorsement of a lifetime for LUCK, Inc.

Afterward, Rick and I made our way toward the eight tables of food and drinks outside the conference doors. There was a huge spread: danishes, donuts, fruit, cereal, grits, coffee, milk, juice, toast, sausage, eggs, and the list goes on. That was just for breakfast. There was an equally spectacular lunch spread. I was beginning to like these functions. After about ten minutes, I leaned over to Rick as we stirred our coffee and asked, "Is everyone staring at us, or is it just my PTSD?" I often tease us about the compulsive hyper-vigilance of post-traumatic stress disorder (PTSD) common to most returned citizens that comes up for us seemingly out of nowhere. It's a way to bring it to light in laughter and jest thereby allowing my brothers around me to open up. It works.

"No, you aren't hallucinating," he chuckled. At that moment, an older lady who I will I call Ms. Smithsonian, approached Rick and began to woo his attention.

"You won't be allowed around children under seventeen because of your criminal histories," she said. I saw a look in her eyes that told me we were dealing with a cold heart. It's strange the gifts and tools one is imparted for survival. "But the seventeen-year-olds? Now *that* is the marketplace you'll be allowed to work with." *What angle does this lady with lips of honey have?* I pondered while Rick continued to do what he does best, network. I watched her body language and simply listened, but I did not care for the energy of Ms. Smithsonian.

She began to unfold a vision of LUCK partnering with a group I will call the Juvenile Adjudicated Complex (JAC) in their "Turning Around" program to mentor and train an at-risk group of seventeen-year-olds who had served a year within the confines of the Wayne County Jail. I was taken aback. In 2015, Seventeen-year-old kids, in Detroit, Michigan, are serving a year within the county jail? I was appalled, for I served a year in the county in 1995 and I, personally, understand the depths of despair that the county jail will impart upon its captives.

I pictured a group structure like in the book, *Lord of the Flies,* where a group of youths left to govern themselves commit atrocities on the most weak and vulnerable of the group. I'd been there. I was them. I *am* them. I knew what they felt, how deeply they hurt, without having met these youths, for confinement within the walls of the county jail, at any age, will leave trauma on the psyche. I could not wait to get my foot in *this* door, both figuratively and literally. I had tearfully prayed for countless nights to have the chance to help imprisoned youths. Now, we were close.

May 5, 2015, Opportunity to Speak at the Same Prison that Released Us

Around the same time, while still on parole, Rick and I were invited back into Jackson Cooper Street Prison, the prison we were released from, as keynote speakers. Ironically, the event was put on by the Latino organization that I helped create while in JCS. At that time, the deputy warden called me and another prisoner into his office. "I need the Latino population to stay busy and not have an idle hand this summer," he said in acknowledgment of the fear that the staff had of a large Latino population with nothing to do. In that meeting, we strategized to create program that had already been approved at other prisons called Latino Americans Spanish Speaking Organization (LASSO). Now several years later, LASSO wanted Rick, Michael Reyes, and myself back into the prison to celebrate Cinco de Mayo with them. Rick and I were asked to speak to the men while Reyes would perform his spoken word poetry. The fact that Rick and I were approved to enter the prison was a miracle in and of itself, for we both were still on parole *and* paroled from *that* prison.

It was an out-of-body experience. One year before, I had been confined within the walls of this present-day slave plantation, and now I was walking back inside to speak life into the men I was compelled to leave behind. The gymnasium was packed with over 300 men in attendance, including Rick, Michael Reyes, and I. And once again we ran into a figure that would forever change my life and the men of LUCK: Representative Harvey Santana. We entered that prison with a mission: leave those men better than we found them. And, that we did. Rick and I passed out LUCK, Inc. pamphlets with one clear message: better yourself and better all those around you. LUCK is hiring all transformed men in the mission to safeguard the community through the transformation of the most at-risk populations. "And," I stated lastly, "we are providing livable wages in this mission." We left the men energized and wanting more for them.

It was a challenge, emotionally, to enter JCS and speak on behalf of LUCK, Inc. because we left that prison as a member, and leader, of ACL, which we grew and expanded exponentially under Rick's leadership and a team effort. Rick later told me, "The staff warned me that the ACL members were going to cause a scene. I didn't say anything to you because I knew you would respond correctly if it did occur." It turns out, James had been telling the men that we once trained, and trained with, that we stole the program and started our own in an attempt to steal the money that was "coming." I laughed, "He is still telling them that he has not received the funding from the state," I responded. "Sad part is, they are still believing it," Rick justly highlighted.

Lus Ybarra, former Latin King gang leader who had served twenty-one years in prison from the age of seventeen for murder and for three other violent crimes he committed while in prison, was quietly sitting in the crowd. Lus was one of my former teachers/mentors at Jackson Cooper Street responsible for influencing my reform. I admired him, thus, that created a space for him to positively influence me during those days that I still embraced criminal tendencies. As I spoke, I looked at him and connected on several occasions. After my speech, I walked up to Lus and we hugged. I handed him a LUCK flyer, then whispered, "Come to us when you get out. We'll be waiting for you." Then I pulled back and looked him straight in the eye. Now, the responsibility to return the mentoring favor was mine and I looked forward to making all debts paid. I witnessed Lus' in an environment that mirrored the culture of hell as he taught men to pursue the path of heaven and, as the great Martin Luther King so eloquently said, "The ultimate measure of a man is not where he stands in moments of comfort and convenience, but where he stands at times of challenge and controversy." I sensed that Lus would be a key component to the LUCK team in the future.

I grew closer with Representative Santana as he counseled Rick and I for almost an hour in the parking lot after the event. "The non-profits of Detroit are going to pull you in to get to know you to see whether or not you are a threat. They will try to steal what you have, your methods, plans, and visions, and then they will spit you out." He warned us of all those wolves in sheep's clothing, and then he named them. That day Representative Harvey Santana began to mentor me and LUCK through the shark-infested waters of Detroit's non-profit and philanthropic world, a world that would do exactly as he warned: pull us close and then try to kill us.

June, 2015, LUCK's First Program with At-risk Youth

After this serendipitous shout out at the conference on raising-the-age, Ms. Smithsonian contacted LUCK later for an introductory meeting with her team who had been trying to connect with the seventeen-year-olds that were being released, and referred, by Wayne County Jail. The team that sat before us consisted of three black men, all with a social work background, and two white women who had, at the least, a Master's in social work. Direct care workers who had been trained in the classroom of social work, desperately vented, "We can't connect with them. They won't open up." Rick, Cam, and I answered question after question. From the onset, the tension in the room could be cut with a knife, though LUCK was quickly becoming accustomed to the animosity that was displayed toward us by individuals such as social workers with the credentials that positioned them to help others.

One of the institutional barriers to entry for the felon is the barrier to certain fields of work, like licensed social work. While we felons were allowed to get a degree in social work, such as Vaughn, the licensing aspect was a different story. Vaughn was locked out of getting a license, but his gift to help the at-risk youth made room for him. The culture of many industries, like social work, are not as diverse in their staff as they could be, however, because of such provisions that preclude the most fallen. And, yet, that is the *very* mission of such a career, or so it should be: to help the most fallen. I understood their position, thus, my mandate for LUCK's trainers to pursue education as an equalizer, a way to level the playing field.

"We are *not* qualified because we went to prison. You got that?" I said to Rick after one particular training session. "We are qualified because of the skills, tools, and coping patterns that we have developed, reinforced, and used to augment our personal and professional success." I drilled this into the men of LUCK's minds. Too many people come home from prison claiming they know best merely because they had been through it. There exists an over 75% recidivism rate, thus, mere experience with prison does not suffice in becoming a transformed man that seeks to reform others. "It's the education. It is the skills and tools that empower us to *respond* better, for conflict is inevitable. How we *respond* to the inner and outer conflicts will determine the quality of our existence," I would reinforce within the minds of the men.

"They've been traumatized and hurt to a degree that unless you have experienced it, you cannot fathom it," I told the JAC staff. I have always been the blunt, direct voice of LUCK whereas Rick is in my life to balance out the discomfort that such comments may ignite.

"We need this partnership so that the youths can see us interacting with your staff, law enforcement, and the like, so that they may be pro-socialized," said Rick with his car salesman's pitch. I smiled inside. *He's selling Bitterleys now,* I thought, in reference to my constant teasing of him over a decade ago in a distant, forgotten world. I first met Rick in level four of the St. Louis Correctional Facility in 2002. "You are a straight up *used car* salesman," I would tease him as we bartered prices on weed. What a different life we live now. I snapped back to the meeting.

When JAC explained that their services included meeting with the youths once a month, taking them to the probation office, and giving them a $20 gift card (when they could), I was taken aback. I was becoming familiar with this "nonprofit" scam: get a grant, write inflated salaries and wages into the grant, and give as little as possible to the vulnerable, disenfranchised youths. "I'm simply suggesting that we meet to train these youths at *least* twice a month. Once a month is a waste of time," I blurted. I had to get it off my chest.

"Okay, we can do that. But your team takes on the expenses for that second day of the month," replied Ms. Smithsonian, qualifying the agreement.

"No problem. We're use to coming out of pocket to help our mentees. This is why it is our *purpose*," I retorted. LUCK had never been paid a penny for training and mentoring the youths of JAC. The friction between Ms. Smithsonian and myself could be sensed, however much suppressed. I *was* the population that she preyed upon.

"Okay, so there we have it. LUCK will begin to mentor and train this group next week. Just a warning: we only have two, sometimes three, participants. There isn't a strong engagement and retention with this group," said Ms. Smithsonian.

"It's okay. If we build it, they shall come," I replied with a wink and a grin. She remained stoic. I didn't know her history or how she had come to be that way, but I felt protective of the kids we were working with. I knew that *those who hurt, hurt others,* and clearly somewhere along the way, it felt to me that she'd been hurt or disappointed enough to have tucked away her compassion. So, we began working pro-bono in partnership with JAC to mentor seventeen-year-old males recently released after having served a year in the Wayne County Jail.

The Juvenile Adjudicated Center was located a few blocks north from the campus of Wayne State University and occupied a building that had formerly been a Detroit Police headquarters. The next week, Rick, Cam, and I sat waiting for the arrival of our first mentee, Devon Freeman, aka "Will," in the JAC conference room where training of all sorts took place. Will was a seventeen-year-old African-American male who was about five-foot-eight with a dark complexion. He was beginning to grow dreadlocks. Though I knew his name, I asked, "What's your name?" to open the conversation.

"They call me Will," he said, with a smile that showed his chipped front tooth. Will looked at me directly in the eye without blinking. I *immediately* knew that this kid not only had strength, but he had that look in his eye of one who could kill. I know that look.

"Who the fuck is *they?*" I challenged him, just a test. I always do it with young, tough guys.

"The streets," he said without hesitation. I liked this kid. He reminded me of myself at that age. Will displayed an air of confidence that displayed strength coupled with humility rooted in pain.

"So, what do you like to do? What is your passion?" I said, in an attempt to understand what he values most.

"I spit, you know. I rap," he said with the confidence of a lion.

"Spit something then," I said, equally challenging. He immediately began to rap for what seemed like almost two minutes. We were blown away at this kid's strength. His words conveyed pain and struggle experienced from a survivor, not a victim. Anyone else facing the pressures of this young soul would have given up long ago. I admired him immediately.

The second kid to join us was clearly under the influence of a heavy tranquilizer of some sort. I did a year in the county at age sixteen and most guys played the "I hear voices" roll so that they could get a script of Seroquel so that they could sleep or numb their emotional pain. It was common for this population to be "tranquilized," and this kid was one of them. "Waddup, my dude?" I asked as he sat down and placed his head on the table. The social worker looked up at me.

"Just leave him. Let him sleep. He's on medication," he said. That kid slept the entire two-hour workshop, thus, we only had one student. And, yet, *despise not the days of small beginnings.*

Despite this, we knew that we were exactly where we were supposed to be. We were in alignment with our purpose and with all that *Is*. Rick, Cam, and I opened every class with an Invocation, a prayer, and closed with another prayer. We stood in a circle and grasped hands as a representation of oneness, of unity. I always prayed in the name of Jesus, my mentor and King, as we fought for territory and to bring a culture of peacemaking by equipping the most violent and aggressive populations with the skills of critical thinking, effective communication, and conflict resolution. Thus, we were fighting to bring the *kingdom of heaven on earth* within the minds, and, invariably, the lives of these youths.

I have fallen in love with what I've been called to do many times over, but that was the first workshop we had as free men. "How do you think it went?" I asked Rick and Cam as we walked to the elevator after that first night's class.

"I think it was phenomenal. Don't worry, they'll come," Rick said, in reference to only two students being in class, with one being tranquilized.

In time, more kids came and more kids stayed. Sadly, there were also more kids who were tranquilized, to life, their trauma, their realities, and their pain, but the greatest misfortune was that they were also tranquilized to their purpose. These youths were not leaving the county jail well, at all.

While trying to help at-risk youth, the reality was that I could barely help myself. Being branded a felon brings many implications not thought of in the "comfort" of the prison cell where rent, utilities, groceries, and the like are not weighing one down. Reentry, just like the prison walls, had its own demons, and, as we slowly discovered, we were ill equipped to battle such foes, let alone even know they existed. We needed help, but the problem was that prison conditioned us to not ask for help.

June, 2015, Meeting the Godfather of Southwest Detroit

Mrs. Duggan and I became close friends. Over the next year, we went to meeting after meeting together and uncovered many of the gaps for returning citizens. She began to see first-hand the social caste that exists for those branded a felon when looking for employment, an apartment, or even post-secondary education. It began with Adrian asking me to take her to meet with a man I will call Hank Vargas, founder and owner of a successful company that employs hundreds and is based in Southwest Detroit's hardened area. He developed several diverse companies that make up one conglomerate that delivers construction services, patented products, material management, equipment, parts, and more. Since Mr. Vargas had a history of hiring gang members, Mrs. Duggan wanted to know whether he was willing to help again with a similar problem: employment of felons.

"Mario, Mrs. Duggan's passion will not allow her to sit idle, but the mayor doesn't want her running around the city trying to help felons, if you know what I mean. So, this has got stay quiet," Adrian said, once again reminding me of the importance of keeping Mrs. Duggan protected at all times by all means necessary and to assure that she would only play a behind-the-scenes role.

"Don't worry, my brother, I got it covered," I told Adrian, always taking the job, whatever it was. At that time, I was still working for the family business. I was compelled to walk out of our workplace several times after such calls in pursuit of purpose. When I left the office to help out Mrs. Duggan, I would say where I was going, but my past transgressions led my family to question the sincerity and truthfulness of what I was saying. My little sister would whisper criticism behind my back that challenged the validity of my "meetings" or my "stories." My mother's love for me would not allow my little sister to fire me, but my mom's understanding of *who* her son was and what lengths he would go to cope, adapt, or survive, frightened her. My mother did not understand that I had gained new coping skills, new response tools. Even so, I had yet to learn how to relate to society, let alone a family.

In the end, my family resigned to my request to be the midnight janitor instead of the receptionist so I could free up my days and, to a large degree, avoid conflict with my younger sister. I cleaned the offices of the family medical practice in the midnight hours for almost a year as I worked as an accountant, went to Wayne State University full time, and poured everything I had, tangible and intangible, into the development of LUCK, Inc. Despite all of this work, I could barely pay my bills or put food on the table.

That day after Adrian's call, I picked up Mrs. Duggan, and we talked the entire thirty-minute drive to Southwest Detroit. Later, I joked with the fellas, Rick and Cam. "Adrian has me driving the mayor's mom to a meeting." We would all chuckle at the absurdity of life. I went from being repeatedly placed in long-term solitary because prison administrations thought I was a threat to the prisoner population and their institutions to being trusted with the mayor's mom. I was humbled and in awe of God's power in my life.

The meeting with Mr. Vargas was enlightening. He definitely liked to tell his story. He is the Chairman and CEO of a corporation with annual revenues of nearly $250 million, employing over 500 people. Vargas was a key figure in a significant gang truce of the 90s that helped reduce chaos and violence in the neighborhoods of Southwest Detroit. His solution was simple. He sat down with the leaders of the most influential gangs in a private meeting and asked them, "What do you want? What will it take to get you to put the dope and guns down and to stop the senseless violence?" The consensus was unanimous: a livable wage with benefits for their families. He gave them just that. Turns out that the men weren't lying; that was all they needed, a chance to do legitimate work in order to provide for their basic needs. In time, one culture was transformed with a generation to follow.

In our meeting with Mr. Vargas, Mrs. Duggan listened and responded, and I sat there quietly. I was just her driver and knew my position. As the *48 Laws of Power's* First Law commands, "Never outshine the master." Mr. Vargas was interesting and charismatic, to say the least. The four of us sat in his office: Mrs. Duggan, Mr. Vargas, his secretary of twenty-five years who I will call Gwendolyn, and little ole' me. I was humbled to witness the dynamic energy of this phenomenal woman who wanted to help the disenfranchised, the same kind of men who her son, Mayor of Detroit Mike Duggan, put away during his decades as a successful prosecutor. Ironic.

Eventually, Mrs. Duggan introduced me and asked that I tell my story. "Unfortunately, at the age of sixteen, I embraced the belief system that it was okay to rob and kill drug dealers," I said as I sat there with the suit, tie, and prestige of a Harvard businessman. I then filled him in on my imprisonment history and my life since my release. The conversation continued and questions poured out. I could tell that Mr. Vargas was impressed.

"You see these?" asked Mr. Vargas as he pulled open a box of strawberry plants that were piled up adjacent to his beautifully crafted wooden desk. I'd been wondering what was in those dirty boxes that sat in the middle of a well-decorated office. "I loved working in the gardens and apple fields as a kid. This was the culture I was raised in. I helped a lot of people from my culture because I have noticed that there is not a lot of help for *my* people, the Latinos. There are programs and funding for black schools and juvenile programs, but the problem is that the ones running the programs are thieves. I will not give money unless it is to help my people." He was clearly passionate about an issue that had been unaddressed for some time. There was an awkward moment, but Mrs. Duggan, forever the statesman, broke the ice.

"Tell me more about these strawberry plants," she said with a smile from heaven. He snapped out of it and grinned. "We have a garden that we are working for the neighborhood off of Jackson Street behind the plant. Would you care to see it?" he asked with a huge grin. We all jumped in our respective cars, and I followed Mr. Vargas and his secretary to the garden around the block. It was a sunny, spring day. "Ohhhh, Mario, this is so good," said Mrs. Duggan, grabbing by forearm. "He *loves* you. Maybe he can give you a job!" she said, as I drove around the block.

"We'll see, Mrs. Duggan," I said with a wink. "Let's stay focused." She is precious. But she had touched, in part, on our vision. We wanted to make a good impression on this man in the hopes of getting me gainful employment, a livable wage with benefits, just like he had given to the former gang members, coupled with a program of substance for Detroit's returning citizens. I didn't just want to get "Mario" a job. I wanted to get jobs for hundreds of "Marios." But Mrs. Duggan was a mother first, and, in a sense, my surrogate mother. She was concerned for me for what might result if the economic struggle that I was facing would overcome my "new self" to the point of resurfacing my "old self." She was my angel.

I took pictures of the three of them in front of his garden, and, in turn, Mr. Vargas took pictures of me with the ladies. Gwendolyn and Mr. Vargas spoke of the great social cause this inner-city garden provided the residents of the neighborhood. "It's great," Gwendolyn said. "The families participate and bring their children. Employees volunteer their time and mentor the neighborhood children. It is such a great bonding experience with the community. Then at harvest, they are able to eat healthy food that many cannot otherwise afford." Up to this point, we had spent the entire afternoon, almost five hours, with our gracious hosts. Eventually, Mr. Vargas and I drifted off to a part of the garden that was out of earshot. "You know, I am exactly like you. I just never got caught," he said. I was shocked. "I'm known as the Godfather here in Southwest Detroit. I had a lot of juice once upon a time. Now those guys are all old and retired from that life. I need a guy who can perform in the business environment *and* the streets, know what I mean?" he said, as he stared into my sunglasses, trying to see my eyes. "I need a man of influence." I didn't flinch. His implications were clear. He needed someone who would do *whatever* he was told, no questions asked. He needed a "button" to push upon his own whims.

He walked me toward the back of the garden where the fence was aligned with the neighborhood behind it. "You see the third house from the corner?" He looked but didn't point.

"The yellow duplex?" I asked.

"Yeah. Those people in there, they're no good. They throw bottles in my garden. They play loud music all day and sell drugs out of that house," he paused, allowing it to resonate. "If I could have that house blown up, I would. The problem is, I don't have anyone I can trust to follow through," he said, turning to me and looking at me for what seemed an eternity.

"Are there kids inside?" I asked.

"No, just partiers," he said nonchalantly. I looked over at Mrs. Duggan. She was smiling and joyful. I looked back at Mr. Vargas. "It was a pleasure to meet you, sir," I said as he reached out and embraced me. Mrs. Duggan and I said our farewells and drove off.

"What an interesting man. I hope he gives you a job," she said.

"Don't worry, Mrs. Duggan," I consoled her. "I'll figure something out." I dropped Mrs. Duggan off in the comfort of her suburban neighborhood and drifted back to Southwest Detroit as I thought about how to approach this situation. I was drowning, and so were the men around me. I was seriously tempted by this powerful man's offer. If I could help make his little "problem" go away, I could prove my worth to him and get my foot in the door.

Loyalty to Vargas would open many doors. I would be able to help the guys get jobs, too. I also understood that such a path would entail closure of the door to God, for a house divided cannot stand. And, yet, as St. Paul said, "I continue to do that which I do not want to do." So, I made a call. I was being pulled between two worlds.

"Wassup, my *hermano*?" yelled out *Serpiente* (Snake) as we called him. Serpiente had served twenty years from the age of sixteen for cocaine, guns, robbery, and you name it. At the time, he was second in command of the gang the Spanish Cobras recognized by Chicago's headquarters and lead by King Chuey, who is still imprisoned today.

"Waddup doe?" I said, grinning ear-to-ear. I had known Serpiente since 2007 when we were both at Ryan Road Correctional Facility. We had a lot in common, from both being imprisoned from the age of sixteen to similar, charismatic personalities. "Let's grab a drink," I said, knowing that he was always great company. Serpiente lived by the mantra, "You gotta laugh to keep from crying."

"Meet me at the spot. I got some Tito's, cranberry, and orange juice on ice with rice and beans cooking." Serpiente was a five-foot-eleven, brown-skinned Puerto Rican who could talk a female corrections officer into cuffing herself.

"I'll be there in fifteen," I said, already close by but wanted to scope out the scene. After being institutionalized, I had learned to circle and stake out locations before going in. I was conditioned to be ready for war at all times, and surveying the land was one the most essential parts of preparation. Coupled with Snake's lifestyle, I did not want to unwittingly walk into an ambush or a drug raid. It was a coin toss with Snake.

As I entered the basement of the three-unit apartment building owned by Serpiente, I could smell the Puerto Rican beans and rice cooking. He already had a drink ready for me and had Salsa music playing on his big screen TV. Serpiente was a hustler through and through. He owned over fifteen properties, all in other people's names, but he was more than that. He was a natural born leader, formed in the fires of hell. He had a good heart and a conscience. I told him all about the conversation with Vargas.

"Shit, that *hermano* will get us all jobs. Let's go," he said, grabbing his keys and turning down the flame on the stove to simmer. "I want you to show me the house," he said. We ran out so he could get back in time to prevent the food from burning. We circled the block, until he got a clearer understanding of the house. "So, he says there aren't any kids in there?" Serpiente asked for the second time.

"That's what he said, but it must be confirmed," I replied . . . again. Serpiente was looking for the go-ahead, *now,* but I wanted to confirm whether or not there were children in the house. I didn't trust Vargas' information.

Early July 2015, Slave Questions the Slave Master

Around the same time, Adrian called. "I'm unsettled that you have not been helped by the people who are supposed to help returning citizens. I want you to go into the Lawton parole office and assess the reentry process. You will have assessed the situation before everyone else, so you will be first to the ball. Whoever is first to the ball, scores." I'm pretty sure the mayor was not necessarily aware that a parolee was going into Lawton to assess the state agency, but I didn't care to ask. I learned a long time ago: don't ask questions when you don't care to know the answer. "Find out the weak spots so we can be ready to meet with Jeff. Mayor Duggan had hired Jeff to create and implement a program to assist in the job training and job connection of returning citizens to the city of Detroit that stemmed from a U.S. labor grant.

"Adrian, bro', you know that I am on parole, right?" I replied.

"Worse, my parole is in the process of being transferred to Lawton because I am moving to an apartment on campus," I said. "Bro', they're gonna crucify me. I can't go in there asking them questions," I said, hoping to preclude myself from this task.

"I know, I know," he said. "Don't worry. As long as you are standing in righteousness, then you have nothing to worry about. Mario, the fact that you have gone through, and, are going through, what you have makes you the *perfect* person to do this assessment and recommendation," he said in his Italian olive oil voice that could sell ice to an Eskimo. I love Adrian. Theresa said I would.

"Okay, okay, I'll do it, but I swear, if I get a parole violation and sent back, you'd better send me money!" That got us both laughing.

It took a while for me to get cleared to enter Lawton for the purpose of assessing them. After all, it was unprecedented for a parolee to enter the back offices of a parole office to assess *them.* At first, the meeting was uncomfortable. The first ten minutes centered on questions about LUCK's vision. "So, you believe that you, that *LUCK,* can do this *alone?*" asked the Lawton supervisor in a negative tone.

"Can you please clarify what *this* refers to?" I asked meekly as perspiration soaked my underarms and my heart beat out of my chest. My PTSD from entering this environment was off the charts. False Evidence Appearing Real (FEAR), will paralyze you, or push you through whatever you are facing.

"Transforming men and changing this system," she retorted.

"Actually, ma'am, my personal transformation did not occur until I broke down the illusionary paradigm of *us versus them.* I would have never transformed had it not been for the organic relationships I developed with the Michigan Department of Corrections staff who pro-socialized me," I said in a tone of gratitude and humility. With a tear in my eye I said, "Deputy Riley and Officer Runyan are like my uncles. Mr. Guthrie is like my brother,"

I said with a sense of sadness at those I had left behind. Those relationships had been my world, but they had been cut off because of "policy and procedure" that does not allow parolees to communicate with staff. Immediately, the Lawton supervisors sensed my sincerity, and the walls of *us versus them* dissipated for them also. We gained an understanding of the seriousness of Detroit's parolee and probationer problem in terms of a lack of good contractors who were following through with their contractual promises.

I stepped out into the sun, looked up, squinted, and whispered, "Thank you, Lord." In the end, I walked out of that Lawton meeting with the start of some new relationships while continuing to destroy old stereotypes and beliefs. I was thankful. It was a humbling experience to go before my captors while still on parole, which, by law, is defined as the least form of *confinement,* but *confinement* nonetheless. The entire two weeks leading up to this meeting created a state of inner turmoil for me that was, at times, unbearable. Your purpose will do that . . . it will stretch you to the point of knocking you to your knees to humble you, to make you listen to *every word that proceeds from the mouth of God.* Your purpose can cause you to cry out, "Please, Father, if it is your will, pass this cup from my lips." And, yet, in the end, you will discover that pain is a necessary process of purification to bring you closer to your truest self . . . God manifest.

While at the Lawton meeting, however, it was revealed to me that James and Tanya had been getting millions to provide job training for returning citizens along with a livable wage job upon release. Apparently, those millions of dollars were lining their pockets instead of going to helping the men with a livable wage job.

Later, I told Rick, "They got the contracts. James has the money." We were sad . . . and angry. Rick had looked up to James. He had given his blood, sweat, and tears because he believed in James's sincerity. From day one, three years earlier, I had told Rick, "I don't trust him. He comes off as a pimp." But without outside volunteers, the program A Chance to Live would have been designated as a gang, or as MDOC would label it, a Security Threat Group (STG). James and Tanya's façade of being the panacea to the prison problem of violence and aggression was allowed by the men who truly ran the organization (meaning us) because their committed presence ensured a platform by which we could better ourselves and better others. "Well, I guess it's time for us to have that conversation with James," said Rick quietly, always the more composed one.

Mid-Summer, 2015, God's Messenger

As the division within narrowed my vision further to the point of blindness, and stimulated by the inability to ask for help, my world began to crumble around me. In the most stressful times of my life, I found myself in solitary confinement. It was there that I found my place beside the Lord. Though I was spiritually stretched beyond measure, I found comfort there. There was something in the solitude that gave me the inner strength to overcome the external storms that life invariably brings to us all. I was determined to do it my way, on my own, where I could be alone and in my comfort zone, so, I broke off my engagement with my fiancée.

"If you ever involve yourself with drugs, I will not be with you." She had clearly expressed this upon our getting to know each other. But the mantra that ate away at my thoughts during the sleepless nights was, "A man provides for himself and his household." At that time, I could not provide for myself let alone a family. I was constantly behind on my rent, my bills, and I still could not consistently pay for my car insurance, let alone groceries. Brenda would come each week with groceries, further compounding my sense of impotence. When a man cannot provide for himself, he is stripped from the intrinsic value of working his garden, of being fruitful and multiplying. I was completely frustrated with *what is* while staying in motion toward what *will be*. Frustrated with the vision that God had imparted upon my most inner being, while everything around me said different. I began to think that perhaps I was delusional, that God had not spoken to me. I would argue with myself, attempting to rationalize and justify my plans. I finally convinced myself that we were better off apart so that I could pursue this dream of making money, even if it meant producing marijuana.

"It's better that we're not together. I will not apologize for how I put food on my table," I said defiantly as tears rolled down my face. She was confused but knew what I was implying.

"I don't understand. I love you as you are," she said in her sweet tone. But I was determined to go it alone and establish my financial independence. Alone. Just like always.

That week as I sat there waiting to get a call from Tina to talk about real estate, I thought about my life and all that I had endured. *For what? What was the purpose of it all?* I bitterly pondered. There was only one other time in my life that I felt this low, and it resulted me trying to take my own life. I am learning that this sense of hopelessness is normal when one is pulled away from one's purpose. Martin Luther King, Jr. attempted suicide on several different occasions. It is a matter of the law of polarities or the law of opposites as some call it. The law asserts that everything is experienced relative to something else, and when there is no "something else," it is not possible to experience what is being experienced. So, in order to experience the heights of God's presence, one must also experience the depths of His absence.

"Good day, Mr. Bueno," Tina said, her phone call interrupting my daydreaming. "I need to speak with you about a possible business opportunity that could benefit us both." I listened intently, for a hustler knows a hustler's language.

"Cool," I said. "When and where do you want to meet?" I was still fixated on the easy cash that a grow house makes.

I met Tina at a house that she was just showing to a potential buyer. I sat in the car, smoking a cigarette as I contemplated where life was taking me when Tina jumped in my car. "Hey, there," she said. "Thank you so much for meeting me on a holiday weekend. So . . . " She paused for what seemed an eternity. "I don't know how to say this, but . . . " Again, she hesitated.

"Tina, would you just spit it out?" I snapped, irritated by life, let alone her wasting my time.

"I have never forsaken business for anything personal, but God has given me a message to give to you, Mario. I have to tell you that He says that you are not listening to Him," she said in fearful yet determined tone. I laughed as I stared out the window, reflecting on the numerous occasions that I have had a message sent to me by a God that is more silent than not. "I'm serious, Mario," she said earnestly. "I'm not crazy, and I'm not making this up." I laughed even harder.

"That's just it, Tina. I know you're not, and I believe you." She looked shock but continued.

"I have struggled for *three* restless nights with this message, not wanting to cross the line of business ethics and practices, but God refuses to let me sleep until I give it to you," she said in relief. "Now if you don't want to listen, that's fine. That's between God and you. But God says that you're not *listening* to Him. That this is *not* your purpose. If you sell drugs, then so will your children. He specifically wanted me to say, word for word, that if you sell drugs, then 'You shall reap what you sow.'" I smiled. God used my most often used Bible verse for those I mentored just to get my attention. "God also put it heavily on my heart to help you achieve your vision of having rental properties. If you are willing to just be a landlord but not use it for marijuana grow house, then we can be partners.

I will work on getting the property, and you help with the manpower to help fix it up.

After we get you a property rehabbed and rented in your name, we will do the same for Cam, and then Rick. This will strengthen your guys' credit. Eventually, we will have four properties, one each, to invest into *one* firm. Then we use the four homes as leverage to begin our real estate investment firm." She wanted to help people like us, and I was humbled. I looked at her for a few seconds then stared back out of the window. I reminisced about the boy who sought his God in the quietness of the night as his mom was on drugs and his dad was non-existent.

"I use to talk to God all the time as a boy," I told her. "I would beg God to save my mom during a time that she could not cope with life. I would talk to Him while on my knees. I think God blessed that little boy because He could hear that little boy's cries. Eventually, though, that little boy stopped praying," I continued, as tears rolled down my cheeks. "But God has sent me many messages throughout my life, and it is true, I have been purposefully ignoring the Spirit. Thank you for your obedience. And, yes, I am ready to listen."

Tina did as she promised. She gave me a list of duplex properties to choose from. They were all in impoverished areas, but I found a nice one. We bought it with her commission from the sale, so basically, she loaned me the money. The duplex was on land contract requiring me to pay only $400 a month while charging $500 per unit. Tina and I fixed up the duplex with the help of Rick, Cam, Tina's parents, and my father. It was a real grass-roots effort. Thus, my two-year goal of obtaining a duplex was manifested by the Grace and Glory of God within less than a year.

CHAPTER 15

IF YOU DO THIS, YOU DENY ME

Late July 2015, Are You Holy?

ABOUT A WEEK LATER, Serpiente called me. "Man, *hermano*, there's three little kids living in the upstairs and two in the downstairs unit. I'm glad I listened to yo' ass," he said. I was relieved. The worst thing in the world would be to harm a child, let alone an adult. The last thing we needed was blood on our hands. We discussed several options from entering the premises and removing the individuals to simply blowing the house up. Regardless of the scenario, there just was not enough information on the dwellers to make an advantageous assumption of risk. In street terms, the juice wasn't worth the squeeze.

"Just let it go," I told Snake, "'cuz we both know they don't stop investigating a murder." That added shock value in case he took it upon himself to try and get the job done.

"You definitely right, my *hermano*," he replied.

"Yeah, let's stay focused, bro'. I appreciate you," I said as I hung up the phone. *Trick no good, Mr. Vargas.*

A few weeks passed, and I went back to Mr. Vargas with a box of Spanish pastries in hand for Gwendolyn and the others. "Oh, Mario, you are so sweet," Gwendolyn said, always so welcoming and warm. "He's in his office. Let me check if he's available," she said, walking gracefully in her golden years. I waited for about five minutes, looking at all of the artwork that the student interns had done to decorate the offices. I was nervous. I was there to tell Mr. Vargas that, number one, I could not take care of that "house situation" because there were children in it, and, number two, I needed a job because I could not make ends meet. "Come this way, Mario. He's ready for you," Gwendolyn said, snapping me out of my nervousness. I walked in to be greeted with a huge smile and an embrace.

"How are you, son?" Mr. Vargas asked genuinely.

"You more than most understand the struggle toward success. New levels, new devils," I replied with a grin, always smiling to keep from crying. He laughed.

"So, how is the queen, Mrs. Duggan?" he asked. His fondness for her was genuine. You can't help but love Mrs. Duggan.

"She's good, Mr. Vargas. She really loved the visit we had here and at the garden," I said, remembering her giddiness on our "field trip" that was to be the first of many. We both smiled and leaned back into our chairs. I scanned his office and lowered my voice. "Is it okay to talk in here?" I asked him. He understood the implication and nodded his head up and down. "There were kids in that house: three upstairs and two downstairs. It took about a month of recognizance to get the data." He remained stoic, not saying a word. Then he pursed his lips and nodded. I continued. "I need a job, Mr. Vargas. I can't get a livable wage because of my crime. I could barely get into school because of my crime," I said, exasperated, as I held an application that I had previously filled out in the hopes that I could turn it into him and possibly get hired on the spot.

"You come to me and ask for a job, but you fail to tell me what problem of mine you can solve. I don't even know what you can do," he said, leaning deeper into his large, leather chair. "Let's start with what do you like to do?" he asked.

"I like to help people," I said, unsure of where he was going with this. Mr. Vargas chuckled lightly and responded in kind.

"So, you like to *help* people," he repeated as he opened his desk drawer searching for a clean sheet of paper. "I'm sorry about the mess. I can't ever find shit in here." He dug around until he found a sheet of paper, and he drew a line down the center. Across the top he wrote, "Pros & Cons." On the side, he wrote "Help People." He looked up. "Do you have any money?" he asked with a serious tone.

"No, sir, I do not. Otherwise I wouldn't be here begging for job," I said in frustration, knowing that I had failed him in not taking care of that "problem" with the house.

"Are you holy?" he asked with a grin.

"Holy?"

"Yeah, like are you like a minister or priest to where you are qualified to help people?" he continued, still grinning.

"No, sir, I am not," as tears began well up in my eyes.

"Well, then, you can't help people," he said as he crossed out the words on the paper "Help People." I lowered my head as I fought back the tears.

"Do you need some money, son?" Mr. Vargas asked, now sincere. I shook my head no.

"Please, son, if you need some money, just tell me. Just ask me," he repeated.

"No, sir, I do not need your money. I appreciate you and your time," I said, looking him square in the eye with the inner thought of what Jesus told Peter: "Get behind me Satan." For I knew, deep within my core, that helping people like me was my calling, my destiny to be fulfilled through my covenant with my Creator whether I had money now or not, thus it was important that focused on vision, as opposed to sight. Sight, that which you can see with your senses is the enemy to vision. Your vision is a preview of your purpose. So, technically, anything that tries to pull you away from your vision is demonic influenced, thus, Jesus' address to Peter as "Satan".

"Let me at least buy you lunch, son," Mr. Vargas demanded.

"Thank you, sir, but I already ate," I replied. I was so conditioned to not accept help from anyone while in prison that it transferred over to the streets. He stood up and walked around his desk as he pulled out huge knot of hundreds, fifties and twenties. He tore off two twenties and put them in my pocket as I stood before him. He grabbed a business card and handed it to me.

"This is my cell phone. Before you do anything stupid, you call me. If you need money, call me," and then he hugged me, as a father would a son.

"Thank you, sir," I said, as I made my way out of his office. I never saw him again. Yet, all was not lost. I still awaited a check for the thesis I was wrapping up and that $2,000 would come in handy. I was two car payments behind and one rent note behind, with the next bill due in a few days, and no money for groceries. All while still having my mother pay my car insurance and phone bill. "As long as our children are in college, we pay for the insurance and phone," she had told me. She could tell I felt undeserving of such gifts. She would pass me off money when I visited her for a fleeting moment, a meal here or there, running just like when I was six-teen but now chasing my purpose, chasing God. She was a mother whose heart had been torn out again and again by a boy blinded by his pain turned into anger. Now she was a mother whose heart was at rest in the knowledge that all things do happen for the good for those who love God and are called to His purpose.

The ethos of "Never ask anyone for help" was taught, condi-tioned, and reinforced for decades in a concrete jungle where prisoners live by a dog-eat-dog paradigm. Now, faced with no money and the belief system that a man must provide and a man does not beg for help, I earnestly finished my thesis so that I could receive the promised $2,000. This was a scholars' program aimed at the disenfranchised populations, those who statistically do not pursue a doctorate degree, for the sole purpose of incentivizing them to undergo the rigorous training and experience that would help push them through to a future doctoral program, thereby increasing diversity within the doctoral field.

August 6, 2015, Twenty Years from the Date, a
Private Mass for the Victim

As usual, I started my fast at 12:00 am on August 6. As I arrived to the Church of Holy Redeemer in the small, tightly knit Latino barrio of southwest, Detroit, I reflected on Samuel. He would have been forty-seven years old, just celebrating his son's graduation. I thought about Samuel's daughter and what quality of life she has experienced as a result of my falling short. I thought of Samuel's nephew, now in prison with a life sentence, and the devastating impact my sins have played on all of those around me. I recalled the covenant I had made with God.

Stepping out of the car, I stared into the bright, blue sky. Then across the parking lot, I saw Brenda, my former fiancée. I had tried to run from her, from her love, by breaking it off. Brenda's love was the first, functional love that I had experienced. As I reflect, I now understand that my running and pushing her away was merely a method of protection; I had developed a sense of non-attachment to that which is not permanent. That begs the question: what is permanent? Aha! *That* is a facet of self-reflection essential for success. Through the stripping of all that I had, through the years of solitary, I sought Spirit in the most stressful of times and learned that Spirit is the only "thing" that is permanent in this world, the unseen from which we came.

Every time I would try to run, Brenda simply responded with love ... always. I had been home only a year as I worked low-level jobs and went full-time at Wayne State University. Brenda, on the other hand, owned and operated a medical practice and was completely from the other side of the tracks, as they say. "Mario, I did not want to love you," she whispered to me late one night in my apartment on Wayne State's campus. It was one of those early rare occasions that I let down my emotional walls that had protected me for so long, even before entering prison. "God told me to help you, to love you, Mario," she would say. "God showed me our life together. I saw our children and your success. Mario, you are going to be great. You'll see. Everyone is going to want to hire you one day." She would tell me this at times when my own family didn't want me to take a leadership role in the family business.

I see now that a lot of my uneasiness with Brenda and her godly lifestyle came from an unconscious sense of inadequacy. Here I was, thirty-seven-years old, and all of my peers were successful in business and their personal lives, and I was a junior in college that could not take care of himself let alone a wife and child. My sense of inadequacy compounded my PTSD, so I secluded myself. I found the most solace in exercising the action plan that was rooted in my vision boards and goals. In the end, no matter what, Brenda and I would end up back together, but only because she was patient, resilient, and forever forgiving.

While I would love to say that I only brought joy into her life, my opinion is that of the inverse. The emotional turmoil of a returning citizen (parolee) who has served decades in prison since adolescence has not been thoroughly researched, but I can tell you from personal experience that the *fight* to survive began when

I exited those prison gates. I was conditioned to survive inside in a hyper-aggressive adult environment from an adolescent age. In fact, I had learned how to survive within a harsh, aggressive, violent environment since the age of three. But Brenda came into my life to teach me about true, unconditional love. For if I am to lead without love, then it would all be for nothing. If I am to bring healing and self-forgiveness to others, then don't I have to experience it first? One can only reproduce what one has experienced. Her vision pulled her through the hardship that I unconsciously interjected into her life. As I reflected, I began to understand this unconscious "not trusting" of her, and little by little, I allowed myself to grow closer. She was teaching me how to trust... that innate awareness that I possessed before the trauma.

Three days after our first break-up, my phone rang. "Mario, I'm sorry. Are you busy?" It was Brenda. I could hear her humility and uneasiness.

"Naw, waddup, ma?" I asked in my usual nonchalant way. She would always say, "I dislike it when you answer the phone like that," another attempt to keep my wall up.

"Can you please stop by my house on your way to work today?" she asked. I allowed for a long pause. I had broken up with her because she was demanding too much of my time, and she did not understand my need to experience certain things— like living on my own, for example. I wanted to get an apartment close to campus, and she thought that she could stop that. "No, I don't want you living on campus with all those girls." But trying to cage the bird only makes the bird fly away.

"Yea, but it's gotta be quick," I said, not wanting to allow an opportunity for us to get back together. I was determined to use the 86,400 seconds that we are all given in a day on me, on watering and fertilizing that Chinese Bamboo tree that requires five years of constant daily nutrients, yet doesn't break ground for five years; but when it does, it grows ninety feet within the first six weeks. That is how I viewed myself those first years out of prison, as that bamboo tree that required nutrients *every single day for five consecutive years*, and, most of all, it required *faith* that eventually, if I didn't give up, I would break ground. I was determined to stay focused. Brenda and every other girl took away from those 86,400 *seeds*.

When I showed up to her house, she shut the door behind her and said, "Now say it to my face. Tell me that you don't love me," she said, with the face of an angel. Of course, I loved her! But what she didn't understand was that the only peace I felt was when I was imparting it. To dive into a relationship would be for self, not for purpose. I was being pulled by two polar opposites: a lower self and a higher self . . . a lower craving and an upward calling. I smiled.

"You know that I love you." She looked up at me and stepped forward.

"Now, tell me that you don't want to be with me anymore, and I will leave you alone forever," she finished with a tear rolling down her cheek. I caught her tear with one finger and stared into her eyes.

"I'm getting my apartment, and I need my space," I said as she broke into a huge grin.

"I will decorate it," she said as she jumped up and wrapped her legs around my waist. Even though I was torn, broken, and not wanting to let down the wall that had protected me all those years, I was tired of that same wall keeping out the love that might exist *for me*. Up to that point in my life, I'd been hurt by every person who had "loved" me, beginning with those who brought me into the world. I was tired of having to protect my heart, my vulnerability to the pain of the past. In a sense, I was imprisoned before my imprisonment, and, indeed, continue to be so. Sometimes we allow our hurting from the past prevent the healings of the present.

I wanted healing, and with every part of her being, Brenda was offering that to me.

She looked so beautifully innocent that day in the church parking lot, trusting her church, an institution, with all of her heart to heal a man's brokenness, *my* brokenness. "*Hola, mi amor,*" she said lightheartedly. I smiled and gave her a peck on the lips as I grasped her hand. We walked into the church where Father Eduardo was waiting. We met several weeks earlier as he agreed to meet with Brenda and her "fiancé" for counseling. I was pulling away, struggling alone in my apartment with the process of becoming the man that I am destined to be. "Let's go to counseling with Father Eduardo, you will like him," she asked meekly. I saw it as a way out. "Let's do it," I quickly replied. Little did I know that she was looking for a way out as well.

We sat with Father Eduardo for almost two hours. He asked question after question until he heard the entire story. He looked at Brenda, "You must give this man space. Do you understand, Brenda, the pain this man carries?" At that moment, I lowered my head and began sobbing. She consoled me as he continued, gently.

"Mario, have you had a private mass for Samuel?" he asked. I shook my head no.

"The Spirit is moving me to ask you would you like to have a private mass for Samuel?"

"Absolutely," I said, humbled by the opportunity.

"Okay." Father Eduardo took out his Apple IPhone and scrolled through what I assumed to be his calendar and said, "How about a Thursday? How does that sound? Those are my days off."

"A Thursday will work, Father," I replied.

"How about August sixth which is in about three weeks?" he asked as he looked up at me.

I paused, lowered my head in reverence and reflection, looked back up at Father Eduardo and said, "August sixth will be twenty years to the day that I took Samuel's life. I fast every year on that day. That day will be perfect," We were in awe of the symbolism and serendipitous irony, or divine providence, depending on your faith.

Holy Redeemer's artwork is breathtaking. I took a deep breath to push me through the moment of spiritual reckoning for the sins of the past, of a lost youth. This was a regular Catholic mass with one exception. The congregation consisted of two. Father Eduardo was determined to bring peace and a blessing upon Samuel's soul. I felt the energy of the Spirit throughout the mass.

In closing, under the Spirit's influence, Father Eduardo prayed over me for a couple of minutes in a quiet tone. I looked up and saw that his eyes were rolling in back of his head and were all white as he mumbled in tongues for what seemed to be an eternity. I was in awe, for I had never experienced such a revelation. Then he opened his eyes and looked down upon me. "I felt Samuel's spirit here today. He is at peace," he said as my tears fell. "Mario, God wants you to know that you are forgiven. He says that you needed this blessing before you go into your journey and that you will have a major impact on the lives of many children."

It was an emotional moment for me. For twenty consecutive years, I have tried to make up for my sin. I have worked endlessly trying to allow God's Spirit to use me in penance for taking one of His sons. Hearing that God forgave me energized my spirit and was a confirmation that what I was pursuing with LUCK was in accord with the Creator.

We thanked Father Eduardo profusely and walked out of the church feeling blessed and highly favored. The sun was still shining as we walked into the parking lot. I shook my head in disbelief of what I had just experienced. I knew Brenda was thinking the same thing.

"Were you surprised that the Padre spoke in tongues?" I asked.

I usually said the word padre in a sarcastic tone, conveying my distrust with most institutions, including my own Catholic church. "No, the Holy Spirit was present. And, anyway, *coño*, I told you that God showed me, like pictures, all your blessings that are coming," she said as she gave me a kiss. I looked back at the church once more with the sun gleaming off of the beautiful windows.

"A major impact on kids' lives, huh? They would barely let me into college, let alone into schools with children," I replied. I forgot that when God is for you . . . who can be against you?

Mid August, 2015, A Broke Published Scholar

The Ronald McNair Scholars Program offered this population of first-generation college bound the opportunity to be mentored and trained in the research and development of a thesis, which would be published, along with the opportunity to present it orally with a PowerPoint, or a board presentation that did not require public speaking. I chose to present my thesis orally at Michigan State University, Wisconsin University, and Wayne State University where I was rated in the top six. The thesis was mandatory and it came with a stipend. The terms of the stipend allowed for thirty percent of it to be paid in the first week of the project in exchange for the student to agree to not work during the ten-week process. That would allow the student to focus their complete attention on the arduous task of completing a thesis in ten weeks. This training showed a statistically significant (positive) difference in the diversity of the doctorate fields. The remaining seventy percent of the stipend was to be paid upon completion and submission of the thesis.

I am done, I thought with relief when I sent the thesis via email. I needed that incentivizing check in order to get through the summer expenses. The challenge of developing a thesis while learning the computer skills needed to do it was a daunting task. There was a heavy learning curve. I made many mistakes, but it was all part of the process. I benefited from a two-hour workshop offered by the McNair Program that equipped me with the skills to use my laptop for the thesis research, the most crucial step of the process. But, my real value came in the form of my mentor, Dr. Valerie Simon of the Merrill Palmer Skillman Institute of Wayne State University who agreed to mentor me through the entire multifaceted phase of the thesis formation process. Dr. Simon met with me bi-weekly and held my hand through an extremely challenging process for any college student let alone one who just returned to society after 19 years in prison.

The fight to advance within that realm strengthened me to the point that I now have enough confidence to have written this book, to write the LUCK curriculum, to pursue a doctoral degree, and to pursue other forms of scholarly writing. I called the office right away after hitting send.

"When can I pick up my check?" I eagerly asked the McNair staff.

"Oh, you won't get the check for at least six to eight weeks," replied the office employee dryly.

"What?? The thesis agreement that we signed said that we would get it this week!" I exclaimed. "I have not been working as much as usual because the requirements of the research program did not allow us to work."

"You should have budgeted accordingly," she replied. Desperation set in as I paced my apartment floor. Pressure. I was feeling it from everywhere. Even at the accounting firm.

Late August, 2015, The Death of a Dream

Since summer of 2014, I had been working between Manuel's two offices, one in Southwest Detroit and the other in Auburn Hills. Manuel and his entire family experienced many challenges, the first being that his mother, who lived with Manuel along with her sister, was diagnosed with cancer. I had been there for six months, and Manuel was in Florida with his sixth wife purchasing a yacht for their retirement. We assume he included her in his vision, yet, one never knows, considering she *hated* the water and boats, and Manuel clearly had a higher-than-normal comfort level with the divorce process.

"Manuel," I said, almost in a panic. "I just arrived at your house, and your mom is as yellow as a yellow crayon." Manuel's Auburn Hills office consisted of the first floor and the basement to his house. He, his wife Mary, his mother, and his aunt, all lived upstairs. "The staff say she's been like this for over forty-eight hours," I continued. "I'm going take her to see Brenda." Manuel knew Brenda better than he knew me. She had worked for him years ago, and he was like an uncle towards her, as well.

"Yes," Manuel said quickly, "take her to see Brenda, and have Brenda call me."

Brenda eventually called hours later with the results. "Manuel, I am so sorry. She has a very advanced stage of cancer, but I think we may have a chance."

Manuel rushed back from Florida to take care of his mother, who was the bosom of his heart. He took pride in taking care of her and her sister, his aunt, who suffered from severe dementia.

Life, as Manny knew it, quickly disintegrated. As his mother was cut open to remove the ball of cancer, the doctors discovered that the cancer had spread; thus, chemotherapy was necessary before the surgical removal of the cancer. Stitched back up from her belly button to her neck, Manuel's mother was fighting to recover from surgery as she was assaulted by the chemotherapy. It was sad. Yet, as Brenda had said, "That lady will outlast all of them. She's a fighter." She was groomed during the Fidel Castro revolution and hardened in the eventual expulsion of many Cubans by Castro, including her and her family. Then, his aunt, his mother's sister who lived with her (in Manuel's house), side by side, passed suddenly, after suffering from years of severe dementia. Within months of this, his grandson was gunned down in the street from an old jail beef. Last but not least, his wife fell ill with a cough and lost twenty pounds in a month only to discover that she had stage-three cancer of the throat.

It was a Wednesday when I had finally had enough. "Señor, I am deeply sorry about your wife. I truly am." I paused as we sat in his garage where we now smoked. Funny thing is, when his mom fell ill with cancer, she criticized the caretaker for demanding that everyone smoke outside. Now, it was *her* asking that we stepped outside on account of *her* cancer. Life is funny like that. Life is definitely the ultimate teacher. "I have worked for you for the past year at ten dollars an hour. I have a kid on the way and, with all due respect, it doesn't really cover gas. I would like to be given a bundle of clients and a salary and eventually purchase those clients as I slowly purchase the seventy-five percent that we discussed," I continued. He nodded in agreement. He was done. Manuel Alphonzo, black belt in Judo and wealthy accountant had been beaten once too often by life. The weight of the world was on his shoulders.

"Monday. We will sit and do it Monday," he relented as he pulled himself up from the garage step that led to his house. I felt a knot in my stomach as he walked away. Here I was fussing over money while this man was struggling to live and . . . watched everyone around him die.

Three days later, Manuel's wife was coughing up blood as Manuel, screaming for help, held her in his arms. She died, choking on her own blood, as he cried out to a God he had claimed did not exist.

Upon hearing the news, I rushed over his house. I held him as he cried, chest dry heaving, as he now realized the depths of his love through the pain. "What am I going to do?" is all he could utter through the sobs.

We drank whiskey and smoked cigarettes as I listened to fond memories of Mary, his sixth wife. Ironically, she was the only one who had ever loved "Manny," as she called him, and never tried to change him. This is why Manuel loved her so. I was sad for this man who appeared lost to his purpose, God and everything permanent.

Now, with his grandson, wife, aunt, and even his dog all-dead, how could I talk again about ownership and business? My mentor was falling apart before my eyes. Over the next few weeks, Manuel's psoriasis became so bad that he looked like a leper with raw skin from neck to toe. He walked with bandages wrapped around him like a mummy. The bandages were stained red with blood and yellow from the puss. It broke my heart to see this once tall, dark, handsome man, who had even been a black belt instructor in Judo, now become a "leper" who could barely walk.

Believing it was stress that had caused his psoriasis flare up, the staff forced Manuel to go to the shooting range and attempt some "normal" activities. I, on the other hand, felt as if I was still getting pimped at ten dollars an hour as he charged clients a hundred dollars an hour for the work I was doing. Little did we all know that things were much more serious than we could imagine.

My stepfather was Manuel's best friend and would visit him often as I worked in the basement. In the weeks after Mary's death, my stepfather brought over a special ointment for Manuel's open sores. "Please, Manuel, do not use that ointment that your friend gave you," he said, referring to a doctor who was a client of Manuel's. "I am afraid that the ointment you are using is neutralizing your immune system, making you susceptible to many risks."

My stepfather returned a week later to check the progress of the new ointment to discover that the jar was still unused. With another jar in his hand, my stepfather set it on his nightstand, frustrated that his medical advice was not being adhered to. They were best friends, and watching Manuel disintegrate destroyed a piece of my stepfather. He would often vent to me in relation to his frustration with Manuel not using the medication. Eventually, I stopped going to the office. I was consumed with the writing of a thesis for the Ronald McNair's Scholars Program, and I was working on the duplex property that Tina and I invested in.

Just two weeks after I stopped working at Manuel's office, I was raking leaves at the investment rental property when I received a call from my mom. "Oh, Mario. It's Manny," she said. "He was rushed to the hospital, and we don't think that he is going to make it." I dropped the rake and fell to one knee as I exhaled. "He's been diagnosed with stage-four skin cancer. The medication he was using for his psoriasis caused his immune system to shut down, which allowed the skin cancer to grow at a fast rate," she said crying. I dropped everything and ran to my car. The hospital was only five minutes from the Detroit rental property that I now owned.

When I entered his hospital room, Manny was covered in bandages from head to toe. Even his eyelids were raw skin. I almost vomited at the sight of him. He was unconscious from the morphine that dripped into his I.V. He was so strong yet now so weak. It was humbling. This one man was the best friend to many, many people and the life force of a company and an entire family.

I lowered my head and prayed. "God, I beg you to save this man. Let not my will, but yours be done." I sat there with Manny in quiet reflection about his loss and mine. I thought this was my shot. There is no way I could do it without him.

Over the next two weeks, I went to the hospital often. Most days, Manny was unconscious from the morphine. He was in such pain that on the days that I arrived during the changing of his bandages, my mother and I would stand outside his door as he screamed out in pain, "*Nooooooo! God, please, noooo!*" I would whisper prayers for Manny as tears fell from my eyes.

Finally, after almost three weeks since being admitted and only two months after his wife's death, I received a call. "Mario," said my mom, "come quickly to the hospital. Manny is calling for you, and we don't think that he is going to make it through the night." I ran out of my apartment to my car in pursuit of one last goodbye.

As I approached the hospital room, my mom was waiting for me. "Oh, Mario, it doesn't look good," she said as I embraced her, able to console my mother more so now than upon my first release.

"It's okay, Mom, God is with us," I reassured her as we walked side by side into Manny's room. Manny was looking around the room, yet, it was as if he was looking *through* us and not *at* us. It was odd. I walked along Manny's bed and asked him, "Do you recognize me, *Señor*?" as I always referred to him.

"Of course, I do. Mario, come closer," he snapped back, again not looking at me, but through me. "I need to know now, do you want my accounting firm? Do you want my shares of the business?"

I was taken aback. I was not prepared for such an endeavor, but I also did not deserve such an offer, such a blessing. I had not earned it, so I lacked the strength to sustain it. Tears poured down my face as I took two steps back. Everyone in the room stared at me waiting for a response. I walked out of the hospital room towards the elevator and went downstairs to the chapel I had seen on my way in. I entered, knelt before a cross, and whispered, "Heavenly Father, the God of Abraham, Isaac, and Jacob, the God of the Anointed Christ, I beg of you, please save this man. I don't want his riches. I desire *him*, Lord, his life. He means so much to us Lord, but not my will but yours be done."

I went back upstairs to find everyone ushered out of Manny's room with the exception of his attorney, his partner who owned twenty-five percent, and his doctor "friend" who had supplied the ointment that froze his immune system, as a witness to what was to occur. Turns out, according to them, Manuel had left everything to his partner, who went from twenty-five percent ownership to now one-hundred percent ownership just like that. Truth is, she deserved it because she earned it. She went through the process to develop the character to sustain such a blessing and I had not. She had been sustaining much of the burden of the business towards Manny's last years. One thing I learned through my reformation is *process.* I feared getting what I didn't earn. For it would violate the law of harvest, *to the measure in which you sow so shall you reap.* It is dangerous to get something that is good at the wrong time.

I walked down the hallway of that hospital more lost than ever. It's funny, when God wants you to do something, He generally does it within the confines of discomfort and insecurity, for both require a resiliency of faith in order to overcome the symptoms of such perceptions and conditions. Pressure. Pressure will either make a diamond . . . or burst a pipe. I was beginning to burst.

CHAPTER 16

"IF YOU DO THIS, THEN YOU DENY ME."

September 2015, "I'm the Heroin King of Detroit!"

I SAT IN MY CHAIR staring out the window of my ninth-floor apartment numbered 911. It held doomsday connotations from either the emergency number 9-1-1 or the day of tragedy this nation will never forget, 9-11. From either perspective, I definitely was in trouble. As a thirty-seven-year-old man, I had never been faced with the trouble of being behind on bills, something so common to the average "free" citizen but foreign to a juvenile lifer such as myself. I lie down and fell asleep from the depression. I awoke approximately four hours later to a slew of text messages, one stating, "This is D. Hit me up." I smiled. I knew that I could get on my feet now. "D" had always been a hustler, a grinder. Years ago, I used to get ten ounces a month from him when we were in one of the prisons in Detroit. I always made money messing with D. I called him immediately.

"Waddup, my dude?" I exclaimed.

"Waddup, bro'? You busy tonight?" D responded.

"Naw, what you got in mind?" I curiously asked. D always had an angle.

"Bro', we gotta sit down and talk. Drinks and steaks on me," he said and gave me the name of a place in downtown Detroit. Living in Midtown, I was only five minutes away. *This is not the path*, I heard. I shut it out. I finished my shower and rushed to get ready. I had more energy now. Hope does that. It pulls you through your challenges. Even hope of this sort. Though that is not faith, for it is tangible. True faith is confidence in what we hope for and assurance about what we do *not* see. I was losing my faith. The struggles of life were blocking me from the knowledge of principles that had sustained me for nineteen years within the belly of the beast. *This is not your purpose* I heard again as I scramble to read the GPS in search of the location "D" had given me. I blocked it out and kept on driving.

Rick and Cam were also struggling to make ends meet, and in relation to their family's expectations. Rick having returned home after 18 years of imprisonment demanded a lot of energy to restore his broken relationships, especially with his two daughters. Cam returned to a family that was struggling to meet their basic needs, thus, he quickly resumed a leadership position within his family economic structure, which placed unbearable pressure upon this twenty-four-year old who had just served five years in prison. The strain of life created tension between us. They put LUCK on the back burner, while I struggled to maintain the faith in a vision that was quickly fading. Temptation became greater as the distance between us grew. I needed them and, they needed me. For *when two or more gather, in my name, so shall I be.*

As I walked up to the structure, I could see that this place was really high-end. "Excuse me, sir, do you have a reservation?" asked the front doorman before he allowed me to enter. I fumbled with my words, feeling completely inadequate as PTSD began to take over my nerves.

"U-m-m-m-m, I don't—"

"Waddup, boy-y-y-y?!" said D, as he appeared and embraced me with a huge hug.

He then engaged in a friendly conversation with the doorman that was clearly not his first and shook his hand as he handed him a folded bill.

I was introduced to the doorman who apologized and said, "Please, sir, any friend of D's is a friend of ours. Come any time." He gestured for us to enter the opened door. I was in shock.

We were led to a table and drinks were brought to us with no wait. We ate, drank, and laughed. The owners stopped by and conversed with D who introduced me to everyone. I felt like I was in the movie *American Gangster*, with D being Denzel and those around us the Italian mob. The only difference was that this mafia was from Albania.

"So, what's the real deal, Mario?" D looked at me, knowing me as a friend and brother. He could sense my inner discord.

"Just struggling financially, bro'. And I refuse to apologize for how I put food on my table," I said more so in response to the incessant thoughts that flooded my mind telling me to turn from this path than to him.

"Money? That's your problem?" he exclaimed. Stretching his arms out wide on each chair next to him and tilting his head back in laughter, he stared directly into my eyes.

"I am the Heroin King of Detroit!" he grinned. It was the same old look from inside.

"I need help, D. I'm ready to work. I'm getting denied everywhere because I am on parole. I barely got into college. I need some work," I said in reference to his product, a clarification not needed between us.

"I got you, boy. I'll show you everything, but you gotta step on this. It's too strong. That is how you will come up. You just gotta find you a few young fellas on the block that are hungry and have the hustla' mentality. Never push it yourself," he said with a gleam in his eye. "Step on it" meant to cut the heroin with something else, like baby laxative, thereby increasing my product amount while avoiding an overdose.

About a week later, D showed up to my apartment to breakdown the details of the operation. My financial situation had not changed, so my basic needs were still in jeopardy. "I'm going to give you small amounts as you get trained in pushing this shit. This is a different devil with a different clientele," he said, sitting in my apartment with his back facing the window. He covered his mouth as he spoke so his lips could not be read. He's always been overly cautious, a lesson learned from decades in a life of crime.

"Cool. Just show me what I need to do," I said, as he broke down a lot of information within a short period of time. As I saw him to the door, I glanced at the cross that I had not bowed down to for over two weeks, hiding from God in shame. I embraced D and told him to go in peace.

As I walked back to my small apartment living room I glanced back at the cross. I immediately fell to my knees and prayed the Lord's Prayer, the Our Father. I began to sob uncontrollably. My tears blinded me and I began to dry heave. I was having trouble breathing as I stood up, blinded by my own the tears. All I could see was the face of Jesus' brownish-bronze skin tone and long, dark, thick hair, staring at me. The dry heaves came harder, and I gasped for air when I heard a soft, tender voice. "If you do this, you deny Me as Peter denied Me." Again, I fell to my knees face down sobbing uncontrollably as my tears soaked the carpet and whispered, "Forgive me Lord."

While still on my knees, sobbing, the phone rang. It was my cousin, Tone, the one who had participated in my indictment and conviction, the one who twenty years earlier had made three statements against me to the homicide detectives. The Lord had put it in my heart to forgive and embrace him a few months earlier when he was battling thoughts of suicide. When he was going through a divorce that entailed five children, he had tried to hang himself. At that point, the Spirit moved me to reach back out to him, after several of his failed attempts, to make amends. The Lord used me that day to pour life back into his heart and mind. The Holy Spirit aided in healing and redemption for the both of us.

I stood up, shook off the tears and answered his call. "Waddup, cuz?"

"Hey, my brother, what's going on? You out partying?" he asked, his spirits high.

"Naw, bro', I don't have much in the way of funds to operate with."

"Actually, that's why I'm calling. Today I figured that if I had saved just $50 for you each week that you were in prison, I could have saved over $50,000 dollars for you. I'm sorry that I didn't do that. But I want you to come over tomorrow because I have a few hundred dollars for you. I know it's not much, but I'm going to start giving you some money from each paycheck." I fell silent. There was only the sound of tears dripping from my cheeks, landing on my desk where I now sat.

"Thank you, my brother. Trust me, the Lord is using you to help others, but especially me," I said as I choked back the tears.

"I just don't want you to stop what you are doing, Mario. You are so inspirational, and you are helping a lot of people. Please, don't let that flame burn out."

Over the next seventy-two hours, my mom, sister, and friend gifted me over $1,200, enabling me to pay my rent and car note. I never asked any of them for help, but each of them said they were moved to give me this money. I never reached back out to D, and he never reached back out to me until several months later.

He explained how a series of misfortunes befell him after that night when he left my apartment. I believe that was a provision of the Lord.

In my eyes, I failed the test posed by the fallen one. In my eyes, it should not have gone that far, where Jesus needed to point out my hypocrisy. As serendipity would have it, I always criticized Peter for betraying Jesus. I looked at Peter as being a coward. And, yet, until that moment, I had never looked at falling short of my purpose, as a denial of the Creator and His will for my life.

September, 2015, My Brother's Keeper II Summit

Even though I view myself as failing God's tests, I continued to be showed favor. I have heard it said, "Favor isn't fair," amongst the religious. God continues to prove that so through my life. Rico Razo is the 6th District's Manager, a position created under Mayor Duggan's administration as a liaison between community and government. I first met Rico two weeks after my release at a small authentic Mexican restaurant in Southwest Detroit. Adrian graciously asked if I would meet with Rico, and I agreed. As I look back, I see how Adrian assisted in my pro-socialization and reintegration by inviting me to meetings that pertained to an issue where he believed I could influence a solution. Adrian visited me the last year that I was in prison, a time when I was at my pinnacle in terms of teaching and being a positive person of influence amongst a group of the most violent men in Michigan.

What I did not see or understand was the influence that was gifted to me, to the men of LUCK and men like them, of connecting with an otherwise disconnected population. Rico and I began to work together on different occasions over the next year, and our working relationship grew into a genuine friendship. Men like Adrian and Rico were men that I wished to learn from. I looked up to them and I wanted my demeanor and my attitude to mirror theirs. Rico and Adrian often asked me if I could attend a meeting here or participate in a project over here. So, it was not unusual when Rico called me to ask whether I could attend an upcoming event. "Hey, there, Mario, how have you been?" asked Rico, his amazingly soft spirit soothing my PTSD in a way that helped me see that which I must become. The rules of engagement were different in this world, and Rico served as mentor as well as a friend.

"Good bro', just grinding. Constantly work or school. My life is based on deadlines," I said with a chuckle, knowing that his life was much the same.

"We are proud of you, Mario," he said in reference to the work of LUCK.

"Thank you, bro', but you know that I am the last one to be proud of. I do what I do because I owe society. I owe the community my life," I replied, as my usual response.

"We're still proud of you," he said with a grin that I could see through the phone. Rico was a class act and a stand-up kind of guy. His "yes" meant yes, and his "no" meant no. He was a straight shooter, and I admired his integrity.

"Thank you, bro'," I said in surrender.

"There is an event for the program launched by the Obama administration, My Brother's Keeper. They asked me whom I think should represent the Latino leaders of Detroit, and I gave them two choices, you being one of them. I told them both stories and they chose you," he said.

"Yeah, sure, no problem. Just, please, send me an email or else I will double book or, worse, forget," I said. He was accustomed to this response.

A couple of weeks went by until the day of the event was upon us. I had no clue what the event was for until I opened the email . . . the day of. It involved a book signing with a group of six famous, successful Black men who were representing the program, including best-selling author, Shaka Senghor, author and minister, Dr. Eddie M. Connor, Jr., and actor and educator, Lamman Rucker. And me! Tonya Allen, President and CEO of the Skillman Institute, served as the moderator. She asked us questions, and the crowd of youths and mentors and agency representatives listened to our insight.

It was a phenomenal experience. In the end, I was humbled to have been asked to participate in the book signing with the other men who had come together to write this one book called *Reach*. The audience members asked me to sign the books and the authors, the successful men above, encouraged me to sign as well. "Sign the book, bro'. Soon you will have yours published," they said, speaking life into my spirit. I signed the books and took photos with the authors of the book.

As the event was coming to an end, Odis Bellinger, a youth leader and mentor from the East Side of Detroit approached me and said, "I was told over a year ago about you. I heard your story and I was told that you were skilled in what you do," he said, shaking my hand. I knew who he was. We had not had a chance to meet, officially, but all things happen for a reason and a purpose.

"It's a pleasure to meet you, officially, Mr. Bellinger," I responded.

"Are you interested in coming into my schools and speaking? I can pay you $35 an hour," he said. I thought about what Father Eduardo had told me just several weeks earlier about how I would have a huge impact on many children's lives.

"Absolutely, just tell me when and where," I responded without hesitation.

"Tomorrow from 8:00 a.m. to 1:00 p.m. I can use you every Wednesday at Detroit Lion's Academy," he said, looking down at me from his height of six-foot-five.

"Only God could stop me from being there tomorrow," I said, shaking his hand and embracing him.

The next day, I showed up at Detroit Lion's Academy around 7:50 a.m. Ironically, the school was just about five minutes away from where I lived. The K-8 school looked like a low-security prison with its chain-locked doors and metal detectors. Sadly, it was reminiscent of a minimum-security prison. I had been texting with Mr. Bellinger so he was already aware that I was on the premises. I approached the door and it opened. "Good morning, Mr. Bueno," said Mr. Bellinger.

"Good morning, sir," I responded.

"The students are going to get a treat having you here," he said. I hoped so. I prayed daily for the Spirit to use me as it sees fit, but especially before a speaking engagement, I prayed deeply for the guidance of spirit. For in a speaking engagement such as this, I was not familiar with my audience and I had one opportunity to make a transformational impression. Talk about pressure.

I spoke to about six classes that day, averaging about forty-five minutes per class. They were a rigid and bitter bunch. You could tell that they had seen too much in their short lives. I walked out of there with my t-shirt soaked under my dress shirt. I was drained mentally, emotionally, and physically. That was my first experience speaking within a school since I was not allowed inside any of them due to my crime. I walked out feeling empty, having given all that I had. I walked out wondering whether the words had any impact.

The next day, I received a phone call from Mr. Bellinger. "They *loved* you, m-a-a-a-n!" he yelled out.

"Really?" I asked sincerely.

"Of course! You know you got the gift," he said nonchalantly. One thing I notice about Mr. Bellinger is that he is not stingy about praising that which deserves it or correcting that which warrants it.

"Thank you, my brother," I said, humbled.

"Make sure you come back next Wednesday," he said. I sat there staring out my ninth-floor apartment window envisioning myself helping the youth, many youths. I remembered again the contract I had made with the Creator so long ago in the darkness of that cell in I-Center: *I challenge you to save me, and I will spend the rest of my days helping kids like me.* I smiled. God had heard my cries. I was not alone. Truth is, I was never alone. God created me for a purpose, and before he made me, He had created the environment from which I would gain the skills and tools to manifest *His* purpose for my life. When I forgave my mother, father, and cousin, I came to the conscious realization that my entire life has been in divine order. It was through this mess that God had formed me into a *mess*enger. That My Brother's Keeper II event that Rico invited me to seemed to open the floodgates for many more chances to speak, especially at schools.

October, 2015, Papito, I Have News . . .

A couple of months after Brenda and I met with Father Eduardo on August 6, 2015, the turbulence that my reintegration entailed screamed louder as I looked all around me at a world I did not know that I did not feel comfortable in, the PTSD, the challenges of being inadequate socially, financially, and ethically, all impacted my ability to be in a relationship. I could not securely attach to anyone emotionally, including Brenda. Living in the apartment gave me my solitude, and yet in that solitude I became obsessed with *my work.* I lived and breathed to *work the garden.* I was completely obsessed with the creation of LUCK, and I put everything to the side in its pursuit, including my health.

So, I broke it off with Brenda . . . again. Our values and what we deemed desirable were completely opposite. She wanted to be on a beach in Miami with her loved ones, and I was obsessed with a vision to build the most efficient stabilization program for at-risk youth and returning citizens. I was obsessed to serve those that hurt like me... and, more importantly, were at risk of hurting others.

Towards the end of my imprisonment, as Adrian began to visit me, he would commend my leadership abilities and my ability to overcome all that I had faced. "You've fought the good fight, Mario," Adrian would say, speaking with a biblical resonance.

"And yet, at what cost? What will be the residual effects on a youth imprisoned within the confines of the harshest adult prisons for two decades?" I replied, asking the ever-present rhetorical question. He would put his hand on my shoulder and say, "We will be here for you, my brother."

Now, a few years later, I was *experiencing* that residual effect I had long pondered. What remained of that boy who was a resilient fighter with tenacity to overcome every obstacle except the enemy within? What remained of that hurt little boy who turned sadness into anger as a way to survive in a desperate attempt to find security, stability, and safety? That little boy no longer needed to defend himself because he was no longer in harm's way, but he didn't know this. Although he remained safe from the harm of others... he remained imprisoned and in conflict with the sins of the past as I, the grown man, sought peace through my purpose.

I pushed Brenda's love away until she could take it no longer. We broke up in a way that a fire slowly dims. The truth is that she was perfect for me. She was just as I had described in that letter to God. But I was hurting, and hurt people, *hurt* people, for we give what we are. My conflict has never been with Brenda. It has always been with myself. As I embrace the old African Proverb "When there exists no enemy within, the enemy without, can do you no harm." But I pushed her away for the second time.

Now, I was in my apartment engrossed in a vision that was written on an oversized dry erase board in the middle of my living/

kitchen/TV room (it was a small apartment). I lived it. I breathed it. I ate it. I slept it. Later, Cam would tell me, "I worried about you when you were in that apartment. We didn't think you were going to make it," he said one day as we sat reminiscing about the struggles. When Brenda stopped coming over, I let the apartment's cleanliness go. I didn't care about anything...except the success of LUCK.

Two weeks after breaking up with Brenda for the second time, I received a Face Time phone call from Brenda. "Hello, am I disturbing you?" she asked politely. She is always polite and polished, the complete inverse of my ruggedness.

"Nah, waddup?" I asked, as I continued looking at my accounting book. I was failing the last Intermediate Accounting class that my degree in accounting required me to take. We were fighting internally at LUCK over lack of resources. We had all been just giving, giving, giving to the point of breaking. The pressure to achieve, to succeed, drove my obsessiveness to the point that I had not been making time for Brenda. And, when I did, the conversation was all about LUCK, about *purpose.*

"*Papito,*" she looked at me with a nervous grin.

"Yes?" I replied, continuing to look at my accounting work.

"*Papito!*" she snapped. My head jerked up to look at her.

"Yes, Brenda."

"I'm pregnant," she said, the nervous grin turning into a fearful, sad look. Brenda had always wanted to be married before getting pregnant.

"Are you sure?" I said, forcing the vomit back down my throat as if I were the one pregnant. I knew at that very moment that my life would never be the same. I knew that my selfishness would now be curbed, for I had committed long ago to my unborn child.

"*Yes,* I'm sure, *coño!*" she shot back revealing her intense fear. I smiled.

"Do you know who the father is," I asked, joking with her as usual.

"Don't make me smack you!" I broke out into laughter as she did also, nervously so. I was completely overwhelmed with just trying to take care of myself. How in the world would I take care of a child? And how was I going to "have her back?" I did not want to get married. I was already married to my *work*. And it was my work that she did not value. She did not understand that to not value *it*, to not value *them*, felt like she was not valuing *me*, for my promise to help all those *like me* is why I do what I do. Brenda did not understand that *I was them*.

Though we were on the verge of calling the wedding off during our separation, the discovery of Brenda's pregnancy helped me decide to get married. The impact on a child of not having a father in the home was, statistically speaking, is a poor starting point. I wanted something different for my child. I wanted my child to know my voice, and in that knowing I wanted my child to have an unshakable confidence that I would never forsake her. We agreed that I would move in with her and her parents at the end of my last semester, the start of the fourth month of her pregnancy.

While Brenda and I were becoming solidified, my business relationships were dissolving before my very eyes.

November, 2015, Rep. Santana's Warnings Prove True

In the meantime, LUCK continued to train and mentor the youths, and by the end of a five-month period, we had grown the group to about ten youths. We continued to supply the meals and beverages at our mandatory second meeting, as we used the curriculum I built week by week. We didn't mind though. We trained inside the prison for free. It was the intrinsic, inner feeding of our spirit that we were chasing. One time, someone asked Rick, "Hey, Rick, do think that you can save the world?"

"I'm not trying to save the world. I'm just trying to save myself," Rick replied, as he choked back the tears. At this point, we had been spending time with the mentees several times a week on the East Side of Detroit in comparison to the JAC's once-a-month program.

Four months into us working for JAC, Mrs. Duggan invited me to an event for her son, the mayor, which I humbly accepted. At the time, I had no idea that the date, two months later, would fall on a day when I was scheduled to train the youth. I *never* missed a day with the kids, so I saw it as an opportunity for the youth to experience something other than the probation office. I emailed Mrs. Duggan, and she quickly responded "Absolutely. And Mike [Duggan] says he'll make time to meet with the kids," she wrote. Mrs. Duggan is a pure soul. I could feel her excitement. So, I called Mr. Jackson, the youths' direct care worker, and laid out my idea. Mr. Jackson engaged the youths by taking them to and from their appointments with probation and the training sessions.

"I have to ask Mrs. Smithsonian for permission," he said.

"Bro', with all due respect, I am being polite by asking. You know that I hang out with these kids every week, apart from training. I pick them up to go places now. Asking permission is simply a courtesy. Please understand that," I said, triggered by the manipulation of the youth. I had already discovered through my building of a close relationship with Devon Freemen (Will) that the staff used the kids to get funding and then provided the bare minimum.

"They try to keep us pilled up, but I don't take that shit," Will had confided in me once. "When they ask me to attend their events, they know I want that money, so I make them give me CVS cards when they want me to meet with them white people that be giving them the money," Will vented the night I took him to his first day of his Internship in Southfield. The JAC was giving kids like Will $20 CVS cards to appear at fundraisers to take pictures. They would pay the kid's family members $200 to show up to say, "My son's life has changed because of JAC's Turning Around program." When I learned of this one night as I drove Will home, I immediately turned on my recorder on my phone. Rick would never believe this. I continued to ask Will questions and the answers broke my heart, just as they did Rick's and Cam's.

"You know, Mario, you the only man that has ever showed me love for no reason. You know that I don't know my daddy cuz he raped my mama?" he said as he stared out the window. "My mama gonna be so proud of me when I tell her what I am doing," he says in reference to his first day at his internship. God connected Will, through me, with an internship at a radio station in Southfield. I wanted his vision of the world, of himself, and of whom he can *become* to be expanded. He stared out the window as we listened to the sounds of 2pac's *Ambitious as a Rida* as I drove him to his favorite Coney Island on Detroit's most violent East Side where we sat, ate, and talked about his future. Every time I took him out to eat, Will only ate half. He took the other half home to his little brother and sister. Little did Will know, he was mentoring me.

The night before, I had been informed by Will that Mr. Jackson and the social worker were talking trash about LUCK and saying how they weren't going to the event. Will wanted to go to the event, so he called me. "Bro', ya'll gotta pick us up 'cuz they lying. They ain't gonna take us. They was laughing, sayin' that you believed them that they was taking us," Will said. Will and I had developed a strong bond that was unbreakable. Mr. Jackson had promised me that he would get the youths there.

"Okay. What time did they say they'd get you?" I asked.

"Five o'clock," Will said.

"Okay, I'll be there at 4:30 and don't be late," I said and hung up the phone.

The next day, Rick, Cam, and I picked up all the youths and

their friends and met up with the direct care worker and the social worker assigned to the youths at the event. This upset them. "Mario, we went to pick up the youths and they were gone. Why didn't you tell us that you were picking them up?" the social worker demanded.

"I'm sorry about that, my brother," I replied. I always called him brother because I couldn't remember his name.

During the event, as the youths congregated together in their comfort zone, their social worker walked up to them and criticized their behavior. "Why aren't you guys mingling and meeting new people? That's why you're here, to build a network," he said, in a condescending tone. I stepped up from behind.

"With all due respect," I said to him and then looked from him to the youths. "You men are here to expand your *vision,* for you can only create and manifest what you can *see.* Don't worry that you're seeking your comfort zone by seeking out each other. That's natural. Look," I said, pointing all around. "They're all in their comfort zones. You're here to expand your vision of what you think you can become," I said and continued to walk about.

It upset me that this simple field trip was made to be such a big deal by the JAC staff. They acted just like the staff in prison: always doing the bare minimum in terms of their job. It was an inconvenience for this social worker to come out on an evening and take some at-risk boys to be culturally and socially oriented. His body language and then the attempted chastisement of the young men said so. That triggered me, because I too was that little boy facing the challenges of grown men.

I walked over to Mrs. Duggan who came up to me with open arms and embraced me. "Where are the boys?" she said with a smile that could soften the meanest soul. I turned, stepping slightly to the side so that she could see beyond me.

"Can you guess which ones they are?" I asked, always my

facetious self. There in the middle of that large building decorated for a king and full of white influential donors was a group of young, black youths all recently released from the Wayne County Jail. Mrs. Duggan and I laughed. The youths were in a new world, and yet, from their body language, laughter, and carefree nature *that* "new world" felt safe. Mrs. Duggan hugged each of them. Then Mayor Duggan came over and was finally introduced to the felon who had stolen his mama's heart.

"This is Mario, the one who was bringing the kids today," said Mrs. Duggan, smiling. The mayor shook my hand, and I leaned in and whispered, "I respect you immensely, not only because of your position, but because of who your mother is. She's phenomenal." I pulled back and the mayor kept the same politically correct grin, not knowing how to respond. I moved out of the way and ushered the young men to him. Rick, Cam, and I stood there and smiled. "These kids will never forget tonight," Rick said.

The week after the field trip to visit with the mayor, LUCK was asked to meet with Ms. Smithsonian and her team. Rick and Cam thought the meeting was at noon instead of 11:00 a.m., so I was the only LUCK member in the meeting. Tension had been brewing for months now.

We wanted to train *the kids* to become mediators because we understand these youths needed to learn the ability to resolve conflict. LUCK's mediation training is prefaced with an arduous retraining of beliefs, values, and attitudes, followed by an extensive six-month training of critical thinking, effective communication, anger management, and conflict resolution. Thus, once mediation certified, these youths would epitomize peacemaking, and, since one may only give what one possesses, the youths would give only peace. JAC, however, simply wanted to collect a check and minimize expenses.

Often the returning citizen and the children of Detroit are

treated as HMO clients: the less resources spent, the more the profit. So, places such as JAC receive a grant (their grant was for $200,000), hire several employees at $40,000-$60,000 and "mentor" the youths by picking them up once a month to take them to the probation office and, maybe, just maybe, give them that $20 CVS card. Those who have failed to walk a mile in the shoes of these youths, of those returning from prison, are taking the resources meant to assist such vulnerable populations reintegrate back into the community and using it for salaries/wages, business operation expenses, meals and entertainment, while youths being released from the county jail get nothing more than a pep talk. The most basic of all needs, a sense of security, let alone soap and toothpaste, are not being met, but we still expect these fallen ones to reach self-actualization. The system has created a façade of helping the disenfranchised youths and returning citizens; the truth is, these "nonprofits" are simply helping *themselves* at the expense and the safety of our communities. For when these disconnected youths and returning citizens lack the basic needs that are essential to living, what do you think they will do? The best predictor of future behavior is the most *recent* past behavior; thus, these ill-equipped populations turn to their only skill-set: crime.

"We have to do more than just take them to their probation office and give them a $20 CVS card," I said, throwing a jab at Ms. Smithsonian.

"How dare you? Do you think this is a game?" she snapped.

"Have you ever seen where these youths live, Ms. Smithsonian?" I challenged, staring deep into her eyes. "Have you ever driven your BMW down Mack Avenue all the way to the east side where these youths live?" I continued. "You haven't, have you? You cannot lead someone from some place that you have *not* travelled, and that is the fundamental conflict: you cannot identify, let alone empathize. It's all about the money to all of you, isn't it?" I declared, as I glared around the room at her "team," if that's what you can call it. Pathetic poverty pimps is what I call them.

"Get out of here!" she yelled. I looked around the table at her team and then back at her.

"Trust me, I've been kicked out of better prisons," I said with a smirk as I stood up and gathered my belongings. "You aren't in this for the right thing, Ms. Smithsonian, and it will catch up with you."

I was cut off with more screams of "Get out!"

"Someone didn't take their Ritalin this morning," I said with a laugh as I walked out the door. It was a nervous laugh, though. I was still on parole, so I did not want any misconceptions in relation to confrontations. Ironically, I was relieved to have gotten all of that off of my chest.

She was the gatekeeper to all of the adjudicated youth in Wayne County. She was the present-day slave master who controlled the destinies of these young slaves within a new Jim Crow, a system in which these youths were now a part of, both tangibly and intangibly, for what was the residual effect of housing the seventeen-year-olds within the harshest form of confinement? My relief came in the form of defending them, and, in essence, defending myself. I was standing up for that sixteen-year-old boy who was listening to that sergeant talk about how grown men were going to rape him once he got to prison. I was sticking up for that kid who couldn't stick up for himself at the time. "You will not take advantage of youths on my watch," I said to myself as I exited the conference room. "Not on my watch."

I was standing in front of the elevator with my briefcase in hand and my coat over my shoulder when it opened, and Rick stepped out. "Guess what? We were just fired from our volunteer work," I said, laughing aloud.

"Yeah, right," he said in disbelief. I filled Rick in with all that happened. We stepped into the elevator and went down in silence.

It was a depressing reality: the only group of young men that we had been able to pour life and knowledge into had now been taken away from us. In a sense, we felt as if our meaning and purpose had once again been stripped from our souls. I felt like I had failed once again. This failure hurt to the core of my innermost self.

"It's meant to be, Mario. I believe that. This must be taking away from something else that we must do," Rick said. No matter how much I have failed, Rick has *always* responded the same. I have never had that in a mentor. Rick has taught me so much in the mentoring of others. "Mario, you were put literally in a dungeon at sixteen. It's going to take some time. Don't be so hard on yourself," he would console me in our talks over the years. Rick had watched me grow up, literally, in prison, and he contributed to that growth to a large extent. I had an "anger problem" you could say, though it was always in response to perceived threats. Thus, there were triggers. The more time I spent out of prison, the more I was becoming conscious of those triggers. "Bro, you *are* these youths. That building," he said as we stood in the parking lot of JAC, "is one of your biggest triggers. You were *them*, bro', and now we are here to help them. It's okay," he said, as a tear rolled down my cheek and then another. "It's okay!" He grabbed me in a big hug. I love Rick like a brother, a friend, and, at times, a father figure. This is what a mentor does. He's there for you to speak life into your spirit when all you feel is death.

November, 2015, Good Intentions Industries of Detroit

Around the same time that we were "fired" from the volunteer work with the Juvenile Adjudication Complex, I had been in several high-level meetings with and spoken in front of a man I will refer to as Mr. Kevin Bitter, the "Change the Story" Program Director with a large organization I will call Good Intentions Industries of Detroit. After a meeting at the Skillman Institute, Mr. Bitter approached me in the parking lot. "My anger management and conflict resolution guy went back to Ford Motor Company. I know that you're an expert in this area, and I want to pay you to come and train my men and women," he said as he asked for my email. I handed him my card.

"I have an expert team that can train the most at-risk populations in anger management and conflict resolution." I was eager to get our team back to training and getting paid to do it was even better. Up until then, our pay had only been intrinsic and non-tangible. To witness agencies getting millions for what we do for free was only sickening in that the agencies weren't following through with their commitment to walk these at-risk populations towards personal and professional success. This was more fuel that pushed us through the challenges that our system has in place to ensure its own survival. For example, the frustrating reality that felons are blocked from being vendors for Michigan schools, regardless of the felony. I was relenting to the possibility that LUCK, or at least I, would not be allowed access to at-risk youth, so I turned my attention to my studies. My reasoning was this: if I must earn a doctorate in the pursuit of transforming this system that is refusing us access, then consider it done.

Around this time, I received a phone call from Brian, the man who had trained me in the art of training other men while in prison. He had recently been released. Rick and Cam could not offer as much to LUCK as I hoped, so Brian added some new energy to an old fight.

One day Brian and I met at the downstairs bar of my Belcrest Apartment building in Midtown Detroit. Ironically, it was "A Chance to Live" that had recommended he contact LUCK. "It turns out that James and Tanya are exactly what we expected. No good." This was all Brian could say about our former mentors.

"Look," I whispered to him as he sipped on his cranberry juice and water. Brian had just come home from doing eighteen years, and he was a militant Nation of Islam follower, so no booze for him. I wondered how long he would last out in Sodom and Gomorra. "I have a vision that involves us doing *exactly* what we did inside: we are to transform the worse of the worst, the most violent, into peacemakers," I said, grinning ear-to-ear. Brian was always a listener, always the statesman. He was full time at Oakland Community College straight out of the gate, just like us. I wanted him in the crew, in the pack. Inside there had been a butting of heads between Rick and Brian, but I didn't care because Rick and Cam were not producing, not contributing—at that point—to LUCK, so I had to bring a power player like Brian on without their consent.

"You are in. I'm currently negotiating pricing on anger management and conflict resolution services that Good Intentions Industries is requesting. I know that as a team we can bill a lot more because the product delivered is much, much more." I leaned forward and whispered, "They cannot do what we did, what we can do. They are lost as to how to solve the violence." I leaned back and grinned.

"Let's do it," he said with a grin.

Rick and Cam were upset that I had brought Brian on without their knowledge or opinion. And, yet, it was challenging to get them to answer my phone calls during this period of time.

Mr. Bitter and I emailed each other back and forth over the next two months until we reached an understanding as to what he was looking for in terms of a service provider for his clients. He explained that the populations would be seventeen to thirty-six-year-old males who were gang-affiliated, either felony probationers or parolees, and a second cohort of adult women of varying ages. The LUCK team met with the Good Intentions' "Change the Story" team and a common vision was created. "I cannot pay you men what you deserve, but I will pay you what I can. You men are destined for high places," said Mr. Bitter eloquently, one of several mentoring moments we experienced with him.

LUCK was to train two cohorts in anger management and conflict resolution every seven weeks. LUCK had its first contract! In actuality, it was a Memorandum of Understanding. Either way, it was a developmental milestone for LUCK. We had populations to train, and we were eager to get back in the classroom.

CHAPTER 17
SHORT-TERM SACRIFICE...
LONG-TERM REWARD

January, 2016, Generational Changes

I TERMINATED MY LEASE at the end of December and moved in with Brenda and her parents. We set the wedding date for February 13, 2016. Well, *she* decided. Seeing how depressed she was getting as a result of *not* being married, which was rooted in her belief that our child would not be as "blessed" if she was born out of wedlock, I conceded, with one request. "I will pay half of the wedding, but I don't want to know anything about it except what day and time I gotta be there," I told her, with a straight face.

"Thank you *papito!*" Brenda cried and leaped for joy. I just wanted my child, forming within her, to not feel an ounce of sadness. From the time I moved in with her, I was able to witness my child being cared for by a loving mother. Brenda would use special headphones for her to listen to sermons about Jesus as she worked at the doctor's office. She would talk to her and soothe her when she displayed her energetic presence early in the womb. As I reflect,

I valued greatly that decision to move into Brenda's house and be present for the struggle that lay before her in bringing our child to this world. Little did I know what additional challenges lay ahead.

February, 2016, A Boy and His Father Seek Reconciliation

At the time I was struggling with the news that I would soon be a father, I was also struggling with my own father was asserting his self into my life. He has been there for me above and beyond since my release. My mother, too, though the unresolved issues between a father and a son are different because the unconscious image of the father inherent within the son's mind can either be empowering or disempowering. My concept of my father needed to be changed through experience. It needed to heal, for my father was no longer that twenty-five-year-old who raised his hand and voice toward my mother, just as I was no longer that sixteen-year-old who raised that pistol at Samuel.

I squared up to fight my own father within the first year of my release, but it was with the haunting images of a little boy's memories that I stood toe-to-toe with him. This time, that scared little boy found the loving arms and compassionate heart of his father, the father he had always prayed for.

"Please, son, just tell me what I need to do," he begged me, as tears rolled down his face. I was squared up to fight as I yelled, "You'll never be around my daughter, you hear me?!" It was Christmas season of 2015. It was his frustration expressed in an aggressive tone at a family gathering that triggered me. That frustration was aimed at my aunt, a female. I let my guard down and began sobbing and my father hugged that little boy who had been searching for his father for over thirty years.

"Please, father, just don't be aggressive in front of me. It triggers me," I said through my tears. I was finally able to understand the root of my anger. It was the beginning of true healing, which created a space for me to offer the same to mentees such as Will.

End of February 2016, A Legacy

Devon Freeman, my first mentee from JAC's Turning Around program, left the program when they gave him an ultimatum: either you are with JAC or with LUCK, in so many words. Needless to say, he chose LUCK because you measure a tree by the fruit it bears. In terms of his basic needs, LUCK tried to make sure that Devon ("Will") was taken care of. I could not expect him to seek self-actualization if he lacked security in his home or was going hungry or was without heat in his home. These are the challenges facing our most at-risk youths and returned citizens. Their most basic needs go unmet as the community agencies that contracted millions to service these populations pat them on the back, hand them a bus ticket, and say, "You can do it." For years, the men of LUCK have pulled from their own wallets to meet the needs of their mentees and clients.

I went to Will's house several times a week as part of our mission to put into motion the law of association. I knew that he could only become better if he *thought* better. Thus, I made it a mission to put myself around him as frequently as possible. I wanted Will to be exposed to his passion, so I landed land him an internship a radio station in Southfield, Michigan. Every Wednesday I drove him to that internship, which lasted about eight months. With his love of music, Will grew from the experience. During one of our drives, I received a call from my friend Adrian at the mayor's office. "Mario," he said excitedly, "how would you like to leave a lasting legacy for the city of Detroit and for returning citizens? Mrs. Duggan says, quote, unquote, that 'You are the one,' that 'You get the job done.' She says that 'You men of LUCK are the real deal.'"

Having arrived at my destination, I pulled over and looked around at the hopelessness of Detroit's east side. I looked at my mentee with the ever-present grin on his face. This kid was resilient. No matter what, he always had a grin on his face and would give the shirt off his back. He was loyal to a disloyal world.

"I simply wish to bring glory to God, Adrian. I only wish to serve. I only wish to help young men like me," I replied.

"Well, just keep doing what you are doing. Stay focused and stay loyal to your vision," he said. Adrian was not only mentoring me, he was checking in on his "investment" of time and contacts, all of which are resources. I understood the message: stay focused. We recognize LUCK's value. And, how could he not? I had nearly killed myself in proving my sincerity. I never said no to an at-risk kid, and I always followed through.

The work I was doing had an impact, but when Rick and Cam joined, the level of impact was noticeably different. Jesus had given us the formula: "When two or more come in my name, so shall I be there." This verse resounded within my psyche during times of internal struggle within LUCK, Inc. This verse was my mantra when others would attempt to persuade me into believing that I alone could follow through with this systemically, transformational phenomena where the problem is transformed into the solution in a magnitude that a culture is transformed.

March, 2016, Gang Prevention from an Unlikely Source

At this time, I was still working for my family. I cleaned the entire office every night in pursuit of school and the development of LUCK, Inc. I had just gotten hired as a part-time direct-care worker for a stabilization program for fourteen to seventeen-year-old at-risk youths on Detroit's east side. That, too, was a midnight job on the weekends, and I was still going to school. I struggled financially, but it was worth it. Choosing the path of righteousness was creating a foundation for me out here upon which I could stand, enabling me to bear the weight load of the blessings that would befall me.

After speaking with a friend, I learned of a job opening as a program director for the non-profit agency that worked heavily for prisoner rights and freedoms called the American Friends Service Committee. The position entailed program creation and implementation for prisoners. It also entailed going back into the prisons, when invited, to run a parole-readiness workshop. I was excited, especially about the pay: $55,000 per year with full benefits for three years. I applied for the job and got through the first two phases of the interview process. Now, I eagerly prayed for a third, face-to-face interview. Such pay would change the quality of my life as I knew it.

A week later, while driving to the face-to-face interview I had long hoped for by American Friends Service Committee, I received a call from State Representative Harvey Santana. "Yo, Mario, waddup? You busy?" Vice-Chairman Santana said in his usually upbeat, assertive demeanor. I had been working with him over the past year in relation to gang intervention and prevention. On one occasion, he had the entire LUCK, Inc. team and a mentee give testimony in relation to the Detroit Public School debate. At that time, the argument was whether the schools needed more money or better staff. The testimony LUCK gave influenced the Appropriations Committee to the extent of doubling what was originally going to be given to the City of Detroit for gang prevention and disruption. I also connected him with high-level gang members who were on the inside, men he would otherwise never have gotten to know without an introduction and a "co-signing," just like one needs who has no credit. In this world, your word is your bond. One of the gang leaders, Romero, is the brother I sold my Corvette to.

About a year after my release in 2014, Rome discovered that I had been released on parole.

"How in the hell did you get a parole?" he asked in disbelief, for Romero knew the old Mario, the hustler, the schemer, the self-serving critical thinker. Romero had yet to meet the new Mario, the disciple, the student of life who sought to impart peace instead of the sword.

"You want to know the secret of getting to come home?" I said and laughed aloud. "The real question is are you ready for such *truths*?" I paused, leaving him with the understanding that this was *not* a rhetorical question. "Rome, I need you to listen very carefully. You do *not* get out of life what you *want*. You get out life what you *are*." I paused for effect.

"I am ready, my brother," he replied.

"Well, then since the student is ready, the teacher has appeared," I continued. "Romero, the *only way* that you will *ever* come home is if *you* become the *exact opposite* of what you *are*." I paused and then continued. "Since you were a youth, you have been recruiting other youths, other young men and women, into a dark world of drug trafficking, murder, and mayhem. You had to be stopped, thus, the universe stopped you. In order for you to ever come home, you must become the inverse of what you have been. You must become the goodness that is at your core, and then you need to recruit others for such a purpose. Only then will the universe deem it necessary for those gates to open. Only then will you be released," I concluded. A long pause ensued. Rome wasn't accustomed be spoken in that tone or in that manner. At that point, I didn't care. I needed him to *truly understand* that I did not come home by tricking the universe; the universe, it turns out, is much smarter than we think.

"You are right," he conceded.

I have been mentoring Romero since that day. He prepared a

five-minute audiotape and asked that I provide it to my boss at the time, State Representative Santana, and the Michigan House Appropriations Committee. As a result of Romero's powerful testimony, the committee *doubled* funding for gang prevention and disruptions for the city of Detroit. Below is a transcription of Romero's audiotape, made in the burrows of a level-five (the highest that exists in Michigan) maximum state prison, Ionia Maximum Facility in Ionia, Michigan.

Romero Silva's Transcript: February, 2016

My name is Romero Silva, Inmate number 295133. I am being housed in a level 5 maximum-security prison due to being designated an STG 2 security threat group gang leader. I've been affiliated with the Latin Count nation for over twenty years now. I was initiated into this gang by the co-founder of the chapter two branch of southwest Detroit, so I am recognized and respected as one of the originals. My reputation in this gang life is solidified but nothing to be proud of. There is no prison in the state of Michigan I can go to and not have to deal with some kind of negative energy due to the reputation I created for myself.

My whole life revolves around gang activity. I was raised into this gang life, and I was taught more about violence and drugs than anything else as a child. I have been in and out of juvenile detention centers, and I entered the prison system at the age of twenty. I have not been home since. I have always had this feeling in my heart that I was destined for something far greater in life than what I have chosen to dedicate my life to. Being a gang member was always something I felt I was misled into but once I took my oath, there was no turning back. I thought that this was my destiny, so I committed and dedicated and sacrificed my all and very easily rose to the top of the food chain where not only was I a member but a leader, a decider, a maker, a changer in laws, politics, conduct, purpose and goals. Thinking I was fulfilling my purpose in life I would make decisions based on mobility and looking for a positive change for the direction this gang was moving in. But no matter what was set in stone, it always ended up with a negative twist. Year after year, I watched so many of my closest associates fall victim to gang violence whether murdered in the streets or coming to prison for homicide. As the years passed, the more I matured, I realized how senseless the gang violence really is.

I'm here today to let my voice be heard. I speak from experience. I speak through pain, through adversity. I was there to help create this madness; now I'm here to help destroy it. I've witnessed the most horrible atrocities that gang life has to offer from people murdered in the streets to innocent people being victimized to inmates being stabbed viciously. The list goes on and on. The saddest part of all of this is watching the youth follow in our footsteps and glorifying this lifestyle. The madness has touched so close to home that my own son was shot twelve times in southwest Detroit in a case of mistaken identity by the same gang that I helped create. This has to end.

Gang violence is a huge problem in the city of Detroit, and it has plagued the public-school systems. To find a solution to this problem, one must understand the roots of this problem. What I understand through experience, the gang mentality is that someone is always looking up to someone. Pee-wees looking up to their elders, elders looking up to their chiefs, and nothing will ever change unless you can change the rules. You can put all of your effort into fixing the public-school systems. You can put all of your effort into reforming gang members in the streets. But you fail to realize that there are one hundred more active gang members waiting to be released from prison to fill their shoes.

The roots of this problem reside right here in this prison system. People like me who are known as living legends in this gang life who have the power to wreak havoc not only in every prison in Michigan, but also in every major city in Michigan. That is where the change has to come from. The MDOC is a breeding ground for gangs. Why? Because we have nothing else to live for in here. The same policy set in place by the MDOC to prevent gang activity is the same policy that has created the most vicious gang mentality I have seen yet. The policy is called STG (security threat group). At any given time, the administration can label you a gang member or a gang leader and place you on STG Phase 2 with as very little as an opinion or a suspicion that you are a gang member. The consequences that come from that is that you are sent to a Level 5 maximum security prison. You are locked in a cell twenty-three hours a day. You only get two one-hour non-contact visits per month. You are only allowed five fifteen-minute phone calls per week. You have no access to an electronic mailing system. Essentially, you are pretty much cut off from family, friends, loved ones and anyone that might have motivated you to do the right thing on your own.

There is no such standard to work your way off of STG. We are told that to be removed we must disassociate ourselves from any gang member or any gang activity, but then we are placed in a cellblock with all STG Phase 2 members. So now we must become anti-social. One example of why I have not been removed from STG is because I have a brother in the prison system who is also on STG and because he calls home to family members, I am being told that I cannot have contact with these same family members. I have not spoken to my own mom in over a year now. Now you tell me, what man will not start going insane? What man will not give up all hope with those kinds of restrictions? We are basically being kept alive in a coffin, and you have inmates who have been on this status for ten years or more now. They have basically turned them into savages. There is absolutely no program set in place whatsoever that give a gang member the opportunity to work his way off STG. And that is when a society can take advantage of attacking the root of the problem.

Create a program to reform gang members. Teach them how to be mentors. Educate them. Equip them with the tools that they need to come home and become a part of something positive in society. Prepare them to fill the shoes of being mentors and role models as opposed to just warehousing them until they get released and fill the position of gang members. Dig deep into the root of the problem and find individuals like me who have a respected name in this gang life who are willing to make a positive change. The same way that gang members listen to us for a negative purpose is the same way that they will listen to us for a positive purpose. We can reverse the process from negative to positive, chiefs to elders, elders to pee-wees. And that is how we can make a deep-rooted change in the streets and public-school systems of Detroit. Thank you for your time.

So, when Representative Santana called me that morning, I was excited to take his call. "Good morning, State Representative Santana. I am actually on my way to the third phase of an interview for American Friends Service Committee," I said with excitement.

"Really," he replied, but his tone was not soothing. "You don't seem like you'd be a good fit there," he said, "but who knows? Maybe you'll bring a different flavor." He continued, "I am looking to possibly hire someone to work on my staff. I need someone to go into all twenty-one of my schools in the ninth district and do a qualitative and quantitative data assessment on the schools. I want to understand everything that's going on within these schools before this Detroit Public School issue comes up in the months ahead. In addition, I want someone who can develop mentorship programs and implement them within those schools," he said and paused. "And, lastly, this person must be able to speak professionally and effectively with school administrators and pillars of the community. I was thinking about hiring Swift," he threw out, as if fishing. I hesitated. "What do you think?" he asked and waited patiently for a response.

Swift was a gangbanger from Southwest Detroit who I had recruited through one of my connections for an event that Representative Santana was hosting at Henry Ford High School. It consisted of a panel of educators and influential politicians, the ones responsible for the fate of DPS, in an educational-type seminar. "Swift," as he is called in the streets, was on parole after having served about five years for robbery. His message involved a failed school system that used social promotion as a means of advancing its students, resulting in "students" like Swift graduating with a fourth-grade reading level. Swift was definitely not *my* first pick for the job.

I liked this Mr. Santana, so I could not bear to see him make a fool of himself. I measured my words carefully. "I *think* you may be able to hire someone more qualified, sir. No disrespect intended."

"Like who?"

"Well, sir, you are talking about scholarly research. You are also talking about the ability to communicate with people in academia," I pointed out. "I don't know a lot of guys like that . . . except me," I almost mumbled.

"I wouldn't need you full time. If you do get that job today, you could do both," he continued. "It's not much more than what you are making now. However, I am giving you an opportunity to chase your passion, to perfect your craft and skill," he said. It would pay just under $35,000 for the year. "But there's one catch. The job ends on December 31st of this year because my term is up." I started to salivate when I did the math: that would be $90,000 for the year. I had only made $20,000 a year up to that point. "Think about it. Get back with me when you hear about this job," he said as I turned up the music and drifted toward the interview.

Life was changing fast. LUCK was a service provider for Good Intentions Industries of Detroit. I was on the verge of being hired to go back into prisons and create programs for prisoners. And now, I was being offered a job to pursue my passion: helping at-risk youth. I sat there listening to the music, remembering the prophecies of the past and simply smiled.

The job would also require that I miss a lot of the Good Intentions' workshops, so I was concerned about having to rely on Rick and Cam to back up Brian. So, before I accepted both jobs, I reiterated several times to Rick, "Are you sure that you and Cam can handle backing up Brian in training these two cohorts if I am tied up in these schools?"

"Bro, don't worry about it. It's no problem, we got your back," he responded without hesitation. "At the end of the day, it's your decision, Mario. We understand either way. But, know this: if you take that legislative aide position, LUCK, Inc. will have an essential key to many doors," Rick almost said in a whisper. We, Rick, Cam, and myself, looked at each other and grinned. "But, you *gotta* take the legislative aide position, bro'," Rick said as he broke out into a huge grin, and we all laughed in praise and excitement.

"In every purpose, God provides a Baker to bring the vision together, a Butler to open doors, and a Financier to fund the project. Fellas, we definitely found the butler," I said, in reference to the story of Joseph in the Old Testament.

I landed the American Friends Service Committee job and began working on March 1, 2016. I also met with Mr. Santana and accepted the terms offered. On March 15th of 2016, I was appointed as a Legislative Aide for the Vice-Chairman of the House Appropriations Committee, State Representative Harvey Santana, only two years home from a nineteen-year prison sentence for murder. I sat in awe not of the miracles, but of the Miracle Maker. I thought of the thunderous voice that scared me out of the shower just weeks before my release: "You cannot fathom the blessing that I have in store for you." Surely that was God.

It soon became clear that Representative Santana needed me much more than he had conveyed, which meant I was at a crossroads with a pregnant fiancée to be concerned about. I was extremely conflicted: on the one hand, I had security in the form of a job with full benefits for three years with the American Friends Service Committee, and that job paid $30,000 more per year; on the other hand, there was a once-in-a-lifetime opportunity for LUCK to positively influence children and the community by gaining access to the schools. It was a no brainer, right? No...not exactly.

As a man of faith, there are times when your vision of who you are to become is clouded by the realities of your present circumstances. My vision imparted upon me by the Creator said that I was supposed to help at-risk youth. But the realities of a pregnant wife and a job that would finish at the end of the year would shake the faith of the strongest of foundations. I had to make a choice, for the quality of the work within the schools would suffer exponentially if I tried to do both. From my perspective, saying no to helping the youth was out of the question. And, from the perspective of strategic positioning for LUCK, Inc., Rick and Cam understood what this opportunity meant.

So, I jumped into the abyss, banking on the legislative aide position and passion to push us toward our purpose. I therefore resigned as Program Director, after only two weeks, from the American Friends Service Committee and embraced the mission before me: help the at-risk youth on the west side of Detroit. I went from being told by the CEO of the Wayne County Juvenile Adjudication Complex that I would never set foot into a school to being appointed and hired by Representative Harvey Santana so that I could literally walk a mile in the shoes of the children. This job came with a salary and insurance, just in time for the birth of my *own* daughter.

Representative Santana introduced me to the principals of every school within his 9th District. "Mario has a story and a skill set to mentor and do interventions for at-risk young males. Please use him as you see fit," was Representative Santana's mimicked pitch, the same one, twenty-one times.

My assignment was to enter the schools unannounced, assessing the entire six-block perimeter from the mindset of a criminal. I used this cloak-and-dagger strategy to get a true assessment, not a façade: the good, the bad, and the ugly. "Now, look," he said to me, "when you go into these schools, you go in there as if you were going into one of those sixteen prisons you were in. Do you remember how you felt? What you thought? How you assessed the danger, the safety, the weak spots in the security?" I was trying to process what he was inferring. "Mario, you not only survived in the harshest environments, but you succeeded. You have the skill. Now think. Close your eyes and envision walking into the school as if you were walking into the prison yard. Go unannounced. Check for weaknesses in the security. Put yourself in the children's shoes. Do a four-block radius check around the school. See what the kids are seeing as they walk with their six-year-old sibling to school," he continued. We visited all twenty-one schools over a two-day period.

I was getting a crash course in *me*, in a skill set that I possessed, but didn't know I had. Representative Santana was *educating* me. He was "drawing out" of me my God potential, my essence. "I am going to pay you to assess the schools, and at the end, you will submit a comprehensive assessment. You will offer your mentorship skills to all principals who accept. And you will perfect your skills as you build your non-profit," he said. I was in shock.

Yet, as I went back to each school, only five of the twenty-one schools within the state's 9th District accepted me. Trained in scholarly research, I used thematic analysis to assess the schools, their environment, and the staff. It was sad. At a time when the Detroit Public Schools were screaming for more resources in mentoring, programs, and staff, Representative Santana was handing over each school a powerful resource in LUCK, Inc., that is, free professional mentors for the most at-risk youth. Mr. Santana continued to send me into those schools that shunned his offer. "Keep doing cold calls. They want to bitch, cry, and complain about no resources then deny the most effective resources they could have?! Keep gathering the data," was his usual response when I would inform him of the principal's refusal to allow me entry to their schools.

What was learned from the data I gathered is exactly what Representative Harvey Santana and the men of LUCK who had experienced the impact of environment on behavior within the prison setting had been saying all along. The problem is rooted in their primary, first, classroom: the home. It was at home where children learn the disempowering coping skills to life's everyday challenges, whether those conflicts are within or without. There existed a significant population within the impoverished schools of the ninth district that involved children entering the classroom (fourth through twelfth grades) lacking the proper social and coping skills for their age. Teachers were performing the duties of social workers, therapists, and the role of parents, before they could even teach the curriculum.

Compounding the problem of the children getting a slow start in life because of inadequate education of life skills at home was corruption within the Detroit Public School (DPS) system. Add to that a racket that Lansing (State Government) was engineering by setting up the DPS system to fail to the benefit of the private sector charter school system, a result of successful lobbying. That is how this thing called our government works: money. Money talks and bullshit walks, and in a city like Detroit, money moves pimp, pastor, and police alike.

There were over fourteen indictments involving DPS principals, administrators, and a seventy-year-old crooked service provider who provided kickbacks for the contracts handed to him by the principals, but who failed to reciprocate with the services that the contract demanded. This robbed the children of basic educational needs and services.

As I walked through the schools and witnessed the apathetic attitudes, aggressive speech toward the children, and a complete brainwashing of precious young minds who were being yelled at to keep quiet in the halls or sit still in the lunchroom for an hour because they no longer have gym, I became disheartened. The schools took away gym, music, and recess, and then forced the children to obey at a desk, obey during lunch, obey on a bathroom break. It's as if our public schools are reproducing brainwashed, obedient servants who will not threaten the status quo compared to affluent, privileged, private schools that teach the kids *how to think* instead of *what to think*. In Michigan, school budgets are based on property taxes, thus further separating the economic disparities and divide.

You can never connect the dots looking forward; you can only connect them looking back. It was not until I began the process of healing with my father that God sent me the most powerful mentor of my life: Harvey Santana. He has expanded, refined, challenged, and nurtured me unapologetically. He literally pulled it out of me. Mr. Santana saw in me that which I could not see in myself. That is the importance of a mentor, a trusted teacher and advisor.

Though I worked full-time for Representative Santana, I continued to lead the growth of LUCK Inc. My vision of employing transformed men to train at-risk populations was slowly coming into fruition. Ironically, God knew what He was doing when I was not allowed entry into social work, for my accounting skills empowered me to work with the tax attorney in the development of the 501(c)(3) status. The business degree positioned me, mentally, to pursue contracting.

Rick, Cam, Brian, and I continued to work the Good Intentions' contract that provided legitimacy for LUCK. My accounting skills and business training was prepping me to represent the transformed men in an arena that was not friendly and required a certain skill. God gave me the vision and forced me to learn the required skills by both opening and closing doors, and it is during this process that one must focus on principles over feelings. We understood the needs of our population, for we were that population, so LUCK provided an extra twelve hours of work, in addition to certificates and refreshments.

We understood two things: 1) It's difficult to mentor and teach a person who is hungry. This is why Jesus turned 5 fish into 5,000; and 2) the more time that we spend with our clients, our mentees, the better the outcomes. We connected with the most disconnected populations, and in that, we found our meaning, our purpose, our *why*. This skill formed and fashioned within Michigan's harshest prisons came at a high price, one most would be unwilling to pay. The men of LUCK have walked that mile in our client's shoes, and then, after that mile, we exited prison and walked a mile in the citizen's shoes who pursued education and advancement. This put us in a position to *lead* the most resistant of populations toward a path of transformation and purpose.

The funds garnered from the Good Intentions' contracting were used to pay the men to train every Tuesday, for an entire year, thus, I was forced to pay them well. I could not expect them to reserve their Tuesday, indefinitely, cheaply. The rest of the funds went towards the mentoring and life coaching of those at-risk youths within the schools that we entered during my tenure as a legislative aide. We purchased over a hundred chessboards for our chess clubs. We purchased and distributed over 500 books in the summer of 2016 in a book club LUCK calls *Real Men Read*. LUCK provided for the movies tickets, popcorn/pop, transportation, and chaperoning for the entire middle school (over 100 students) to attend the showing of the movie *Birth of a Nation*, a powerful movie for these disenfranchised youths. One thing for sure that the Wayne State University School of Business was teaching me: invest in your company by valuing your product. Our product was the transforming of the most at-risk populations.

Summer of 2016, Forty Days in the Desert

In time, as the bills piled up and the demands of life increased, Rick began to get more contracting with his painting company. With Cam as his right-hand man in the painting company, their training and commit to LUCK grew weak and distant. Brian and I were left to become creative and consistent. Training was our passion, our purpose, so we took advantage of any and every opportunity to shift and shape the minds of those that we once were. Brian, imprisoned for eighteen years from the age of eighteen, and I have experienced a different, not necessarily more intense, just differ-ent, pain threshold and unique trauma, the easement of which is only brought about by reaching out to those who are hurting with similar pain. We felt compelled into that training workshop with an agenda in mind, with a sword in the form of words whose point had been sharpened for several days. These were our gifts turned into skills while in prison. We had been doing this for free for over a decade; thus, to be paid for it was divine.

Yet, Rick and Cam brought other gifts turned into skills within that same hardened environment, so God has continued to pull them toward their purpose that parallels and empowers LUCK's. Eventually, however, Rick and Cam completely walked away from LUCK, Inc. Five entire months passed without communicating with my confidants who co-founded my only reason for existing at the time: LUCK, Inc.

Rick and Cam had assumed that I had positioned myself as the sole owner of LUCK, but I had filed as a non-stock (non-profit) status company, which entailed no "possession" of ownership. In addition, the funds being paid from Good Intentions were being distributed according to one's work. Also, they were upset that Brian was getting paid more than them, and, yet, Brian had been doing more work at that time than Rick and Cam combined.

"LUCK is a non-stock company, a concept you obviously don't understand," I would argue. "You don't get *dividends* or a higher pay just because you co-founded LUCK. You must do the work. Period," I would say, unyielding, for my purpose was bigger than their agenda or egos.

The stress of lacking resources as we pursued our purpose created a lot of tension amongst us. I was becoming angry and bitter that I was doing most of the work in the building of LUCK. While Brian assisted in the pre-development stages of the Conflict Resolution curriculum, for the most part, the responsibility was on my shoulders to create the rest, in addition to filling out the paperwork needed for the filing of the 501(c)(3), nonprofit status. While I understand that God has placed me in a position to do more since I *owe* more, I have, at times, failed to recall that inverse relationship of blessing and burden, leading me to still fall short. I *know* that my *cross* is justifiably heavier, but I am human, and, in that, exists fallibility.

I built the curriculum, drafted the extensive paperwork for the filing of the federal 501(c)(3) status, accepted *insecurity* as I represented us in the legislature, and shared the training and facilitating responsibilities with Brian during this short but dark period in LUCK's development. Finally, Lus came home, another one of my trainers from inside, so he was able to make that essential third pillar to our proverbial stool.

Upon Lus' release, I drove two hours out to see him in Adrian, Michigan, and handed him a LUCK one-sheet, which was simply an informational brochure that explained who LUCK is and what we do. As we sat at his kitchen table, his humble father cooked tacos for a house full of Lus' nieces and nephews. "We need you, Lus. Detroit needs you. The children who are carrying guns and embracing this lifestyle that *you* once promoted . . . *need* you." I planted a mustard seed that night. I walked away from Lus with another whisper to God. "Thank you, God. The team is coming together."

In time, Lus moved out to Detroit in pursuit of his purpose— that is, to train and mentor the at-risk populations that LUCK was seeking to influence, just as he had done inside with ACL. Lus struggled as he worked in barbershops, barely making ends meet because of the process that one must endure in developing loyal clients. We didn't yet have enough money to hire him, but he followed LUCK whenever we were in need. He sacrificed his secure job in a factory that was in the same town where his entire family lived, the family who had awaited his return for over twenty-years. He gave up all of that to pursue meaning and purpose, for that internal peace that he could only get from imparting peace upon others. A fair sentence for so much harm that he, and all of us men of LUCK, had handed out to others, whether directly or indirectly.

Lus saw what *his Garden of Eden* looked like and he wanted to get back to that place where one is in complete alignment with the presence of God to help bring forth the kingdom of heaven on earth. Lus was at every training session for Good Intentions and shadowed me through the rest of my legislative experience within the schools of Detroit. Through hardship and struggle, he *became* the effective mentor and facilitator "out here" just as he had been inside. He also mentored me as I was feeling the overwhelming stress of a soon-to-be father.

The pressure of knowing that I would not have a job come the midnight hour of December 31, 2016, pushed my limits throughout the year beyond what I knew was possible. For example, Brenda went into labor the evening hours of Friday, July 8, and it lasted until midnight of July 10, which was a Sunday. I was by her side every moment. I had to replace one midwife and help coach my wife through a strenuous birth. My daughter was born with the umbilical cord wrapped around her neck twice. She was purplish-colored and had to be resuscitated. Even then, still, that Monday morning I went to both schools where I was scheduled to train and mentor. "I am shocked to see you here, my brother," said Brian, a LUCK employee, friend, and my trainer while inside prison.

Just that past Friday, Brian and I had argued as we exited Cody

High School. The pressures of family, school, work, and personal life were wearing on us. While I was actively pursuing contracting for LUCK, I still included Rick and Cam in the vision. This weighed heavily on Brian, but the vision God showed me included all of us. As we walked in different directions towards our cars, Brian and I raised our voices at each other in frustration. We hadn't said a word to each other, until then.

"I won't have a job in four months, which means no insurance for my daughter," I said, forgetting about last Friday's argument just as Brian had, "Let's transform some minds," with a high five. I loved that about Brian. He was always emotionally mature enough to rise above the conflicts and be reasonable. "I want our product to be the blue magic in the movie *American Gangster*. Denzel focused on having the best product. If we focus on the product, then it will sell itself. As it is written, *your gifts will make room for you*. So, too, will our product make room for us. I want our effect on these populations to be so great that we have to turn contracts down because the waiting list is so long."

We walked into Cody High to train and mentor some of the most at-risk and hardened high-school students in one of Detroit's most impoverished and violent neighborhoods. As we walked, I felt lighter, calmer. God saw my daughter through that challenging birth, I thought, relieved and in a state of gratitude. With that obstacle behind me, I now focused on the mission at hand: positioning LUCK to safeguard the community by employing transformed men with the required skills to shift disempowering paradigms and belief systems in impoverished neighborhoods.

Fall of 2016, LUCK is a Threat to Market Share

Prisoners, returning citizens, and public-school children are cash cows for the for-profit and non-profit worlds. In Detroit, greed transcends color, as Dr. Michelle Alexander eloquently depicts in her page-turner, *The New Jim Crow*. It truly is about the "haves versus the have nots," and not black versus white, where principles and government agents continue to be indicted on fraud, embezzlement, and white collar unarmed robberies upon populations so vulnerable that they have been given socially recognized "help" that translates more into words than anything tangible. Somehow the millions that are sent from the legislatures to the non-profits and contracted companies never make it to the returned citizen or the school children in Detroit. In 2016, approximately fourteen principals in Detroit were indicted for embezzling money designated for their school children. If the money is not directly embezzled, it's lost in administrative salaries, wages, and expenses, aka "miscellaneous." Turns out that Rep. Santana was right. It wasn't necessarily the lack of resources, but the use of those resources that resulted in the Detroit Public Schools being in the condition they were in. The kids and the returned citizens were getting pimped six ways from Sunday. Thus, it would be disadvantageous for any crook that was stealing from the children to allow former crooks too close to the crime scene. It was no wonder that LUCK was being blackballed from the Detroit Public Schools. Of course, in public it was because of the felony stain on our records, but in private, the real felons had yet to be revealed.

LUCK, Inc. was trailblazing the way through new territories in terms of reentry and offender success. And with all success, as my mentor Rep. Santana says, comes enemies. One minute LUCK was receiving an award from Good Intentions Industries' "Change the Story" program as "The Most Effective Conflict Resolution & Anger Management Team in the Nation" to the next moment being fired from servicing that very organization. When the program participants and the staff at "Change the Story" complained about LUCK's absence, they were told that LUCK was too expensive.

Little did they know that LUCK had never set a price. We even offered to train the cohorts *pro bono* simply because it is the cross that we must bear, it's the cross that brings us peace. Despite our clear impact, LUCK was let go due to "budgetary cuts" at a time when violence and murder were rampant in the streets of Detroit.

The truth is that LUCK is *the product* delivering *the product,* and in the Detroit non-profit scene, that's likened to the prostitute becoming his or her own pimp. As the *48 Laws of Power*'s first law states: "Never outshine the master." But outshine we did. You cannot lead someone from someplace that you have not travelled, and this is exactly what the non-profits of Detroit were attempting to do. At the best of times, LUCK was able to use the Good Intentions' funds to reward its trainers with good wages and have resources for the children that we mentored in the 9th district public schools that accepted us as I continued to expand our network through my legislative position. At the worst of times, Bitter was trying to divide the co-founders of LUCK by offering Rick a job after ending our services. According to Rick, after he politely declined, Bitter responded, "I'm not trying to start anything between you and Mario, but is it because you're scared to go out on your own?" It was not simply the strain of losing the Good Intentions' contract, but the inconceivable challenges of reentry and family reunification that brought LUCK, Inc. to the precipice of dying before it had even walked.

Winter of 2016, The Mediators Need Mediation

The job with Representative Santana had been extremely overwhelming, pushing me to the breaking point. The work was extensive and the pay little. I took a short-term sacrifice for a long-term reward that only I was shown. Thus, as the farmer watered his Chinese bamboo tree for the third, fourth, and fifth year without it breaking ground, so, too, did I continue to pour into LUCK Inc., literally, all that I had.

It seemed that the closer I got to my purpose, the more challenging it got, from my wife telling me that LUCK had been a waste of time and money to facing unemployment once Representative Santana's term was up. Deep inside, I craved the security that a steady job would provide. I quietly prayed that prayer that Jesus prayed. "Father, if it is your will, please pass this cup from my lips." For the first time in decades, I was afraid. The month of December was constant pressure, all rooted in lack of resources, both tangible (job, money, housing, transportation, etc.) and intangible (skills and tools to respond effectively to the stressors of life). One day a few weeks before Christmas, my wife said, "Imagine if you had devoted all this time to the accounting firm instead of LUCK." Or even more undermining was her response to my excitement when I told her that I had applied to Wayne State University's Latino and Boricua (Puerto Rican) studies department. All they wanted was for me to recruit and retain Latino students. I would have loved to recruit my own people towards advancement.

"What other applications have you put in, *mi amor*?" was Brenda's response, gently yet assertively. Comments like these tore at my very essence, for they challenged the whispers I heard from the Spirit when I begged God, on my knees, for a glimpse of direction, a hint of what to do to please Him. The only answers I had gotten thus far had been to pursue the mission of LUCK.

Yet, LUCK, Inc. as we knew it was falling apart. Rick and I were on the verge of a lawsuit against each other as he tried to get a payout to leave. "Just give me $2,000, and I will walk away with no legal action," he sent in a text message.

"Is that all you're worth? Is that all your *purpose* is worth?" I responded in text. I admit, it got ugly, and, yet, that is what brothers, and especially brothers who are business partners, do sometimes. They fight.

After a public statement by Rick on social media clarifying his separation from LUCK, Mrs. Duggan contacted me immediately. "Mario, I've been gone to Florida for two weeks! What in the world has happened?" she asked with fear in her voice. Mrs. Duggan loved LUCK and the men of LUCK. She breathed life into both.

"Rick has been acting like an ass for a few months," I snapped. "I just hadn't said anything. We don't need him," I said half-heartedly. My very essence knew that God had included him in the equation, in the vision imparted upon me. So much so, that as Rick sent insult after insult during his absence from LUCK, I continued to draft the Strategic Plan and Program Proposals that included Rick and Cam. This caused tension between Brian and me, which led to mediation between us that was governed by Lus. Turned out, both Lus and Brian were giving me an ultimatum: either let Rick and Cam go, or they were leaving LUCK. That mediation between Brian and I occurred just days before Rick released the social media announcement stating he was no longer with LUCK.

"Whether he is in or out, this *must* be settled," she continued. "Now should I call him to set up a meeting, or do you think Adrian should?"

"Adrian," I replied meekly. "Rick likes Adrian, and he may think that you aren't neutral when it comes to me." She agreed. Within hours, Adrian intervened and demanded a meeting of the men of LUCK.

We all agreed to meet in the lobby of a remote hotel. It would be Lus, Rick, Cam, Brian, Adrian, and me. "I figured this would be a good spot to meet," said Adrian as he shook my hand and gave me a long embrace. "How do you feel?" he asked.

"I try not to," I replied. "I try to just go with the facts. And the fact is this motherfucker thinks that he can steal this company out from under me after I gave it my blood, sweat, and tears for *three* straight years!"

"I know, I know, but I need you to remain calm, Mario. Do you hear me?" asked Adrian, much taller than me, looking down and deep into my eyes.

"Okay, okay," I promised Adrian as we made our way to the area designated for this mediation. Ironically, despite the fact that we teach mediation, this was the last option that we exercised. It was a humbling reality.

There were many underlying issues on each side. At first, the meeting went from bad to worse. Later, Adrian confessed, "I thought LUCK was over." But we hung in there and did our best to practice what we preach. First, Rick and Cam acknowledged the sweat equity that I had poured into LUCK. In other words, they *validated* my truth. Hearing this helped to calm me down. "Mario, I know that you have sacrificed *literally* everything for LUCK." Then Rick used his assertive communication training to tell me what he wanted without finger-pointing or blame. "I just want more transparency, more involvement," said Rick.

"Rick, I've said it before, and I will say it again, to you and to everyone, my vision for LUCK has always been one that involves it continuing to exist in our absence, when Mario doesn't exist, when Rick doesn't exist, when Cam doesn't exist, LUCK, Inc. *will* exist. LUCK must continue for the betterment of the community. I did not start my own painting company or my own t-shirt company to pay my bills like you guys did. But I can no longer sustain LUCK on my own," I said, looking the men around me in the eye as I choked back the tears.

Then we took it to the next level, the hard work of getting at the real feelings beneath the anger.

"I had a daughter on the way when I chose to put LUCK, Inc. first, even at the sacrifice of what was best for her," I said as a tear rolled down my cheek. "Rick, the truth is you have had an influence on my life that I can never repay," I said looking into his eyes. "You vouched for me when I had no credibility to stand on, but you have hurt me. I feel betrayed. You were duplicitous with the information regarding the contracting and the request for proposal," I said and glared into his watery eyes. "Even still, the vision that has been given to me includes you, thus, it is not my choice but God's. You are a leader . . . so lead," I finished as Rick wiped away a tear.

"I love you, Rick," I said and then turned to Cam. "And I love you, Cam. But I need you both to get into the game because I can't do it without you." We all embraced and made a commitment to LUCK and to the creation of a better process in its development and expansion.

Mrs. Duggan, of course, was in pure joy upon hearing of the news. I simply sent her a picture of all of us together, mentored by Adrian who continues to be a light upon LUCK's path toward transformative progress. In the end, effective communication *does* work in reaching understanding.

January, 2017, LUCK Lands Contracting

The first contract with the Detroit Employment Solutions Corporation (DESC) was for LUCK to train and mentor (up to) 600 returning citizens. It was a blind-bid process that resulted in two service providers standing after the initial Request for Proposal shakeout, a proposal that took me four consecutive non-stop days and a miracle of insurance coverage. As irony would have it, A Chance to Live (Tanya and James) was LUCK's only serious competitor for the bid. Called in for follow-up questions in relation to the request for qualification/quote that I submitted on LUCK's behalf, we walked into the downtown board room of the DESC where Tanya literally acted as if she were seeing a ghost and James was cool as ice, as usual. "Mario, Brian, well, hello, there," Tanya stuttered in shock. Clearly, LUCK and A Chance to Live had been kept in the blind that we had both been invited to the same meeting. "Well, well, hello there," I said as I embraced both in due respect. Brian was reserved, yet respectful as always.

The meeting was run by then acting president Jose Reyes. It was clear that LUCK's work as service providers for returning citizens over the past few years spoke volumes. A Chance to Live spewed rhetoric as the men they were contracted to serve suffered from the lack of essential basic needs, let alone an empathetic ear to provide faith and action. At one point as we were negotiating over pricing, I said, "We have been doing this for free for over a decade, helping men like us transform. I used to chase money. Money is not the concern. If it were, then someone would probably be tied up and in a trunk right now." As we walked out, Brian and I stayed after making small talk with the security guard working the front desk. As Tanya walked by she motioned me over.

"Mario, don't you dare do this work for free." My so-called mentor was now trying to counsel me. I stared deep into her eyes with pity.

"I'd do it for free just to make sure that you two crooks don't get it," I countered. She just didn't get it, did she? Her "clients," our "clients" are us, the men of LUCK. We were those men. We are those men. LUCK men had literally walked that proverbial mile, and in that pain, we found our passion to help those like us simply so they could choose better . . . be better. In the end, we were contracted to assist high-level parolees reintegrate back into the community, another prophecy fulfilled.

Cam, Rick, Lus, and I carried the baton, as Brian was engrossed in an internship at a successful law firm during his days as a paralegal. His nights were consumed as he pursued a Bachelor's degree from the local college. We set up systems and positions. Then we brought on a team of men who have been doing this work with us for years, the peacemakers of Jackson Prison yard, the same men that the Chance to Live organization had shunned upon their release.

In the end, we trained and mentored over 300 returned citizens over the 2017 contract with the DESC, connecting over 100 parolees with jobs. In addition, LUCK contracted a transportation service company that provided the transport to and from work for those high-risk offenders that lacked transportation. LUCK also provided the work attire (steel toe work boots, uniforms, clothes, etc.) for most of these men and women. All the while, LUCK was paying out of pocket for the aforementioned expenses. What was LUCK's contract for then? To motivate, mentor, and provide family reunification therapy, which LUCK fulfilled.

However, it's challenging to mentor an at-risk young man who has an empty stomach. It's also impossible to connect such a man with a job when he has no transportation, no license, no money for work attire, etc. LUCK filled the basic needs of the client before attempting to expand their vision of themselves, and then coach them towards that vision. We were successful in mitigating unnecessary violence and harm upon the family by simply being there for people who had no one to turn to, no helping hand to guide them through the maze of the criminal justice system upon release. We mentored and coached men who had served forty-nine of the last fifty years in prison, men who became our family, men who now serve LUCK, Inc.

The second contract was for a middle school in River Rouge, even though LUCK had never volunteered time or skills in a River Rouge school. The Detroit Schools denied our service vendor status because of the crime that I had committed at the age of sixteen, but they accepted our services for free. But to me, competition in this Detroit racket called the non-profit world was a no-no. The River Rouge Request for Proposal was twenty-nine pages and took me nine days to complete. By the Grace of God, it was successful.

LUCK was determined to transform this at-risk middle school's culture within two years. Another challenge met and another prophecy fulfilled: we were going to have a generational effect on these children's lives. LUCK was now positioned to employ the transformed men that were with them in Jackson Cooper Street in the bold mission of reducing the violence and victimization, first in the City of Detroit and, then, the rest of the inner cities in America.

LUCK continues to grow, for the trained Peacemakers continue to come home from prison. The harshness has served as a process of purification that has catapulted these men, these imprisoned apostles, to a spiritual awareness likened to a sage. While the program at Jackson continues, its validity and effectiveness does not. In time, as we men of ACL were being released in droves, James' true intentions to not hire any of the men he had trained were made known, and this did not sit well with the men still inside.

Yet when the men of ACL call me, I always say the same thing. "It's a platform for you to become that which you were destined to become: a citizen." I even proselytize those men who call me and choose not to participate in programming like ACL. "It will give you skills and tools that you *must* have out here in order to succeed. Never forget: it is not *what* you get but *who* you become that will determine your destiny." The men listen because I have been where they are.

The other men of LUCK are full-time college students who desire to give more, and therefore, need to absorb more. We are determined to reduce senseless victimization through the educating and life coaching of the most at-risk. We have partnered with agencies that share a vision of peace and prosperity by transforming the problem into the solution.

Home now for more than three years, LUCK, Inc. has made an impact on the Detroit community. It has become clear that the men of LUCK, Inc. connect with an otherwise disconnected population. In pursuit of transforming the criminal ailment of selfishness, rationalization of criminal behavior, and a complete inability to empathize that enables a criminal mind to victimize others, LUCK life coaches have devoted their lives to training and mentoring populations that they were once a part of. The work continues to grow, and now, LUCK is reinvesting in its own vision by hiring more transformed men in the fulfillment of the contracts.

May, 2017, Restoration and Healing

As LUCK continued to expand its reach, we innovated and adapted to the needs of the clients. It was clear long ago that entrepreneurship would be the path for reformed criminals like us because we had the raw material needed such as the ability to take risks. Our only shortfall comes in the form of not knowing any better. Once taught the skills of business, finance, and psychology, coupled with an increased ability to be emotionally intelligent, returned citizens possess the drive, stamina, and chip on their shoulder to prove to the world, including them, that they are, indeed, somebody.

So as co-director, Rick sent me to Texas to review an entrepreneurship training for felons. On May 5, as I sat at the breakfast table in the hotel reading a new book, my phone rang. I looked and saw that I had two missed calls from Tracy, Damion Todd's friend who would sometimes send messages from Damion who is still in prison after thirty years from the age of sixteen. Damion was soon to be re-sentenced under the new Juvenile Lifer Law. I immediately picked up.

"Waddup Tracy?" I said, hoping to hear that Damion would soon be coming home.

"Hello, Mario?" said a timid voice. "You may not remember me," she said gently.

"Oh, shit, are you Tracy from back in the day? Samuel's Tracy?" I said in shock, hoping it wasn't.

Tracy was my victim Samuel's girlfriend. She had testified against me twice, once in each murder case. She had been on the phone with Samuel when I paged him from Jay's house hours before the murder. She would barely look at me in court, and when she did, I saw the pain that I had imparted upon that innocent soul.

"Yes. You remember?" she asked, timid yet a little more firmly.

"Tracy," I humbly expressed. "Every breath I take I do so in order to make up for all the pain and heartache that I caused you and his family. I beg that one day you may forgive me. Not for me but for yourself. I already hurt so many people and to not forgive me simply means that my shortcomings are still hurting you. I don't want to hurt anyone any more, Tracy. I am no longer that sixteen-year-old boy who is angry and hurting," I said. I listened to almost ten seconds of silence in fear of what was to come.

"About two years ago I saw your picture on Facebook with a Bullock Marshall. I was scared that they let you out and angry. I was confused because *you killed Samuel*, my boyfriend, and now you were in this picture with my other friend, Bullock. So now I was afraid that you might harm him as well," she finally expressed, as the pain that I had caused this woman so long ago surfaced. "I've been watching you for over two years, Mario. I called you to simply say I am very proud of you and that *I forgive you*." Tears fell upon the book that I was reading. To hear my victim's girlfriend say that she forgave me *and* that she was proud of me was priceless. In that one act lays the essence of God ... *pure love*.

Later that month, Tracy met me at LUCK's event where we hosted over 100 returned citizens on parole and flew in the New York Time's bestselling author Shaka Senghor at LUCK's expense to speak life into the minds of the parolees. LUCK's desire was to expand the vision and potential the parolees possessed to become greater. At the end of that night, Tracy looked at me and said, "I met the real Mario today, and I like *that* Mario."

"Oh, Tracy, how I wish I would not have taken Samuel's life, but I'm not that boy any more. I don't even remember that boy. Today, you see Mario the man, a man who understands his purpose and his reason for being." I hugged her, bringing restoration and healing to the once broken pieces that still lingered within us.

Tracy soon became a family member of LUCK, Inc. She even employed us as we slowly developed a construction company called Rebuilt Solutions: Rebuilt Properties by Rebuilt Men. She even employed us to paint her parents' home, a sign of her trust in who we'd become and in LUCK, Inc.

After our contract with DESC ended, Rick and I had to lay off the entire team. We held the meeting in the Level One Bank conference room as we explained the unfortunate news and handed each man a check. "This is only temporary, fellas. In the interim, we are blessed to have an opportunity for some of you men to canvas for the mayor's re-election, and others will be hired by the Detroit School of Digital Technology, a partner of LUCK's that is helping the returning citizens and veterans in Southwest Detroit." In addition to that last check, Rick and I decided that as a bonus and an investment in our team that we would have the entire team trained in Restorative Practices with a concentration on schools, the first of its kind in Michigan. I told Rick that I wanted to put Tracy on the team. I knew the pain that such training would unravel if Tracy was on our team but didn't want to shy away from the growth that I would undergo. Empathy awareness training is a powerfully transformative tool, and, to a certain degree, having Tracy in the group would be just that for the LUCK men, especially me.

"Absolutely, my brother," Rick quickly responded. "I think that would be good for both of you. It will bring a lot of healing."

Rick was correct, as usual. The training consisted of thirty-two hours, four consecutive eight-hour days, and unending workshops and group projects that focused on *how you feel,* exactly that which I try to avoid.

On the third day, the instructor put a group together that consisted of a female Wayne County sheriff, Cam, and Zeek, another LUCK coach. The instructor appointed the female sheriff as the Restorative Justices Coordinator who was to run a mock circle. Restorative Practices uses the powerful symbol of the "circle" because it implies community, connection, inclusion, fairness, equality and wholeness. Circles have evolved in every culture resulting from the natural formation of people sitting around a fire, providing the best way to effectively distribute access to heat and light. When schools and other groups arrange people in a circle, there is no fire but instead an issue or topic that is relevant to everyone gathered.

In this mock circle, the "coordinator" (female sheriff) had created a simulated issue that was a normal facet of everyday challenges in the lives of students: the loss of a loved one. The sheriff asked, "If you could bring anyone back to life, who would it be and why?"

I immediately looked at Tracy. We locked eyes, and she tried to comfort me from across the room but to no avail. Tears welled up in my eyes. The first person to speak was Cam. My mind raced and all I could think of was the greatest regret of my existence: taking Samuel's life. One tear fell and then another.

I don't recall what Cam said, but I snapped out of my daze as I noticed it was now my turn to respond to the question. I looked at the "coordinator" and back at Tracy, now understanding that the sheriff had no idea about my connection to Tracy. I lowered my head as the tears fell and said, "If I could, I would bring Samuel back, even at the cost of my own life, because I am the one who took his life." Roy, the instructor, put one hand on my shoulder as the exercise continued.

Later, the female sheriff apologized when she discovered that Tracy had also been a victim of my crime. "I am so sorry, Mario. I had no idea."

"I needed this. Tracy needed this. Your circle was effective," I reassured her as we hugged. Just as mediation worked in prison, Restorative Practices works in the community by bringing new information to old wounds through a healing process that brings victim and perpetrator towards wholeness.

Thus, Tracy and the LUCK Team were trained and certified in Restorative Practices aimed at transforming the inner-city schools. Both offender and offended, perpetrator and victim, can be transformed into peacemaker and victor. God is good.

August 2017, "Mario is going to Blackball LUCK, Inc. from Detroit"

The funny thing about real mentors, those authentic and genuine trusted teachers and counselor, is that they will generally tell you what you *need* to hear and not what you *want* to hear. It has been written that a wise man learns from another's mistakes. Therein lies the value in mentoring relationships. While you can lead a horse to water, you cannot make him drink. So, too, with mentorship. The onus is on the mentee, the "student," to be open and ready for the teacher.

Our contractors, DESC, had walked away owing us $180,000 with no contract renewal. In the final meetings, we were told, "You didn't manage your budget for the contract correctly." With a Bachelor of Science in Accounting from Wayne State University's varsity league business program, in terms of business, not much gets past me.

"Excuse me, sir, we were awarded this contract at a $400 per client, per month, price. That is it. $400 a month will prevent a high-risk parolee from re-offending because LUCK goes that extra mile. After signing that contract, you handed us a list of 300 men with the mission of reconnecting and mentoring them at all costs. We did that and then some. And, now, going on three months without pay, you say that we went outside the scope of the budget?" I asked.

Of the $5 Million Labor Grant for "reentry," LUCK received $127,000 to reconnect with 300 parolees that they had completely lost track of in a program designed to increase offender success. Though the contract required LUCK to service these high-risk parolees through June 30th of 2017, when LUCK was approaching the $127,000 threshold in February of the same year, we were told, "Continue servicing these parolees. We will find the money. You guys are too important in protecting the community, and we cannot just stop servicing these parolees." In the end, LUCK was strung along for three months with no pay as we paid a team of fifteen parolees to protect the community. LUCK never received the money, even after producing the hard evidence of services rendered. Standing in front of a debilitated building in Detroit's Southwest Latino district, Lus, Rick, and I were helping clean several homes that needed to be boarded up as we awaited a contract renewal that never happened. Once again, the poverty pimps of Detroit one... and LUCK zero. Then the phone rang.

"It's Adrian," Rick said as he puts him on speaker phone and put his finger to his mouth to let Lus and me know to stay quiet.

"Rick," yelled Adrian, "thank you for taking my call. Do you have a minute?"

Of course," as Adrian began a twenty-two-minute tangent on how "Mario is blackballing LUCK, Inc. because of his abrasiveness. He is short-tempered, and he offended many important people in his speech at that Ceasefire event. He owes them an apology."

I listened to the entire conversation without uttering a word. Truth is, the rhetoric that Adrian was spewing came first-hand from the very men who were trying to destroy LUCK. But in their ignorance, they strengthened us, for it is written: "What

my enemies meant for ill, God meant for good." Adrian's senti-
ments were resonating from a speech I had been compelled to give,
against my own will, several months earlier for a program called
Ceasefire, which is intended to reduce the gun violence in Detroit's
most violent zip codes. Ceasefire targets specific gang members
who are on parole or probation and requires them to report to
a "Call In," a meeting with Detroit's Federal Prosecutor Barbara
McQuade, Police Chief James Craig, and Mayor Mike Duggan. In
reality, Ceasefire is merely a type of dragnet used by law enforcement to trap perpetrators in the most gun-related violent zip codes
in Detroit. I can't say I blame them, for it's a last-ditch effort to
curb the rampant violence, crime, and victimization within the
most impoverished Detroit neighborhoods. Yet, these people are
victims themselves of systemic genocide on the minority have-nots.

LUCK had been volunteering pro bono for three years, trying
to impart a positive influence on this subject matter for which
we held proverbial doctorates. Since Ceasefire targets those with
probation or parole status, these people are the same population
that LUCK tries to positively influence in our mission to keep the
community safe.

Unfortunately, Ceasefire of Detroit was not aiming at providing more resources to these offenders who were struggling with
reintegration. They faced socio-economic challenges rooted in a
lack of pro-social skills and a support base that could guide them
through the painful process of reform. Resources were only given
to those who assisted in the investigation and criminal prosecution
of prospective offenders. Thus, the funds were being used to coerce,
bribe, or extort those in legally and economically vulnerable positions to attempt to close cases.

Now two years later, I could no longer jeopardize LUCK's brand
by associating with an organization that was trying to incarcerate
instead of rehabilitate. So, I submitted an assessment of Ceasefire

to the mayor's office explaining that LUCK could not associate with the program any longer because it threatened our brand value, our ability to connect with otherwise disconnected populations. To associate with such a task force was not only deadly to LUCK's brand value, but, in reality, it was potentially deadly to the men of LUCK who intervened in the streets of Detroit.

Right after I submitted this assessment, LUCK was called in. "Please continue working with Ceasefire as we try to modify it in a way that is protective of the community," they asked. So, we acquiesced, for protecting the community is our purpose, our why for living as we bear the guilt of past transgressions. We volunteered because we desired to mend that which we had helped to break. Our vision was nothing short of a community that is whole, sound and complete.

Over a year had passed since that promise. LUCK continued to volunteer in the green room, and, periodically, Rick and I were asked to be speakers in the part of the program known as the "Voice of Redemption." This placed us right after the chief, federal prosecutors, law enforcement, and the mayor of Detroit. I viewed our role as the "Voice of Redemption" as likened to that of Nat Turner in the story of *Birth of a Nation* called to tame and control the slaves. Ceasefire's prosecutorial prowess had worsened since Obama had granted them two full-time prosecutors.

With all this in mind, I received a text from the Ceasefire coordinator in February of 2017 asking if I would be the Voice of Redemption at an upcoming Ceasefire "call-in" meeting with mandated (forced) attendance of thirty of the allegedly most violent, directly or indirectly, perpetrators in the most gun-related violent zip codes for that month. While there is a dire need to aggressively pursue a remedy for the violence that is permeating Detroit, the method of using more stick than carrot is madness. They were calling in men who did not have their basic needs met, including employment opportunities and nurturing mentorship. All they were offering were threats that if they did not put down their guns, the very instruments that safeguarded their lives and "entrepreneurial" pursuits, that they, their friends, their families, and anyone who tried to help them would face imprisonment. I knew men who carried guns because they were more afraid of their "neighbors" than the police who could put them in jail. As Tupac so eloquently put it, "I'd rather be judged by twelve than carried by six." It's planting tomatoes and expecting onions. It's just not rational, for universal law mandates that every thought, word and deed has within it its equivalence in seed form. Thus, when you beat someone with a stick, eventually, you will be beaten with that same stick. What if instead we nurture these men who are broken from early childhood trauma, suffering PTSD from a hyper aggressive environment, and who embrace anti-social paradigms that reward such behavior and ensure survival in their world? It is easy for us to say, "Put down the gun." My question is, what are we guiding them to pick up?

At first, I refused to be used to manipulate a vulnerable population who simply lack social skills, tools, and meaningful opportunities. Ceasefire may be likened to the tree yelling at the fruit. Every agency that participates is merely the arms of the body of a system designed to imprison and exploit human capital, or chattel, as the constitution so eloquently classifies felons turned slaves. The 13th amendment brandished a person convicted of a crime as a "felon" and forever place that individual into a social caste system that, in Michigan alone, is conveyed in over 900 laws, restricting those in Michigan from places such as industry and housing. The felon is the freed slave forced to hover into a lower socio-economic status as disposable cheap labor for the haves. "I am not missing a day of helping our clients for them to use my gifts to promote their program, a program that does *not* work as I explained to them in the assessment. And they have the audacity to ask me to come the day before to *practice! Practice!*" I said to Rick. At that time, we were a service provider for the Detroit Employment Solutions Corporation (DESC) I said this knowing that Rick would try to talk me into doing otherwise.

"The men mandated to be present *need* to hear from you, Mario," was his usual tagline to pull me toward a speaking engagement I did not support. "Don't go there to practice but to work and service our clients. Don't miss this opportunity to speak to these men. They need to hear your message." Once again, Rick reminded me of my purpose. A true friend is, in a sense, a mentor, for a mentor is a trusted teacher and counselor.

"Alright, but there's no damn way I am going to practice a speech. I *am* the speech. I don't do this for money, like it's just a job, pimpin' the system like them," I retorted. Since Rick agreed about the practice, the following day I sent a text explaining that I could not attend the practice because I was working. At the time I sent the text, I was in LUCK's satellite office in Southwest Detroit helping a parolee with his federal student aid application so that he could begin college. I was told that I would probably not be able be the Voice of Redemption since I missed practice but to come anyway.

On the day of the big speech, I showed up in case they could not find a replacement or were going to forgive the absence from "practice" the day before. I sat in the green room watching as the LUCK men spoke to the arrivals who were mandated to be there by their probation and parole officers. "You should go out there. They're ready for you," the Ceasefire coordinator whispered as he tapped me on the leg. *Hmm, so they are gonna let me speak.* I nodded, smiled, and made my way to the "community circle" area where the community at large, the "pillars" of the system, would encircle these thirty men and wave their fingers at them with threats of imprisonment if they did not stop the violence.

I had to speak after Chief Craig, Detroit's Chief of Police, the federal prosecutor, federal agents, the mayor, and Mr. Bitter, Good Intentions' "Change the Story" director, the same man who gave LUCK their first memorandum of understanding for training probationers and parolees in anger management and conflict resolution. He was also the same man who gave us an award for LUCK's work, then cut our contract and offer Rick a job. We trained fourteen cohorts of men and women and grew close to their staff and clients, including Bitter. Yet in the end, *The 48 Laws of Power's* First Law remained true: "Never outshine the master."

Their tone was demeaning, to say the least. And Bitter triggered me by wooing those in attendance who controlled the purse strings and disrespectfully ignoring the same men of LUCK, Inc. who used to serve him. Having experienced, and to some degree still experience, a system that bars you from gaining entry into livable wage jobs, I understood that these "dogs who eat dogs" were simply the outcome of a much bigger dysfunctional mindset that permeated an entire culture that was systemically created. How can the tree chastise the fruit for its likeness and quality? Whether we embrace this reality or not, the soil does effect the seed. The environment in which these men live, unfortunately, requires completely different rules of engagement than a peaceful suburb does. And, it is intentionally designed to be so. Thus, for the "tree branches" to be yelling at the fruit was personally offensive. To lighten up the mood, I began with an unwelcome joke that would, I would soon discover, be used against us. "I did not prepare tonight to speak. Honestly, I thought I would not be allowed because I did not show up for *practice*. Practice. Come on, *ma-a-n*, practice. *Are you serious?*" I said with my closest resemblance to basketball phenom Allen Iverson when asked in a press conference why he was benched for the game (not showing up to practice). Recognizing the connection to the infamous press conference, all thirty men burst into laughter. Horrible start, right? The captive "slaves" have connected with freed "slave." I continued to talk about passion and purpose.

"I have heard it said tonight," I began, "that you all aren't *real* men." I paused for effect. "I'd venture to say that you men are more real than most so-called men in this room. The only challenge is that you lack the pro-social skills, tools, and understanding to resolve everyday conflict, as the gods that you are. Your biggest problem is that you don't understand the self-governing power inherent within every single cell in your body. For you to have to be *told* what to do by any man, including the chief of police," I said as I glanced behind me to point him out, "is a disgrace. For you all are created in the image and likeness of a God that is a Creator. Your only problem is that you are creating unconsciously. It's unforgiveable for you not to live up to your god potential and protect the very community you live in."

The effect was transformational to say the least, with the prover-bial Saul turned Paul reprimanding the very type of man he once was. Tee Grizzley, the formerly incarcerated Detroit rapper, was in the group of the men mandated to attend that day. Afterward his parole agent introduced us. "He wants to volunteer at one of the schools you go into. He likes what you do," she said. I stared at him with no clue as to who this young man was. Later, I found out his influence and his accomplishments in the music industry. Several months later, Tee Grizzley came with us to River Rouge Middle School where LUCK Inc. was training and mentoring at-risk youth. The other men also, as always, embraced the message and me. "You the realist, O.G. (Original Gangster)," was the usual comment after such speeches. "The other motherf----s are fake as hell," they would say in reference to those that spoke before me. *This* is why I don't practice. I *am* it.

My joke, the reference to not showing up for "practice," in

other words, not following "protocol," was the very excuse the chief of police used to ban me from ever participating in Ceasefire again . . . as if *that* was a punishment. Do you think the *chief* ever made it to practice? Not a chance.

The saddest part was not that my speech blackballed the trainers of LUCK from participating in the green room where the mandated parolees and probationers would hear from those who truly cared. The saddest part was that those responsible for safeguarding Detroit were so blinded by ego, politics, and self-serving thinking that they could not truly hear those who have walked a mile in the shoes of the "sinners" and the "saints."

Rick hung the phone up after talking with Adrian and looked at me. "I am so sorry, bro'. I am so sorry that you had to listen to that and not be able to respond, not be able to defend yourself." I looked at him and Lus with tears in my eyes. I didn't know why Rick didn't vouch for me, but in the end, it didn't really matter. What mattered to me, just as in the beginning, was LUCK's continued existence to protect society from angry, broken, and misguided men and women.

"Effective immediately," I replied, "I resign as co-director. I delegate my power and responsibilities as president to you, Rick. I will sweep and mop floors rather than allow LUCK to die under my leadership."

Rick tried to get me to reconsider. "Bro', you are upset right now. Just give it a day to think about."

The worse part about the entire conversation was not that I was unable to respond to defend myself. The worse part was that even if given the opportunity, I had no foundation to stand on. Over the past year, reintegration had gotten the best of me. Inside those prison walls I not only survived through aggression . . . I excelled. Learning to resolve conflict peacefully within the confines of a hyper aggressive environment does not mean that I surrendered the ability to become aggressive. On the contrary, it meant that I was now aware of it, and with new skills, I was able to learn and become different. Again, *process*. I had the temperament and experience of leading men on a battlefield. The problem was, the battle we were now in was different and it required different skills in its resolution and engagement. What our foes did for LUCK was heaven sent. They positioned us to where our gifts would be utilized for the whole and not just the part. Titles mean nothing, for he who is first shall be last, but he who is last shall be first. So, I humbled myself and sought to make amends.

Weeks later, I joked with Adrian as I hit him in the ribs with my elbow. "I heard every minute of that conversation, and I am sorry that I have created a space where you weren't comfortable speaking with me about that," I said, putting my head down in sorrow for the struggles I have had in responding to those I love the most.

"Aw, little brother, I love you so much. You are on the right path. Keep going and don't stop!" said Adrian as we hugged. Adrian has been there for me in moments that were unbearable, as my other mentors have been.

December, 2017

It's ironic, but the old adage that says, "When one door closes, another opens" still holds true. Even though I was blackballed from speaking to a room of 100 people regarding the mission to safeguard the community, God placed me on a larger platform, influencing over a million viewers as the co-host of a TV show called Main Street. It broadcasts from WHPR 33, Comcast 91 every Tuesday live at noon. On the show, my expertise in both the criminal justice system reform and the economy are highlighted. In addition, LUCK has been awarded a new contract with Service, Employment, and Redevelopment (SER) Metro for the servicing of high-, mid-, and low-level parolees toward reentry success. Also, we are collaborating with Junior Achievement, partnering with Citizens Alliance on Prison and Public Spending (formerly CAPPS, now called A Safe and Just Michigan) and several churches in the safeguarding of the community through successful, proven reentry services and practices.

Being process oriented is essential for all success, especially that of reentry. Some areas of our lives require more time and healing...more "process." While I co-host Main Street, a show that focuses on real economic challenges, I continue to sign contracts and employ men, enroll in graduate school, work for the legislator, start a bookkeeping and taxation firm, and, of course, publish a book. At the same time, I am also experiencing the darkness of unhealed familial relationships, post-traumatic stress disorder (PTSD), re-integrative social challenges, and, of course, the challenges of starting over at the age of thirty-six with absolutely nothing but a bad name rooted in terrible, adolescent decisions decades earlier.

I've come to understand that the pain is simply me mourning Samuel. I mourn him, the man whose life I stole, and I have come to accept that it is not only okay for me to mourn him, but good and just. For my every breath is in conscious acknowledgement that Samuel breathes no more.

God Speaks to All of Us. Are We Listening?

I often think about what God had told me two weeks before I was released from that prison in Jackson, Michigan, the only time I have ever *distinctly* heard His voice: "You cannot fathom the blessings that I have in store for you." You are correct, my Lord. I cannot fathom, for your thoughts are not my thoughts, nor your ways my ways.

It has only been four years since my release, and yet it seems a lifetime. I have so much more to learn that at times I cry in frustration for who I *am* compared to who I am to *become*. The visions that have been bestowed upon me, the whispers that I have heard in the darkest moments have brought me to today. From witnessing my father harm my mother, my womb, my security, to watching her chase drugs, to being abandoned by my father, to becoming so angry that I sold drugs and took Samuel's life, to solitary confinement that forced me to my knees to nineteen long years in and out of Michigan's most notorious prisons ... *all* of these things were necessary to help turn a boy into a real man, shaped in the image and likeness of the Creator who can finally give more to those around him than he takes. I cry out to be this man, now and always. In the night, I cry out to the spirit of Samuel, "Forgive me, my beloved brother. I didn't know any better, therefore, I couldn't *do* any better." My tears wet the same ground that tasted Samuel's blood, and it is just. For men who have harmed their community to the extent to which we have, we serve a just sentence, and it is just that we only experience peace when imparting it. It is a penance imposed upon us returning citizens, upon the men of LUCK, Inc., and we carry our cross understanding that "To the measure in which you give shall it be given unto you, pressed down, shaken up, seven times seven."

As I look back at my path, I see it is interwoven with relationships like a spider web, each relationship a strand that is tied, however indirectly, to another. As a boy, I prayed to a God I could not see for a mother I could not bear to look at and for an absent father who had once been the bosom of my heart. Those unanswered pleas pushed me into a belief that I was alone and that *I had to do everything... alone.* This lead me to feel disconnected to those around me, to my community, to the world. It was this faulty paradigm that led me to abandon the core values of humanity and harm all those who stood in my path, especially Samuel. This boy turned man was then buried deep in the darkness of America's most notorious prisons only to discover that he was never alone. I was able to turn from a "mess into a messenger" because of the numerous transformative relationships I forged on the path toward purpose. It was only when I was humbled to the point of realizing that *I could not do LUCK, Inc. alone* that I experienced true power, for when two or more come together, in harmony, in the Creator's name, he is in the midst of them. I have come to realize that who I am, who I am becoming, and what I am to accomplish is all a result of the many people who have crossed my path, good and evil, friend and foe, for all things happen for the good, for those who love God and are called to His Purpose. I now have the conscious realization that we are all connected, whether we accept it or not. I now understand the mysterious universal principal that whispers in the night, "What you do to another . . . you invariably do to yourself."

1979 My father and me

1995, Me at 16

1995, Aug. 10th- Me seen hear being indicted
for Felony Murder & Armed Robbery

1998, Me in Carson City Prison

2002- Me at URF Prison

2004 - Macomb Correctional Facility

January, 2014, My release
from Jackson prison

February, 2014, Me and Adrian Tonon

2015- Me, Adrian, & Rico Razo

October, 2015, Me and
Mentee "Will" Devon Freeman

May 2016, Graduation with a BS in
Accounting, Wayne State University

July, 2016, Me and Mayor of
Detroit, Mike Duggan

2016, Me as Legislative Aide in
Michigan House of Representatives

2017 Me, Rick and Cam

2017- Me and Former State Rep. Santana

March, 2017, LUCK Team

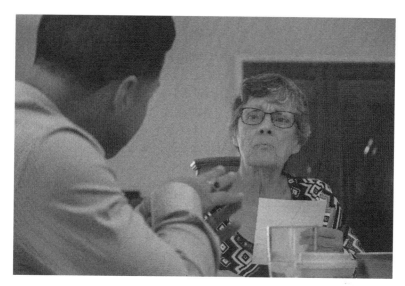

August 2017, Mrs. Duggan and me discussing
strategy to reduce violence in Detroit

August, 2017, Lus, Cam, Congresswoman
Brenda Lawrence, Me and Rick

September, 2017, Me with LUCK clients
(122 years cumulative incarceration time)

September, 2017, Mentee Ryan, Tracy (Samuel's girlfriend) and Me

September, 2017, Ryan Mack, Robin Barnes,
and Me, Hosts of Main St.

October, 2017, Me training in privatized juvenile prison

REFERENCES

Beale, C. (February, 1996). *11* (2), pp. 2-3.

Beale, C. (2001). Alburquerque: Rural Sociological Society.

Briefing Fact Sheet, 1. (2014). *Facts about prisons and prisoners.* Washington, D.C.: Sentencing Project.

Burch, T. (2015). Skin Color and the Criminal Justice System: Beyond Black-White Disparities in Sentencing Skin Color and the Criminal Justice System. *Journal of Empirical Legal Studies,* 395.

Chappell, C. A. (2004). Post-Secondary Correctional Education and Recidivism: A Meta-Analysis of Research Conducted 1990-1999. *Journal of Correctional Education , 55.2,* 148-169.

Frankl, V. E. (2006). *Man's Search for Meaning.* Boston: Beacon Press Books.

Haney, C. (2003). Mental Health Issues in Long-Term Solitary and "Supermax" Confinement. *Crime & Delinquency , 49* (1), 132.

Haney, C. (1998). The past and the future of U.S. prison policy: Twenty five years after the Stanford Prison Experiement. *The American Pscyhologist* (7), 709-727.

Hoyt, E. S. (2002). *Reducing racial disparities in juvenile detention.* Baltimore, MD: Annie E. Casey Foundation.

Huling, T. (2002). Building a Prison Economy in Rural America. (M. M. Chesney-Lind, Ed.) *From Invisible Punishment: The Collateral Consequences of Mass Imprisonment* , pp. 1-2.

James B. Luther, P. E. (2011). An Exploration of Community Reentry Needs and Services for Prisoners: A Focus on Care to Limit Return to High-Risk Behavior. *AIDS PATIENT CARE and STDs* , *25* (8), 476-477.

Justice, C. F. (2001). *Abandoned in the back row: New lessons in education and delinquency prevention.* Washington, D.C.: Coalition for Juvenile Justice.

Kirk, D. S. (2016). Prisoner Reentry and the Reproduction of Legal Cynism. *Social Problems,* 222-243.

Martin Forst, J. F. (1989). Youths in Prisons and Training Schools: Perceptions and Consequences of the Treatment-Custody Dichotomy. *Juvenile and Family Court Journal,* 1-14.

Poe-Yamagata & Jones, M. (2000). And justice for some. *Building Blocks for Youth.*

Samuel Yockelson, P. M. (2004). *The Criminal Personality Volume I: A Profile for Change.* Lanham: Rowman & Littlefield Publishers, Inc.

Senghor, S. (2016). *Writing My Wrongs: Life, Death, and Redemption in an American Prison.* New York: Convergent Books.

Teplan, L. (1990). The prevalence of severe mental disorder among male urban jail detainees: Comparison with the Epidemiologic Catchment Area Program. *US National Library of Medicine* , *80* (6), 663.

Uggen, S. W. (2010). Incarceration and Stratification. *Annual Review of Sociology,* 387-406.